Critical acclaim for *Best Dives of the Western Hemisphere:*

"A marvelously clear and vastly informative book. The best coverage of the subject matter I've seen, and incredibly easy to read—both in text and diagrams. Essential for the serious or beginning diver."
Dr. Susan Cropper, DVM
Society of Aquatic Veterinarians

"Don't plan a dive without it! Before you and your buddy plan your dive make sure you consult this little gem of a book. Its creators and contributors from the world's scuba diving community will guide you to and through some of the best dives of the Western Hemisphere. Concise and informative...one of the few bargains of the 90's."
Wendy Canning Church
President, Divers Exchange International

"Having travelled extensively throughout the Caribbean, I know the value of reliable destination information. *Best Dives of the Western Hemisphere* provides such information, and I highly recommend this well-written book for all divers."
Rick Sammon
President, CEDAM International

"...a scuba enthusiast's encyclopedia—every coral reef, ship wreck and exotic fish has been identified for the edification of expert and novice divers alike."
H.V. Pat Reilly
Travel Journalist

"Interesting and informative—you have provided the right amount of detail and objectivity to help scuba divers and snorkelers get what they are looking for in dive travel."
Bill Smith
President, Brazilian Scuba and Land Tours

"Written with every water lover in mind including the snorkeler, the novice diver and the well seasoned scuba enthusiast. It helps to safely open a new world of discovery to anyone with a facemask and a desire to look beneath the water's surface."
Barbara Brundage
President, Pacific Stock Photography Agency

". . . a full library of Western Hemisphere destination guides—in a single indispensible book. What a terrific idea!
Dee Scarr
Touch the Sea

ACKNOWLEDGMENTS

High-spirited enthusiasm is the magic which separates ordinary from excellent. The authors and editors wish to thank all of BEST DIVES correspondents, dive reporters, and travel contributors (identified throughout the book) for sharing their talent and effort.

A special thanks to Claudia Sammartino, Gold Quill, Ltd.; Nick Lisa; Anita and Ken Liggett, Underwater Sports of NJ; Bill Smith, Camille Mancuso, Maria Shaw, Eliot Tozer, Susan Abrams, Myron Clemente, Mina and Bill Hueslein, Tom McKelvey, Peggy Becker, Pat Reilly, Mary Mahoney, Nadia and Jim Spencer, John Buckley, Melissa, Rene, Lauren, Marlene and Bob DiChiara, Louise and Dave Perlstein, and Michael Hunter.

NOTE: Every effort has been made to obtain accurate and up-to-date information for this publication. Correspondents include a select group of top divemasters from across the Western Hemisphere. Considering the sheer magnitude of the research included in this publication all information cannot be confirmed immediately prior to press time. This publication is intended only as a guide. Additional information should be obtained prior to visiting each area.

Diving is an inherently dangerous sport. Ocean and weather conditions can change dramatically during the course of a day. Extreme caution should be exercised. Accurate weather and sea condition reports should be obtained immediately prior to entering the water. The authors, contributors, and publishers of this guide assume no liability for its use.

BEST DIVES OF THE WESTERN HEMISPHERE

Jon Huber
Joyce Huber
Christopher Lofting

HUNTER
PUBLISHING INC

Hunter Publishing, Inc.
300 Raritan Center Parkway
Edison NJ 08818
(201) 225 1900

ISBN 1-55650-250-8

Printed in Singapore through Palace Press

Photo Credits

John O'Rourke: 10. Divi Resorts: 13, 259. Unexso: 27. G. Binanzer: 19,
21, 35, 39. Sophie Aksell: 44. M. Young: 46, 48. R. Ryel: 54. B. Peavy:
61. T. Grasse: 62. D. Batalsky: 90. Brazil Tourism: 98, 101. Bermuda
Tourism: 68, 70, 73, 75. Mina Hueslein: 104. Cau Pissurno: 102, 107,
110. Tedeschi: 115, 124, 125. A Flinn: 144, 148. Cohen Assoc.: 138, 151.
BBD&O: 130. U.S. Dept. of the Interior: 156, 159, 161. James Spencer:
168. Secty de Tourismo de Mexico: 172, 173. Dietmar Reimer: 180, 184.
Richard Ockelmann: 209, 210, 212, 214, 215, 217, 218. Nick Lisa: 223,
225, 226, 230, 237, 241, 245. Hawaii Visitor's Bureau: 229, 231. Michel
Verdure: 251, 255. USVI Div. of Tourism: 267. All others by Jon Huber

Maps by Joyce Huber.

CONTENTS

Using This Guide

Quick reference symbols are used throughout this guide to identify diving and snorkeling areas. Each area has been given a rating of from one to five starfish by prominent divemasters of the area.

Starfish Ratings

☆☆☆☆☆   **Five Starfish.** Best of the best diving; best visibility, best marine life, best wreck or reef or kelp dive.

☆☆☆☆   **Four Starfish.** Fantastic dive. Outstanding in marine life or visual interest.

☆☆☆   **Three Starfish.** Superb dive. Excellent visibility and marine life or wreck.

☆☆   **Two Starfish.** Good Dive. Interesting fish and plant life; good visibility.

☆   **One Starfish.** Pleasant dive. Better than average.

Map symbols

Dive site   Shipwreck

Snorkeling area   Airport location

Quick Reference Symbols

 Good area for scuba diving.

 Good area for snorkeling.

 Good area for underwater photography.

 Boat access only.

 Beach access possible.

 Protected, no spearfishing or coral collecting.

INTRODUCTION

Considering that two-thirds of the earth's surface is covered by water and that the Western Hemisphere technically takes up half the world, you might wonder how we could possibly cover all the the best SCUBA and snorkel diving of such a large area within the covers of this book. So let's start by defining what we mean by the best dives. Our selection of the Best Dives was based on a number of factors found both beneath and above the surface. We were looking for more than clear water, spectacular coral formations, abundance of marine flora and fauna. Of course, these factors were vitally important. But we considered the totality of the dive trip experience. There was a time when good diving meant an arduous, uncomfortable, often long trip to a remote location with inferior accommodations, shoddy and sometimes dangerous dive operations. Those pioneer days are fortunately behind us. While the free spirit of exploring virgin undersea wilderness still exists, we no longer have to suffer the inconvenience, the discomforts and the physical risks we once did. Finding great diving does not mean living the life of a beach bum, unless you want to. As diving became a major travel related industry, the quality of the hotels, dive operators, restaurants and other facilities followed. Comfortably appointed yachts now take divers to the outer limits of barrier reefs and remote destinations. No longer is it necessary for those non-divers in our midst to sit on shore with nothing to do but wait for us to return and recount our undersea adventures.

Top rated dive areas are quickly realizing that divers, as enthusiastic as they are about their sport, now are seeking a more well-rounded and sophisticated travel experience.

Therefore, to qualify for the "Best Dives" designation, an area had to offer not only interesting and top-rated dive locations, but a whole lot more as well. No matter how terrific the diving was, it did not make our list if it also did not provide the most modern facilities and equipment, manned by trained dive professionals. Comfortable, clean and attracive hotel accommodations conveniently located for the diver were also important in determining our selections. Restaurants, other water sports, entertainment, sightseeing and other attractions were also important. All of the locations were personally visited and inspected by the authors or members of the Diver Advisory Board. If your personal favorite did not make our list, why don't you tell us about it, and we will take another look for the next edition. In the meantime, we submit for your approval 200 Best Dives of the Hemisphere—those diving-oriented destinations on this side of the globe that, in our opinion, have it all.

PLANNING YOUR TRIP

To plan your "best dive" vacation, consider first the type of dive trip that interests you most. Then check the best time of year to go. A week of bad weather or rough seas can turn any "best dive" into a worst dive vacation. While no one can guarantee the weather, each chapter discusses local weather patterns and suggests a best time of year to go. Finally, consider your budget.

PACKAGE AND GROUP TOURS

Hundreds of dollars may be saved by choosing a package tour, offered by airlines, resorts and dive operators. For tours to remote locations see the chapter Live-Aboards and World Wide Expeditions. Off-the-beaten-track expeditions are offered by specialty organizations like CEDAM (Conservation, Ecology, Diving, Archaeology, Museums) which features programs as varied as an underwater archaeological dig on an ancient shipwreck or a mapping tour of the Galapagos. For information write to Membership Chairman at CEDAM International, Fox Road, Croton NY 10520.

Many dive clubs and dive shops across the U.S. are offering group dive vacations to their customers. These provide an excellent opportunity for new divers, singles, and first time travelers.

BUDDIES

Divers' Exchange International, in Boston, maintains a computerized member list of divers and snorkelers around the world. A member seeking a buddy can easily be teamed up with one or more fellow divers living in a selected destination or with someone who is interested in traveling to that destination at the same time. Membership fees are $25 per year. This is a great idea for business travelers, singles, or couples where just one person dives. For additional information write to Divers' Exchange International, P.O. Box 2382, Tisbury MA 02568.

INSURANCE

Many types of travel insurance are available covering everything from lost luggage, trip cancellations and medical expenses.

Trips purchased with some major credit cards include life insurance.

Divers Alert Network (DAN) offers divers' health insurance for $25 a year plus an annual membership fee of $15. Any treatment required for an accident or emergency which is a direct result of diving such as decompression sickness (the bends), arterial gas embolism or pulmonary baro-trauma is covered up to $15,000 with a 5 percent deductible. Air ambulance to the closest medical care facility, recompression chamber care and in-patient hospital care are covered. Non-diving travel-related accidents are NOT covered.

Lacking the ability to pay, a diver may be refused transport and may be refused treatment. For more information write to DAN, P.O. Box 3823, Duke University Medical Center, Durham NC 27710. ☎ 919-684-2948

International SOS Assistance is a medical assistance service to travelers who are more than 100 miles from home. For just $15 for 7 days SOS covers air evacuation and travel related assistance. Evacuation is to the closest medical care facility which is determined by SOS staff doctors. Hospitalization is

NOT covered. Standard Blue Cross and Blue Shield policies do cover medical costs while traveling. For information write to International SOS Assistance, Box 11568, Philadelphia PA 19116. ☎ 800-523- 8930. Lost luggage insurance is available at the ticket counter of many airlines. If you have a homeowner's policy, you may already be covered.

DOCUMENTS

Carry your personal documents on you at all times while traveling. Be sure to keep a separate record of passport numbers, visas, or tourist cards in your luggage.

DRUGS

Penalties for possession of illegal drugs are very harsh and the risk you take for holding even a half-ounce of marijuana cannot be stressed enough. Punishment often entails long jail terms. In certain areas, such as Mexico, your embassy and the best lawyer won't be much help. You are guilty until proven innocent. Selling drugs is still cause for public hanging in some areas.

CAMERAS

Divers traveling with expensive camera gear or electronic equipment should register each item with customs *before* leaving the country.

SUNDRIES

Items such as suntan lotion, aspirin, antihistamines, decongestants, anti-fog, or mosquito repellent should be purchased before your trip. These products are not always available and may cost quite a bit more than what you normally pay for them at home.

SUNGLASSES

Tropical sunshine can damage your eyes. Both sunglasses and a hat should be worn. Corning Glass has recently developed two lines of sunglasses especially designed to filter out the harmful rays of the sun called *Serengeti Drivers* and *Serengeti Solar Barriers*. Both darken with exposure and are also useful on overcast days.

DIVER IDENTIFICATION

Most dive operations require that you hold a certification card and a logbook. A check-out dive may be required if you cannot produce a log of recent dives.

GEAR

Uncomfortable or ill fitting masks, snorkels, and other personal diving gear can make your dive trip a miserable experience. You can greatly reduce the possibility of these problems by buying or renting what you'll need from a reliable dive shop or specialty store before departure. Sandy Mills, spokeswoman for The Parkway System, a major dive equipment manufacturer in South Amboy NJ, suggests carrying an extra mask strap and snorkel retainer in your dive bag.

PACKING CHECKLIST

Snorkelers' Warm Water
Packing Check List

___ MASK
___ SNORKEL
___ FINS
___ FLOTATION VEST
___ REEF GLOVES
___ MESH CATCH BAG
(for wet gear or
shell collecting)
___ FISH ID BOOK
___ SUNTAN LOTION

___ SPARE STRAP
___ SPARE SNORKEL
___ RETAINER RING
___ PROTECTIVE CLOTHING
(against sunburn)
___ PASSBOOK OR
REQUIRED ID
___ SUNGLASSES
___ U/W CAMERA & FILM
___ HAT

Warm Water Scuba
Packing Check List

___ MASK
___ SNORKEL
___ FINS
___ REGULATOR
___ DEPTH GAUGE*
___ BOUYANCY
COMPENSATOR

___ SPARE SNORKEL
___ RETAINER RING
___ SPARE STRAPS
___ SUBMERSIBLE
PRESSURE GAUGE
___ WATCH/BOTTOM TIMER*
___ WEIGHT BELT (No lead)

___ WET SUIT, SHORTIE
   OR LYCRA WET SKIN
___ WET SUIT BOOTS
___ MESH CATCH BAG
___ U/W DIVE LIGHTS
   (Primary and back up)
___ DRAMAMINE or other
   seasickness preventative
___ GEAR MARKER
___ DIVER CERTIFICATION
___ CARD (C-card)
___ DIVER LOG BOOK
___ SUNGLASSES
___ SPARE MASK STRAP

___ DIVING KNIFE
___ DE-FOG SOLUTION
___ REEF GLOVES
___ CYALUME STICKS
   (chemical light sticks)
___ U/W CAMERA AND FILM
___ FISH ID BOOK
___ DIVE TABLES
___ PASSPORT or proof of
   citizenship as required
___ DIVE TABLES
___ SUNTAN LOTION
___ HAT (with visor or brim)

Cool Water Diving
(eg. Brazil, Channel Islands)

___ 1/4 INCH WET SUIT, FARMER JOHNS OR VEST
___ WET SUIT HOOD
___ WET SUIT BOOTS

Must be packed in an air tight container

BAHAMAS

When you say "the Bahamas," you're talking about an archipelago containing more than 700 islands, cays and outcroppings that stretch in a broad arc from just 50 miles off Florida's coast southeast to the waters off Cuba. This sun-drenched chain from Walker's Cay in the north to Great Inagua in the south, is actually the visible portion of two barrier reefs (the Little and Great Bahama Banks) which wander through 500 miles of tropical ocean and cover 100,000 square miles. The dense coral reef system that fringes the islands is home to hundreds of historic wrecks, mysterious blue holes and vacated movie sets. Every year, more than 3 million pleasure seekers visit the Bahamas. For divers its enormous appeal is variety; whether looking for spectacular drift dives, shallow wrecks, lush coral reefs, a quiet island retreat, or the excitement of casino gambling and nonstop nightlife.

You'll find what you want in one of three general areas, each offering its own delights. Old world charm and new world glamour combine in Nassau, the capital city of the Bahamas, and in its world class resorts, Cable Beach and Paradise Island. Grand Bahama Island offers modern resorts in Freeport/Lucaya and the rustic charm of old settlements such as West End. The Family Islands, formerly called the Out Islands, are Robinson-Crusoe-style hideaways with exclusive resorts

Area Contributors: Jeff Prahm, Andros; Win Chesley, Harbour Island; J. Friese, Long Island; John Englander, UNEXSO; Bill Huslein, BDWH.

Long Island

which attract international travelers. The Bahamas offer every style of dive vacation, from sophisticated to simple, from exotic live-aboards to discount dive packages. And it's easy to get there, via frequent flights by major airlines or on the national flag carrier, Bahamasair. On inter-island air services you can combine a visit to Nassau or Freeport with a visit to The Family Islands. On some of the latter, one or two main dive resorts serve as activity center, dive shop, restaurant and hotel.

The climate of the Bahamas is idyllic, the mean temperature in January about 77° F and in August, 89° . The difference between the warmest and coolest months is only about 12°.

British tradition is still very much alive in the Bahamas. English is the official language (spoken with a musical lilt). Cars are driven on the left, and Bahamians still stand on ceremony every day during changing of the guard.

BAHAMA ISLANDS

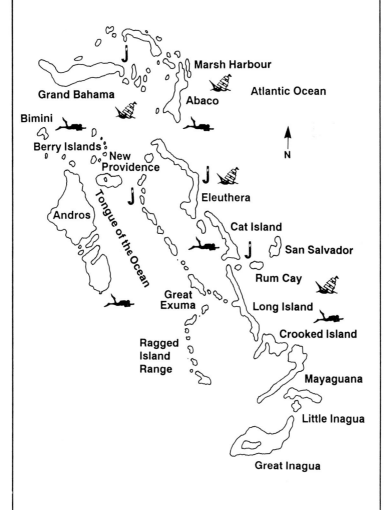

Grand Bahama

Marsh Harbour

Atlantic Ocean

Abaco

Bimini

Berry Islands

New
Providence

N

Andros

Tongue of the Ocean

Eleuthera

Cat Island

San Salvador

Rum Cay

Great
Exuma

Long Island

Crooked Island

Ragged
Island
Range

Mayaguana

Little Inagua

Great Inagua

Sightseeing

In Nassau, Cable Beach, and Paradise Island you can enjoy topside scenery and attractions by taxi, bicycle or horse-drawn surrey complete with fringed top. To get a personal view, ask for a driver who is a Bahamahost. Bahamahosts are certified by the Bahamas Ministry of Tourism and are extremely knowledgeable about native history, folklore, flora, sports and just about everything else.

There are than 200 tennis courts, including almost 100 in the Nassau/Paradise Island/Cable Beach area. There are championship golf courses, four major casinos, more than 30 major annual fishing tournaments, marinas for motorboating and sailing, and airports for private aviators.

Dining

Bahamian cuisine also shares an African accent. Some dishes are simple, using ingredients such as corn meal flour. Others are more elaborate, using tropical spices and fruits, such as soursop, tamarind, coconut and banana.

A staple of the Bahamian diet is "Johnny Cake," a rich pan-cooked bread much like cornbread. The recipe arrived with early settlers who may have called it "Journey Cake" because it fed them during their journey.

Conch (pronounced "konk"), a mollusk whose pink-lipped shells are often heaped along Bahamian beaches, is as integral to the Bahamian diet as the hamburger is to America. Culinary variations on conch include conch fritters, cracked conch, conch burgers, conch chowder, conch salad, and scorched conch.

ABACO

The Abaco Islands are the northernmost group in the Bahamas chain. Most of the diving activity takes place around Marsh Harbour, Walker's Cay, and Treasure Cay.

Best Dives of Abaco

☆☆☆☆**PELICAN CAY NATIONAL PARK.** This   2,000-acre National Underwater Park offers endless mazes of coral tunnels, walls, pinnacles and remains of modern and ancient wrecks.

The park is shallow and ranges in depth from breaking the surface to about 30 ft. The marine life is spectacular with eagle rays, jacks, angels, critters, huge groupers, and colorful sponges.

☆☆☆*USS ADIRONDACK.* A Federal-era battleship resting in 30 ft of water, offers both snorkelers and SCUBA divers a look at the remains of the superstructure and some interesting antique cannons. A host of colorful reef fish inhabit the area around it.

Abaco Dive Operators

DIVE ABACO. This shop is located in Marsh Harbour at the town marina. Owner Skeet LaChance offers easy diving on the inside of the Barrier Reef. Write to: P.O. Box 555, Marsh Harbour, Abaco, Bahamas. ☎ 800-468-9876 or 809-367-2787.

BRENDAL'S DIVE SHOP. Brendal's is located on Green Turtle Cay at the Green Turtle Club and Marina. This operator, catering to novices as well as experienced divers, conducts visits to Pelican Park and the Coral Catacombs. Dive packages with lodging at the Green Turtle are available. Write to: Brendal Stevens, Green Turtle Cay, Green Turtle Club and Marina, Bahamas. ☎ (U.S.) 800-468-9876, 809-367-2572 or (FL) 305-833-9580.

WALKER'S CAY RESORT. Located at the northern end of the Abacos, this resort and dive center, the only one on the island, offers guests private air charters to and from Ft. Lauderdale. Access to most of the dives, which are at the upper end of Barrier Reef, is by boat. Exotic accommodations are available in a scattering of lovely villas and cottages.

Write to Walker's Cay Resort, 700 SW 34th St., Ft. Lauderdale FL 33315. ☎ (US) 800-327-3714, (FL) 800-432-2092 or 305-522-1469.

ANDROS

Andros is the largest of the Bahama islands, over 100 miles long, yet the least populated. It is fringed by the second largest barrier reef in the Western Hemisphere. The following dive sites are all within 10 minutes by boat from the Small Hope Bay Lodge on the north eastern coast of Andros. Superb visibility and calm seas, ranging from flat during summer months to 2 - 3 ft during the winter, are the norm.

Best Dives of Andros

☆☆☆☆☆BRAD'S MOUNTAIN is a top spot for SCUBA divers of all skill levels. A huge mountain of coral rising from a depth of 50 ft to a peak at 20 ft is carved with tunnels, caves and crevices. Masses of fish inhabit the area, including spade fish, Bermuda Chub,parrotfish, grunts and angels.

☆☆☆☆☆THE BLUE HOLE is a huge bell-shaped crater, perhaps 300 ft across, which drops off to great depths. It is in the middle of a 50 ft coral garden. Divers who swim around its perimeter at a depth of 100 ft can explore magnificent natural formations, huge rock pillars and deep shafts which lead to inland blue holes. Huge stingrays glide by amidst super-sized midnight parrotfish, snapper and large crabs. Not recommended for beginners.

☆☆☆☆**THE BARGE,** an LC landing craft that sank in 1963, is a delight for a novice diver with a new camera. Sitting in 70 ft of water the wreck is home to a bevy of friendly morays and grouper. They will greet you at the anchor line, eat from your hand and offer you a tour. Pretty coral formations are found here also.

☆☆☆☆**GIANT STAIRCASE.** Advanced divers will enjoy exploring this wall, which slopes down at irregular angles and, as the name implies, looks much like a giant's staircase with the final step dropping off 6,000 ft into the tongue of the ocean. The wall starts at 90 ft. A variety of corals surrounding a huge sand patch adorn the top of the wall where garden eels peer up from time to time. (They retreat back into the sand when you get too close).

☆☆☆☆**TURNBULL'S GUT** is a fascinating wall dive. From the top, at a depth of 80 ft, the wall plunges into a wide canyon (the gut) which extends laterally 100 ft to a spectacular 6,000 ft drop in the Tongue of the Ocean. The wall is alive with lettuce corals, black coral, vibrant sea fans and sponges and the "gut" is plentiful with fish and large rays. This dive is recommended for those with some experience.

☆☆☆**THE _MARION,_** a sunken barge 100 ft long and 40 ft wide, is a fun dive for those of all skill levels. With a huge tractor and a crane nearby the wreckage lies in a large sand patch surrounded by a really pretty coral garden. Residents include spotted grouper, parrotfish, southern sting rays, garden eels, and nurse sharks.

☆☆☆☆**THE DUNGEONS** are a series of caves weaving in and out of the wall at the Tongue of the Ocean. Some, formed by interconnecting pillars of coral, wind into the wall for 100 ft. Groupers, silversides, rays and shark are found here. Advanced divers only. Depth range is from 70 to 90 ft.

Best Snorkeling Sites of Andros

☆☆☆☆☆**TRUMPET REEF** is a beautiful forest of elkhorn, staghorn, brain and soft corals. Trumpet fish are everywhere joined by beautiful queen and French angels, schools of grunts and yellowtail. Snorkelers and beginning divers get hooked by the bounty and beauty of marine life here. Depths range from two to 15 ft.

☆☆☆☆**LOVE HILL** is a lush coral garden with a shimmering white sand bottom from which huge thickets of elkhorn and staghorn grow. Multi-hued soft corals and gorgonians are in abundance as are a full range of tropical fish and marine animals. Depths are two to 15 ft.

Dive Operators and Accommodations

SMALL HOPE BAY LODGE is a divers' resort offering resort courses, reef tours and accommodations with a congenial atmosphere. Guests stay in one of 20 comfortable cabins at the water's edge. ☎ (U.S.) 800- 223-6961; in Miami, 305-463-9130. Write to P.O. Box 21667, Fort Lauderdale FL 33335.

ANDROS BEACH HOTEL, featuring a choice of hotel rooms, cottages or a villa, sits on a lovely beach. Andros Undersea

Adventures dive center, on the premises, operates a fast 40-ft custom dive boat. For details ☎ 800-327-8150 or write to P.O. Box 21766, Ft. Lauderdale FL 33335.

BERRY ISLANDS

Located just north of New Providence, The Berry Islands are a group of small islands and cays, many privately owned. Chub Cay is the undisputed diving and snorkeling center here.

Best Dives of the Berry Islands

☆☆☆☆**THE FISHBOWL.** The best dives in the Berry Islands can be found on the barrier reef at the northern end of the "Tongue of the Ocean" at Chub Cay. This wall dive which starts at 50 ft is called "The Fishbowl of The Bahamas" because of the myriads of fish and marine animals that adorn the valleys and ridges.

☆☆☆**ANGELFISH REEF.** As the name implies, this reef's residents include innumerable French and queen angels, many of which will pose for a video or still photo. Grunts, rays, turtles, eels, and barracudas are found swimming among the staghorn, elkhorn and brain corals. The average depth is 50 ft and visibility is usually good.

Best Snorkeling of the Berry Islands

☆☆☆**MOMA RHODA REEF.** The walls of this shallow reef are splashed with a profusion of colorful sponges, starfish and

Wreck of the Comberbach

corals. At averages depths of 15 ft, snorkelers and SCUBA divers delight in exploring the coral mounds and crevices where schools of sergeant majors, rays, grunts, hogfish, groupers, jacks and yellowtail parade.

Berry Islands Dive Operator

The CHUB CAY CLUB, on Chub Cay is a well planned self-contained dive resort that caters to the special needs of the underwater photographer with a full service photo lab and custom dive boats. ☎ 1-800-327-8150 or write Undersea Adventures, P.O. Box 21766, Fort Lauderdale FL 33335.

BIMINI

Bimini, just a quick flight from Miami, offers divers some interesting wall and reef dives. For the experienced diver drift dives on the Bimini Wall offer some nice sights; for the novice or snorkeler Rainbow Reef is the favorite. A fabulous display of fish awaits divers at the *Sapona,* a shallow freighter wreck.

Best Dives of Bimini

☆☆☆☆☆**THE NODULES.** This is a fascinating web of coral structures: ledges, tunnels, overhangs, caverns, swim-through chimneys,and towering coral heads all lavishly decorated with gorgonians, sea fans, sponges and invertebrates. Schools of copper sweepers, sergeant majors, grunts, groupers, snappers and lobster inhabit this reef. Average depth 70 ft. For experienced divers.

☆☆☆☆**TUNA ALLEY** is a special coral passageway frequented by migrating tuna along with large groupers, angelfish, and stingrays. Fabulous visibility. Average depth is 50 ft.

Best Snorkeling of Bimini

☆☆☆**SUNSHINE REEF** plays host to masses of butterfly fish, angels, parrotfish, lobsters, moray eels, grunts. At noon, the rays of the sun penetrate the sparkling surface, splashing a wave of magnificent color and light across these lovely coral gardens. This is a good spot for photos. Average depth: 15 ft.

Dive Operators of Bimini

UNDERSEA ADVENTURES offers complete dive/accommodation packages in cooperation with the Bimini Big Game Fishing Club and Hotel. ☎ 1 800-327-8150 or write P.O. Box 21766, Fort Lauderdale FL 33335.

ELEUTHERA

Eleuthera is composed of three islands: Spanish Wells, tiny Harbour Island, and a small cay called Current. Spanish Wells, one of the smallest but most progressive islands in the Bahamas, offers some of the most famous and interesting shallow wrecks and dive sites in all the Bahamas.

☆☆☆☆☆**CURRENT CUT,** a narrow ocean cut between Eleuthera and Current Island, serves as the major link between Eleuthera Sound and the open sea. Tide changes cause

Hull of the Comberbach

millions of gallons of seawater to whip through this narrow gap at speeds of 7 to 10 knots, visibility ranging from 50 to 80 ft. Divers "shooting the cut" can join schools of horse-eye jack, eagle rays and barracuda as they sail by at exhilarating speeds. Depth in the center is 65 ft, with sharp, smooth, vertical walls on both sides and large potholes lining the bottom.

☆☆☆**EGG ISLAND LIGHTHOUSE REEF.** Located due west of Egg Island in 60 ft of water are 35-ft-high coral heads rising from a sandy bottom. Grouper, squirrel fish, glasseye snappers, jack, crevalle jacks, amberjacks, blue chromis, wrasse, parrotfish, and surgeon hang out here. The reef is dense with varied corals and pretty sponges. Visibility is good. A photographer's paradise.

☆☆☆☆**THE GARDENS.** A favorite among photographers, this reef is outside the Cut and due west about one mile. It is a rainbow of corals and sponges and home to large schools of surgeon fish, parrotfish, blue chromis, queen and French angels. Crabs, shrimp and lobster are abundant and giant manta rays are frequently sighted here.

☆☆☆**MILLER'S REEF** is located just off the east coast of Harbour Island. This area is a maze of coral archways, canyons, caves and pinnacles at depths from 50 to 100 ft. Schools of grunts, hogfish, turtles, angels, barracuda, and lobster, chubs, and jacks along with macro critters reside in the reef.

Best Snorkeling and
Shallow Dive Sites of Eleuthera

☆☆**MYSTERY REEF.** Three miles outside of Current Cut, in the direction of Egg Island, is a group of six coral heads located in 25 ft of water. The heads, which sit in the middle of a sprawling sand patch, are 10 to 20 ft high and loaded with all types of exquisite corals and fascinating marine life.

☆☆☆**FREIGHTER WRECK.** Approximately five miles from Current Cut lies the rusting hull of a 250-ft Lebanese freighter which caught fire and was purposely run aground. The wreck sits perfectly upright in 20 ft of water with most of her structure above the surface. Her keel is broken at mid-ship, making salvage an unlikely prospect. Although the propeller was removed by scrap metal salvors, furnishings and ship's parts are scattered around the hull. Large parrotfish, glasseye snappers, and watchful angels are attracted to the wreck.

☆☆☆**DEVIL'S BACKBONE.** North of Spanish Wells island is a long stretch of shallow coral reefs known as Devil's Backbone. Here great clumps of razor sharp elkhorn coral rise from the bottom to the surface and are often awash at low tide. This treacherous barrier reef is a graveyard for ships and a paradise for snorkeling and divers, with wrecks providing dramatic backgrounds for diver portraits.

☆☆☆☆**TRAIN WRECK.** Perhaps the most unusual shipwreck in all the Bahamas is the remains of a steam locomotive, lying in 15 ft of water. Still in the barge, which sank during a storm in 1865, it was part of a Union train believed captured by the Confederacy and sold to a Cuban sugar plantation. The wreck site also contains three sets of wheel trucks believed to be part of the same locomotive, and wood beams half buried in the sandy sea floor. The wreckage which is slowly settling in a garden of elkhorn and brain coral formations, offers some great angles for wide-angle photography.

☆☆☆☆*CIENFUEGOS* WRECK. Just a few hundred yards away from the Train Wreck lies the *Cienfuegos* wreck, the twisted remains of a passenger steamer that sank in 1895. Part of the Ward Line of New York, this 200-ft-long steel hulled ship crashed into the reef during a bad storm. All passengers on board survived and her cargo of rice was salvaged. The remaining wreckage lies in 35 ft of water with some sections at a mere 10 ft. Prominent features are two giant heat exchangers, a big boiler and the main drive shaft. The wreck, looking much like an undersea junk yard with jumbled steel plates, broken ribs and twisted steel beams, makes for a fascinating dive.

☆☆☆POTATO AND ONION WRECK. The *Vanaheim*, an 86-ft coastal freighter, was carrying a cargo of potatoes and onions when she crashed into Devil's Backbone in February, 1969. The force of the heavy seas during the storm pushed her over the barrier reef into 15 ft of water—an easy dive. Surrounding the wreck are very pretty reefs.

Dive Operators and Accommodations

SPANISH WELLS BEACH RESORT has 21 ocean front rooms and seven cottages directly on the ocean. Complete dive/accommodation packages available. ☎ 800-327-5118 U.S., 800-432-1362 FL or write Win Chesley Associates, 820 N. Fig Tree Lane, Plantation FL 33317.

EXUMA

The Exumas stretch more than 100 miles, from New Providence to Long Island. There are close to 200 miles of coral reefs, all magnificent and alive with marine life. Average depth on these reefs is 35 ft, making them ideal for divers of all skill levels as well as underwater photo enthusiasts. Following are just a few of the dive sites.

Best Dives of Exuma

☆☆☆☆**CORAL REEF AND STING RAY REEF** are adjacent to Uly Cay, just north of Stocking Island. Here an array of fish, elkhorn and soft coral patches is home to trumpet fish, barracuda, turtles, and large schools of grunts and yellowtail. Depths range from 20 to 40 ft.

☆☆☆**CONCH CAY** is a northern dive area offering shallow walls and wide ledges for easy exploration. Marine life offers the big attraction here—huge turtles, rays and occasional sharks. The reef is shallow ranging in depth from 6 to 20 ft.

☆☆**LONG REEF** sits at the southern tip of Stocking Island and is a maze of staghorn and elkhorn coral. Queen triggerfish, angels, grunts, hogfish and turtles are in residence here. Depths are 25 to 60 ft.

☆**LOBSTER REEF,** situated in the Eastern Channel just north of Man of War Cay, features huge coral masses teaming with lobster as well as hogfish, snapper, angels, sergeant majors and morays.

☆☆☆**CRAB CAY BLUE HOLE** is just off shore and south of George Town. Starting at a depth of about 35 ft this mysterious blue hole offers a more sensual diving experience than most sites. The unusual current in the area creates a twirling drift dive with fish and critters racing by.

Dive Operators and Accommodations

THE PEACE AND PLENTY HOTEL in George Town on Great Exuma specializes in diving packages and offers spacious modern accommodations. For reservations, contact Win Chesley Assoc. at 820 N. Fig Tree Lane, Plantation FL 33317. ☎ 800-327-5118 U.S., Telex 529782.

GRAND BAHAMA

Grand Bahama Island is the home of Treasure Reef where over a million dollars worth of treasure was discovered in 1962 and is the home port of the Underwater Explorer's Society (UNEXSO) in Freeport/Lucaya. The Gulf Stream passes through many of the best dive sites around the island, providing visibility that can exceed 200 ft at times. Dive sites are close (most less than 15 minutes from shore). Depths on the reefs surrounding Grand Bahama range from 15 to 75 ft.

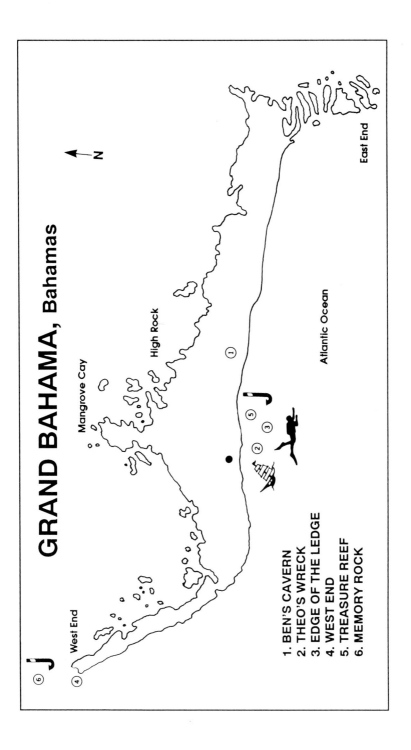

GRAND BAHAMA, Bahamas

West End

Mangrove Cay

High Rock

East End

Atlantic Ocean

1. BEN'S CAVERN
2. THEO'S WRECK
3. EDGE OF THE LEDGE
4. WEST END
5. TREASURE REEF
6. MEMORY ROCK

N

The Dolphin Experience

One of Port Lucaya's more exciting attractions is The Underwater Explorers Society's Dolphin Experience. Visitors— via headsets and underwater microphones—learn about dolphins and listen to the variety of sounds they make as they "talk" and navigate. Participants can sit on the dock around the dolphin enclosure, put their feet in the water and allow the dolphins to brush against them.

Six bottle-nosed dolphins have been trained to frolic with divers in the open sea. Even swimmers and snorkelers can wade out to join the dolphins in shallow water. According to Jeanne Schultz, director of operations for the program, "The dolphins allow themselves to be freely touched and petted. They seem to look forward to human company." Dolphins in training are released on a weekly basis.

Best Dives of Grand Bahama

☆☆☆**BEN'S CAVERN** is an extremely popular dive destination because it gives divers an opportunity to go cave diving without going into a cave. This inland cavern developed centuries ago, when the level of the sea was much lower than it is now. Giant stalactites grew down from the ceilings and stalagmites grew up from the floors. The level of the ocean rose, flooding the cavern.

The ceiling of Ben's Cavern collapsed years ago resulting in a crystal clear inland pool. Divers entering this pool are able to explore the cave formations without losing quick access to the cavern opening above.

The pool in Ben's Cavern is about 50 ft deep. At approximately 35 ft (sea level), divers swim through a halocline (a transition zone of cool fresh water to warmer salt water) where vision is blurred for a few feet.

Ben's Cavern is located in the Bahamian "bush" about 20 miles east of UNEXSO. There is a parking area close to the cavern opening, and a spiral staircase leads down to a dock-like entry point at the side of the pool. Only two dives are made weekly to Ben's Cavern. Reservations should be made well in advance. ☎ 1-800-992-DIVE in the U.S. or 305-761-7679.

☆☆☆**THEO'S WRECK** is the favorite dive of Grand Bahama. This 230-ft steel freighter sits in 100 ft of water and is dramatically perched on a ledge which drops off to 2000 ft.

☆☆☆☆**EDGE OF THE LEDGE** sits less than a mile out from the Lucaya beach. Here the continental shelf abruptly drops off from a depth of 80 ft to more than 2,000 ft. The face of this wall is deeply pocketed with coral overhangs and covered with fuzzy sea whips and blood-red sponges.

Best Snorkeling of Grand Bahama

☆☆☆**TREASURE REEF** is the site where more than $2.4 million in Spanish Treasure was discovered in the 1960s. Thousands of reef fish inhabit this area, including large schools of grunt, snapper, goatfish, and sergeant majors. Depths range from 4 to 15 feet. Elkhorn and staghorn corals, gorgonians, and colorful seafans decorate the bottom.

☆☆**MEMORY ROCK** offers a look at spectacular brain, pillar and star coral formations. Friendly fish and usually calm seas make this a favorite snorkeling and photo spot.

Dive Operator

UNEXSO, short for the Underwater Explorers Society, is world renowned for expert diver training and unusual underwater activities like the Dolphin Experience (see above) and Marine Identification Workshops, during which the resident naturalist will put you on a "first name basis" with dozens of marine creatures. Reliable dive gear rentals are available as are reef tours, video and still camera rentals, E-6 processing, and multiple dive packages. ☎ 800-992-DIVE for further information or write UNEXSO, Box F-2433, Freeport, Bahamas.

Accommodations

LUCAYAN BEACH RESORT & CASINO. This dive resort offers snorkeling and diving in the crystalline waters with UNEXSO. The rooms are luxurious. ☎ 1-800-992- DIVE or write to UNEXSO.

LONG ISLAND

Long Island, home of the Stella Maris dive community has long been revered as a mecca for reef explorers. It is the Bahamas' only island with significant high terrain. The island also boasts miles of snow white beaches, shallow reefs, drop-offs, crystal clear waters, and a profusion of marine life.

Best Dives of Long Island

☆☆☆☆☆**STELLA MARIS SHARK REEF.** This is one of the most exciting dives in the Bahamas... no snorkeling allowed! Upon entering the water, divers are greeted by 7 to 14 sharks, who stay with the divers for the entire dive. Among them are gray tipped reef sharks, bull sharks and a very tame nurse shark. A single hammer-head makes an occasional ap-

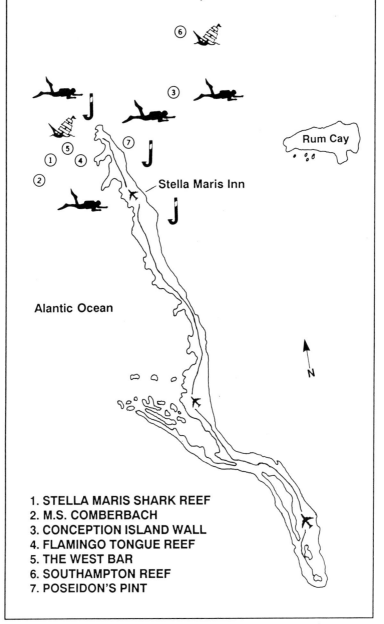

LONG ISLAND, Bahamas

Rum Cay

Stella Maris Inn

Alantic Ocean

N

1. STELLA MARIS SHARK REEF
2. M.S. COMBERBACH
3. CONCEPTION ISLAND WALL
4. FLAMINGO TONGUE REEF
5. THE WEST BAR
6. SOUTHAMPTON REEF
7. POSEIDON'S PINT

pearance. The drill is simply to sit still on the ocean floor and watch Stella Maris divemasters feed the sharks. The sharks stay in the "circus ring" but there are unmatched photo and video opportunities for the viewers. This is the only dive of its type in the Western Hemisphere. Divers are warned not to travel about during the dive nor visit the reef without the guides. Sea conditions are sometimes choppy. The depth is about 30 ft.

☆☆☆☆☆CAPE SANTA MARIA. This is a deep reef with a drop-off where the prime attraction is the wreck of *M.S. Comberbach*, a 103-ft steel freighter which had been especially prepared for safe diving before sinking. The hull is intact and sits upright on its keel so the interior can be easily explored. Located just one mile from shore. Recommended for experienced divers.

☆☆☆☆☆CONCEPTION ISLAND WALL. This is one of the most beautiful reefs in the Bahamas. Gigantic coral heads climb from a depth of 90 ft to 55 ft and the wall, which drops in straight ladder-steps, is covered with a lush carpet of corals and fantastic sponges. The site is just 300 ft from the beach. Conception Island is an underwater park and a bird and turtle breeding area.

☆☆☆FLAMINGO TONGUE REEF. This reef, which gets its name from the thousands of Flamingo Tongue shells along its bottom, is six miles from Stella Maris Marina and is within a half mile of the shore. It is a great spot for beginners since the reef is only 25 ft below the surface and the seas are almost always calm. Snorkeling is fairly good here.

Best Snorkeling and
Shallow Water Dives

☆☆☆**THE WEST BAR.** This is a lovely, pristine coral garden in the shape of a bar some 600 ft long and 300 ft wide. It is within half a mile of two beautiful beaches. The reef has a superb variety of brain and staghorn corals along with soft corals and towering pillar corals, all at a depth of 15 ft in the lee of the island. Visibility is excellent.

☆☆☆☆**SOUTHAMPTON REEF** is the site of a wrecked ocean freighter that sank some 80 years ago. The 300-ft hull has been flattened by time and the ebb and flow of water, yet it still offers dramatic photo possibilities. Prominent are huge engine boilers, the shaft, propellers, and anchors and lots of ship's debris. Thickets of elkhorn and staghorn surround the wreck, providing refuge for huge grouper, sleeping nurse sharks, and large parrotfish. The average depth is 25 ft. Sea conditions range from dead calm to rough. One drawback to this dive is the three-hour boat ride from Long Island (Stella Maris dock).

☆☆☆☆**POSEIDON'S PINT** is a beautiful snorkeling reef accessible from the beach or by boat (a three- or four-minute ride) from the Stella Maris docks. Access depends on the weather. The gardens sparkle with dramatic displays of massive brain, elkhorn, and staghorn coral. Eagle rays, sand rays, tarpon and crawfish are in residence here. Depths range from three to 30 ft.

Stella Maris Shark Reef

Dive Operators
and Accommodations

STELLA MARIS INN, the largest SCUBA resort on Long Island, offers rooms, cottages and luxury villas all situated high atop the hillcrest of the island's east shoreline and featuring breathtaking views of the ocean. The shoreline is rocky with several hiking paths which will bring you to secluded picnic and sunbathing areas. The dive operation is top-notch, offering guided reef and wreck tours. Non-divers and snorkelers get special attention too with a wide choice of beaches, cruises, and even a glass bottom boat. Great dive packages are available. ☎ 800-426-0466 or write to Stella Maris Inn, 750 SW 34th St, Suite 215, Ft. Lauderdale FL 33315.

NEW PROVIDENCE ISLAND

New Providence is the location of Nassau, the capital of the Bahamas, and Cable Beach and Paradise Island, two world-class beach resorts. This island offers casino gambling and a multitude of nightlife activities in addition to virgin reef diving and snorkeling. The island is best known as the sub-sea movie setting for Disney's *20,000 Leagues Beneath the Sea, Splash,* and *Cocoon,* and the James Bond thrillers, *Thunderball, Never Say Never, For Your Eyes Only* and most recently *Jaws IV.* Diving around New Providence offers steep walls, drop-offs, caves, shallow reefs, ocean holes, and wrecks.

Best Dives of New Providence

☆☆☆**THUNDERBALL REEF.** Named for the James Bond film, this beautiful shallow reef offers good visibility and a very photogenic setting for shallow water dives and snorkeling. It is a short boat ride from Athol Island. Although small in size this spot is alive with gorgonians, staghorn, and elkhorn corals. The reef is densely populated with tropicals, queen angels, lobsters and other small critters. Sea conditions are calm with little or no current. Depths 10 to 30 ft.

☆☆☆☆**GOULDINGS CAY.** Located off the west end of New Providence, this tiny island shelters a very pretty coral reef which was used as the setting for the films *Cocoon, Never Say Never, 20,000 Leagues Under the Sea* and *Splash.* The area encompasses several acres and offers both shallow snorkeling sites and deeper dives. Eagle rays, turtles, old wreck sections, schools of tropicals, morays, and acres of elkhorn make this a favorite dive area.

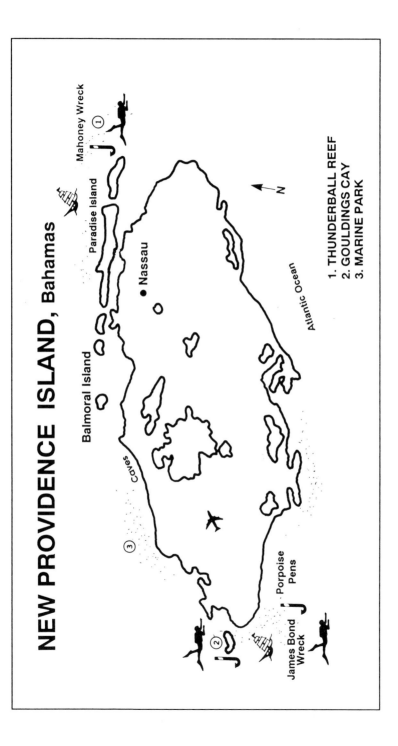

NEW PROVIDENCE ISLAND, Bahamas

Mahoney Wreck

Paradise Island

Nassau

Balmoral Island

Caves

Porpoise Pens

James Bond Wreck

Atlantic Ocean

N

1. THUNDERBALL REEF
2. GOULDINGS CAY
3. MARINE PARK

Dive Operators and Accommodations of Nassau

DIVI BAHAMAS BEACH RESORT . This new dive resort houses a spectacular new Peter Hughes dive operation which is located on South Ocean Beach at the West End of Nassau. ☎ 800-367-3484 in the (U.S.) or write Divi Resorts, 54 Gunderman Rd, Ithaca NY 14850.

SMUGGLER'S REST DIVE RESORT is a small resort offering comfortable cottages and a full service dive operation. Located on the south coast, its dive boats are within minutes of the barrier reefs off the west and southern shores.

SAN SALVADOR

Miles of virgin shallow reefs, walls and new wrecks are yet to be explored in the waters around San Salvador, truly one of the diving jewels of the Bahamas. It is so remote the sole dive resort on the island, Riding Rock Inn, points out that it is NOT IN SOUTH AMERICA in their promotional material. On the shore visitors delight in miles of white sand beaches including the site where Christopher Columbus first set foot in the New World. Most dive sites start between 35 and 40 ft. A wall runs the entire 12 miles on the leeward side of the island.

Dive Operator and Accommodations

RIDING ROCK INN offers divers all the comforts of home in a relaxed casual atmosphere. This plush resort has 24 air-conditioned double rooms, conference center, pool, restaurant, and marina. The dive shop is well equipped with daily E-6 film processing, equipment rentals and a friendly professional staff. The resort also has tennis and bicycling equipment for guests. ☎ 1-800-272-1492, 305-761-1492 or write to Out Island Service Company, Inc., 750 SW 34th St., Suite 206, Ft Lauderdale FL 33315.

Flamingo Tongue Reef

BAHAMAS LIVE-ABOARDS

BLACKBEARD'S CRUISES offer a relaxing week of sailing, snorkeling and diving among the Bahama Family Islands including one night ashore. Three 65-ft passenger sloops are available, each crewed by two captains, a first mate, dive instructor, cook and four deckhands. Guests choose single or double space bunks. Cabins are fully air conditioned. Dress is casual. Boarding in Miami. ☎ 1-800-327-9600 or 305-888-1226 or write to P.O. Box 66-1091, Miami Springs FL 33266.

***SEA FEVER* DIVING CRUISES** are tailored for diving the Bahamas. Captain Guarino hosts 22 divers to the Family Islands and remote cays. The *Sea Fever* is a 90-ft custom-hulled live-aboard. ☎ 1-800-44-FEVER or 305-531-DIVE or write: Captain Tom Guarino, P.O. Box 39-8276, Miami Beach, FL 33139.

***BOTTOM TIME* ADVENTURES** operates two first-class floating dive resorts, *The Bottom Time I*, a 65-ft motor yacht and *The Bottom Time II,* an 86-ft Catamaran. Tours visit remote out-island destinations as well as familiar dive spots. ☎ 800-345-DIVE or 305-561-0111 or write: P.O. Box 11919, Fort Lauderdale FL 33339.

FACTS.

RECOMPRESSION CHAMBER. Located on Grand Bahama Island.

GETTING THERE. Several direct and connecting flights to Nassau and Freeport are scheduled daily from U.S. gateway cities by Bahamsair, Piedmont, Eastern, Pan Am, or United Airlines. Air Canada operates from Toronto and Montreal, Air Jamaica from Chicago and Toronto. Daily flights are also available from other Caribbean islands, Great Britain, and Europe.

Bahamasair flies from Nassau to Andros, Abacos, Eleuthera and Exuma daily. Chalk's International serves Paradise Island, Bimini and Cat Cay from Florida daily.

PRIVATE PLANES. Airstrips serving light planes are scattered throughout the Bahamas. Private aircraft pilots are required to obtain a cruising permit before entering Bahamas airspace and should contact the Bahamas Private Pilot Briefing Center at ☎800-327-3853. Excellent plotting services and charts are also available through AOPA, 421 Aviation Way, Frederick MD.

DRIVING. On the left. If you drive a motor scooter a helmet is required.

DOCUMENTS. United States law now requires citizens to carry a current passport to re-enter the U.S. To enter the Bahamas U.S. citizens and Canadians need proof of citizenship and a return ticket.

CUSTOMS. Under current (United States) regulations, each visitor is allowed to return home with up to $400 worth of merchandise duty free, provided the resident has been out of the United States for at least 48 hours and has not claimed the exemption within 30 days. A flat duty of 10 percent is levied on goods valued over $400. Each adult may bring back 200 cigarettes, 50 cigars or one quart of alcohol duty free. Purchases costing up to $25 are exempt. Canadians may take home $100 worth of purchases duty free after 48 hours and up to $300 worth of goods after seven days. Each person leaving the Bahamas must pay a $5 departure tax. Children under the age of 2 are exempt.

VACCINATIONS. Vaccinations certifications for smallpox and cholera are needed for persons coming from an endemic area.

CURRENCY. The Bahamian dollar is the monetary equivalent of the U.S. dollar. The $3 Bahamian bill, square 15 cent pieces and fluted 10 cent pieces are popular among souvenir hunters.

CLIMATE. Average year round temperatures range from 70 to 85 ° F. The rainy season lasts from early June through late October. Islands toward the south end of the arc have warmer weather.

CLOTHING. Casual. A light jacket or sweater is needed in the evening, especially during winter months. You may want to dress up in the evening for some hotels, restaurants, and casinos in Nassau and Freeport. The Family Islands are very casual.

TIME ZONE. Eastern Standard. Daylight Saving Time is also used during the summer months to coincide with the eastern U.S.

ELECTRICITY. 120 volts AC. No adaptors necessary for U.S. electrical products.

SERVICE CHARGES. The standard tip is 15 percent. Some hotels and resorts add a service charge to cover gratuities.

RELIGIOUS SERVICES. Houses of worship of many faiths minister to visitors and Bahamians. Check with your hotel for individual island churches.

ADDITIONAL INFORMATION. Write to The Bahamas Tourist Office, 255 Alhambra Circle, Suite 415, Coral Gables FL 33134 or telephone the Bahamas Sports and Aviation Centre ☎ 1-800-32-SPORT.

BARBADOS

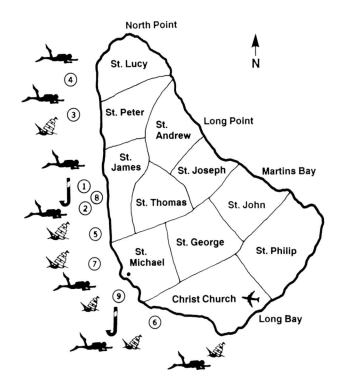

1. DOTTINS REEF
2. SANDY LANE
3. THE PAMIR
4. BRIGHT LEDGE
5. THE STAVRONIKITA
6. FRIARS CRAIG
7. BELL BUOY
8. FOLKESTONE PARK
9. THE BERWYN

BARBADOS

Barbados is a tiny island just 21 miles long by 14 miles wide rising bravely from the floor of the Caribbean Sea about 300 miles from Venezuela. It is the farthest east and the most isolated of the West Indian islands.

Set amidst this visual feast are first-rate dive resorts, vibrant nightlife, duty free shopping, and a full range of delightful dining spots. A well rounded selection of water sports and other leisure-time activities makes Barbados a best choice for couples and families.

Divers, both novice and experienced, are advised to visit Barbados between April and November when you can expect fabulous visibility on the barrier reef and calm seas. This all changes from December through March. A "North Swell" decreases visibility near the shore and to some degree on the outer reefs.

During Spring, Summer and Fall the island's shallow shipwrecks offer a multitude of dive experiences. Most of the best wrecks are found on the offshore barrier reef which extends along Barbados' windward or western coast.

Although visibility is best on the barrier reef, Barbados offers snorkelers miles of white powder sand beaches, and shore access coves with a wide range of corals and friendly fish.

Area Contributors: Dave Farmer, divemaster at Dive Barbados and Jolly Roger Watersports, Bridgetown Harbor; Michael Young, Peter Hughes Diving, Divi Southwinds; and Jeffrey Krames, BDWH.

Independence Arch, Bridgetown

Best Dives of Barbados

☆☆☆☆☆**DOTTIN'S REEF.** Located a half mile off the coast of St. James Parish on the west coast, Dottin's Reef drifts along the shore from St. James to Bridgetown. It is considered to be the prettiest reef in Barbados. Visibility is generally 100 ft. Coral canyons and walls average 65 ft in depth with some drop-offs to 130 ft. Calm seas.

☆☆☆**SANDY LANE.** This is a deeper area off Dottin's Reef, generally done as a drift dive. Walls drop to a maximum depth of 90 ft. The reef, bristling with coral heads and dotted with sponges, is also very pretty here. There are some large fish, coral heads and sponges. For experienced divers only.

☆☆☆WRECK OF THE *PAMIR*. This 150-ft ship was sunk in 30 ft of water by the dive shop operators of Barbados to form an artificial reef. Located just 200 yds off shore, it is easily accessible from the beach and is very open and uncluttered. It is habitat to swarms of small fish. The superstructure of the ship breaks the surface so it can also be visited by snorkelers. Dive operators request no spear fishing or collecting. An excellent dive for novices.

☆☆☆BRIGHT LEDGE is a reef dive on the northernmost end of the west shore. The reef is very narrow with deep water on either side and for this reason is not suitable for novices but is generally a safe dive. Average depth is 60 ft. The area is particularly good for photography. Because the reef is about three fourths of a mile off shore, you'll encounter some very large fish, turtles and rays.

☆☆☆WRECK OF THE *STAVRONIKITA*. To create an artificial reef, this 360-ft freighter, *Stavronikita*, was sunk by the government. The ship was gutted by fire ten years ago and had to be towed in from the open sea. The hull sits in 130 ft of water, the deck at 80 ft. Although the depth discourages most novice ocean explorers, the wreck is quite beautiful and has become a haven for fish making it very appealing to underwater photographers. Nearby in shallow water lie the *Conimara,* an old P.T. boat and the *Lord Combermere*, an old tug boat—both in 30-40 ft of water. Visibility varies. Good photo opportunities abound here as well. The wrecks can be reached from the shore after a 600-yd swim.

☆☆**FRIARS CRAIG** is a good dive for the novice although strong current may be occasionally encountered. This is another purposely sunken wreck. It lies in just 60 ft of water with the bridge at 30 ft, making it somewhat more accessible than the *Stavronikita*. A short 600-yd swim from the southwest corner of Christ Church Parish will put you over the wreck and an adjacent reef, Castle Bank. Exercise extreme caution and check the current before diving.

☆☆☆**BELL BUOY** is a popular reef dive. Located just off St. Michael's Parish on the southwest end of the island, the reef has varied depths with some areas where a wall drops off from 40 to 70 ft. Explorers will find some nice large brain coral heads as well as thickets of staghorn, sea fans and sponges here.

Diving Barbados

Best Snorkeling Sites of Barbados

☆☆☆**FOLKESTONE PARK** is the favorite snorkeling site in Barbados. This area is quite pretty and is teeming with tame fish. An underwater trail has been marked around the inshore reef. It is also the favorite area for boaters and jet skiers so the swimming and snorkeling area has been roped off to insure safety. The sandy beach here, with a coral reef on either side, is quiet and pleasant. A 200-yd swim will take you to a raft anchored over the wreckage of a small barge sitting in 20 ft of water.

☆☆☆**WRECK OF THE *BERWYN*.** This old French tug boat, which is totally encrusted with coral and loaded with small creatures such as sea horses and frogfish, is a favored snorkeling photo site. It sits in Carlisle Bay on the southern end of the island's west coast and the visibility is good and sea conditions very calm. The wreck is 200 yds from shore. The bottom is flat and sandy.

Dive Operators

Dive shops offering snorkeling and diving trips are located along the west shores.

DIVE BARBADOS has locations at both Jolly Roger WatersportsCenters in St. James parish. Dave Farmer, BDWH contributor, is Divemaster. ☎ 809-436-6424 or 809-428- 9033.

EXPLORESUB is located in a small cove on the edge of the Divi Southwinds Beach Hotel property on the southwest coast of the island.
    Divemaster Michael Seale offers personalized reef and wreck tours for groups and individuals. Resort courses. St. Lawrence Gap, ☎ 809-428-3504. After 6, 428-4465.

Barbados flying fish, found only in the waters of Barbados

ADDITIONAL DIVE SHOPS from north to south are **HEY-WOODS**, in St. Peter Parish, **BLUE REEF WATERSPORTS** at the Glitter Bay Hotel in St. James ☎ 809-422-3133, **LES WOTTON DIVING SCHOOL & WATERSPORTS** in Black Rock, St. Michael ☎809-422-3215, **SANDY LANE WATERSPORTS. VILLAGE WATERSPORTS, WILLIES WATERSPORTS**, St. Michael ☎ 809-425-1060.

Accommodations

Most hotels and nightlife are found on the south and central western coast of the island.

DIVI SOUTHWINDS BEACH HOTEL sits on a half-mile of white sand beach near the St. Lawrence Gap. It is surrounded by 20 acres of tropical gardens and features 166 guestrooms. ☎ 800-367-3484, 607-277-3484, or write Divi St. James, 520 W. State St, Ithaca NY 14850.

DIVI ST. JAMES is a luxury resort for adults (16-up) only. Features are 131 air conditioned guestrooms and suites with ocean or pool views. Gourmet meals are served at Sand Dollar, an elegant beach side restaurant; refreshments are offered at a swim-up bar adjacent to the twin pools. ☎ 800-367-3484, 607-277-3484 or write 520 W. State St., Ithaca NY 14850.

CORAL REEF is a luxury beachfront resort with its own dive shop (Les Wooten's Watersports) and featuring a nice pool, shops, and gardens. Reserve through your travel agent.

FOR APARTMENTS, AND HOME RENTALS contact VILLAS AND APARTMENTS ABROAD, 444 Madison Ave., NY NY 10022. ☎ 212-759-1025.

Sightseeing

Ride on an electric tram into Harrison's Cave to explore beautiful underground water falls, Mirror Lake and The Rotunda Room where the walls of the 250-ft chamber glitter like diamonds or view exotic tropical birds and native monkeys at the Wildlife Reserve at Farley Hill, St. Peter. History buffs will delight in finding 17th-century military relics like antique cannons and signal towers all around the island.

Dining

West Indian specialties and native seafood dishes like grilled flying fish and lobster are featured throughout the island. Restaurants range from small home front rooms to large luxury hotel dining rooms.

JOSEF'S, located in the St. Lawrence area, serves fabulous gourmet fish in a grand native home setting. ☎ 809-428-3379.

FOLKSTONE RESTAURANT AND BAR offers casual beach-side dining at very affordable prices. Located at the Folkstone Park in St. James.

GIGGLES BEACH BAR, north of Folkstone Park, is a great place to unwind after the dive.☎ 809- 422-5643.

PISCES RESTAURANT located in the St. Lawrence Gap is noted for West Indian specialties and fabulous rum pie. ☎ 809-428-6558.

Creole cuisine lovers be sure to try the **BROWN SUGAR RESTAURANT** in St. Michael. ☎ 809-426- 7684.

FACTS

RECOMPRESSION CHAMBER. Located in St. Annes Fort, St. Michael. Contact Dr. Brown or Major Gittens at ☎ 436- 6185.

GETTING THERE. British West Indian Airlines (BWIA) offer regular service from London, New York, Miami, Boston, Baltimore and Toronto. American Airlines from New York. Caribbean Airways serves London, Frankfurt, Brussels with connections to St. Lucia. Barbados' Grantley Adams International Airport is modern and well kept. Steamship services are Moore-McCormack, Holt and Harrison, Alcoa, and French Lines.

ISLAND TRANSPORTATION. Taxi service is available throughout the island. Note: cab fares should be negotiated before accepting service. Auto rental: Avis—airport; Budget—St. Michael; Hertz—airport; National—St. Michael. Motorbikes may be rented from Jumbo Vehicles ☎ 426-5689.

DRIVING. Traffic keeps to the left in Barbados

DOCUMENTS. Canadian and U.S. citizens require a birth certificate or passport and return ticket in order to enter Barbados. Entry documentation is good for six months.

CUSTOMS. Personal effects of visitors, including cameras and sports equipment, enter duty free. Returning U.S. citizens may take back free of duty articles costing a total of $400 U.S., providing the stay has exceeded 48 hours in length and that the exemption has not been used within the preceding 30 days. One quart of spirits per person (over 21 years) may be carried out duty free. Canadians may claim up to $100 Can. each calendar quarter. After seven days they may claim up to $300 Can.

CURRENCY. Barbados dollar (BD)= $1.98 U.S. BD = $1.43 CAN.

CLIMATE. Temperatures vary between 75° and 85° F. Average rainfall is 59 inches.

CLOTHING. Lightweight casual clothing is recommended. A jacket for men may be desirable for visiting nightclubs or dressy resort restaurants. Swim suits, bikinis and short shorts are not welcome in Bridgetown shops or banks.

ELECTRICITY. 110 AC, 50 cycles.

TIME. Atlantic Standard (EST + 1 hr.)

LANGUAGE. English with a local dialect.

TAXES. A 10 percent tip is added to the bill at most hotels. A sales tax of 5 percent is also added to hotel and restaurant bills.

RELIGIOUS SERVICES. Anglican, Baptist, Catholic, Methodist, Moravian, Seventh Day Adventist, Jehovah's Witnesses.

FOR ADDITIONAL INFORMATION: Barbados Board of Tourism, 800 Second Ave.,NY, NY 10017, ☎ 800-221-9831, Telex: 023-666-387.

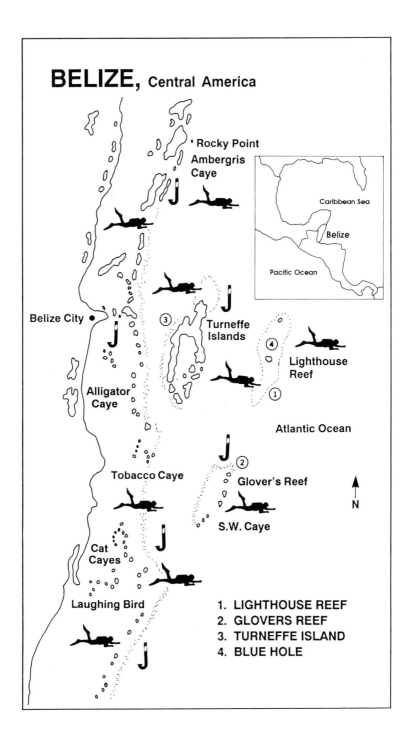

BELIZE

Until quite recently, almost no one knew about the spectacular diving off the islands and atolls of Belize. Today an ever increasing number of novice and accomplished divers are finding their way to this tropical wonderland. Here, only 2 1/2 hrs from the United States, they are discovering one of the finest diving areas in the world. Belize lies on the Caribbean coast of Central America between Guatemala and Mexico. Its 17,000 square miles include dense tropical jungles, a coastline of mangrove swamps, mountain ranges with peaks over 3500 ft and 266 square miles of offshore islands surrounded by dense coral reef. Although its accommodations and facilities are considered somewhat primitive by some (no TVs, automobiles or phones on most of the islands), Belize offers the intrepid visitor an exotic adventure exploring virgin reefs and uncharted islands and cayes. Many tours to Belize are labeled "expedition" rather than vacation.

The best time to visit Belize is during the dry season, from February to May.

Fabulous diving is found everywhere on the Barrier Reef which stretches 175 miles, the entire length of the coast. Then there are three fantastic atolls that provide another 180 miles of living reef.

Area Contributor: Tommy T. Thomson. Reproduced in part, with permission, from *Belize Currents Newsletter*.

East of Belize City and beyond the barrier reef lie the Turneffe Islands, a large group of low islands bordered with thick growths of mangroves. They are very close together and at some points are joined by stands of mangrove. Diving is excellent, considered by many to be better than the diving off the barrier reef, because of the clarity of the water and abundance and diversity of marine life.

South of the Turneffe Islands is Glover's Reef, formed by coral growing around the edges of a steep limestone plateau. The result of eons of growth, it is a spectacular diving spot with more than 25 coral species to be explored and walls of fish to watch.

Further east and to the north is Lighthouse Reef, the outermost of the offshore islands within the Belize cruising area. It is a circular reef system featuring several islands and small cayes. Half Moon Caye National Monument, a nature preserve and bird sanctuary, is a beautiful spot made even more beautiful by a charming old lighthouse. Near the center of Lighthouse Reef is the Blue Hole.

Historically speaking, Belize is widely accepted as the birthplace of the culture that culminated in the classic Mayan Civilization. It was a major trading center for the entire Mayan area. The traveler interested in this culture will find pre-Columbian treasures everywhere.

Best Dives of Belize

☆☆☆☆☆THE BARRIER REEF. Diving along the main barrier reef is confined mostly to the massive canyons formed by large ridges of coral rising from a sandy bottom that slopes downward. These canyons are found outside the reef at depths of 50 to 100 ft. The reef is usually no more than 3/4 of a mile from the shore line of the cayes.

Belize sunset

Diver on Barrier Reef

The canyons are filled with caves and tunnels teeming with life. Schools of snapper, grouper and nurse sharks are quite common. The occasional hammerhead or blacktip shark gives divers a thrill.

The abundance of other marine life along the main barrier reef is remarkable. It is not unusual to see a school of porpoises or huge turtles. The spotted eagle ray is often seen in groups of three or four while the rare mantas usually travel alone.

Schools of amber jack and lone barracudas commonly swim in the open water away from the coral. Morays are found in all areas of the reef.

THE ATOLLS. The diving off Lighthouse Reef, Glover's Reef, and Turneffe Island is spectacular. The reefs are in a practically virgin state, and visibility is over 150 ft. The atolls stand over vertical shafts of rock and coral that drop dramatically to a depth of 4,000 ft. The coral walls that encircle them are almost completely vertical and awesome to see. The tops of these walls begin in only 30 ft of water.

The sea life is even more varied and beautiful than that along the barrier reef. Groupers, snapper and hogfish of tremendous size seem almost tame. The coral growth is as phenomenal as it is varied. Basket sponges are big enough to sit in; gorgonians are everywhere; tube sponges grow to over three ft; and there are thick growths of black coral.

☆☆☆☆**THE BLUE HOLE.** From the air it looks like an apparition. The cobalt blue of the Caribbean abruptly changes to an azure blue circle. The heart of the circle is an indigo blue. It is the Blue Hole of Belize.

The Blue Hole is located in the Lighthouse Reef Formation about 40 miles off the coast of Belize. It is an almost perfect circle, 1,000 ft in diameter in the midst of a reef six to 18 ft below the surface of the Caribbean. Inside the shallow reef, the walls drop suddenly to a depth of 412 ft, almost completely vertical for the first 125 ft. Here they turn inward and slightly upward. Before you is an awesome underwater "cathedral" with alcoves, archways and columns. What you see is a huge now-submerged cave with 12- to 15-ft stalactites hanging from the ceiling. This is a sight that few have had the opportunity to experience.

A WORD OF CAUTION... THIS IS A DECOMPRESSION DIVE. EXPERIENCED DIVERS ONLY !! Nearest chamber is in Miami.

Best Snorkeling

Good snorkeling can be found in many areas of the barrier reef. Our vote for the best is around Glovers Reef where you'll find an immense lagoon sparkling with multi-hued corals beneath a rainbow of reef fish.

Dive Operators and Accommodations

Most of the dive resorts and inns are located on Ambergris Caye, a 15-minute plane ride from the International Airport. San Pedro, the only town on Ambergris Caye, is intriguing to those looking for an exotic, off-the-beaten-path hide-away.

RAMON'S REEF RESORT is located in San Pedro, Ambergris Caye and offers 20 private thatched-roof bungalows, furnished with double beds and full baths.

For reservations ☎ 601-693-1304 or write P.O. Box 448, Meridian, MS 39301.

VICTORIA HOUSE, a beachfront resort located on Ambergris, is somewhat more elegant than Ramon's Reef Resort, and more expensive. ☎ 713-529-6800; local 026-2071; or write to Victoria House, Ambergris Caye, Belize, Central America.

PARADISE HOTEL is at the north end of San Pedro village and features a relaxing tropical atmosphere. Rooms have ceiling fans, air conditioning, TV and kitchenettes. Restaurant. Local ☎ 026-2083.

THE PYRAMID ISLAND RESORT sits on Caye Chapel, a three-mile, privately owned island rimmed with miles of beautiful white beaches all lined with towering palm trees. This hotel offers 32 beachfront air-conditioned rooms each with private bath, two villas, a full service marina on the leeward side, and a fantastic circular restaurant and bar where you can see the coral reef. ☎ (U.S.) 1-800-325-3401 or 606-329-2660; radio VHF 14-6500/Marine Bank 68; telex 371 255 PRICO; or write P.O. Box 192, Belize City, Belize, or P.O. Box 1545, Ashland KY 41101.

ST. GEORGE'S LODGE is the only commercial establishment on St. George's Caye. The lodge, which is beautifully handcrafted of exquisite local hardwoods, houses the dining room, a rosewood bar, secluded sundeck and 12 private rooms cooled by tradewinds. Book through your travel agent or write (airmail) St. George's Lodge, P.O. Box 625, Belize City, Belize, Central America. Allow two to three weeks for a response.

TURNEFFE ISLAND LODGE is the ultimate outpost for divers. Not for everyone, this lodge accommodates 16 guests in quaint bungalows with private baths and showers. No phones. It is a private resort, American-owned and operated, located approximately 30 miles from Belize City. The entire island is

Big eye snapper

Grouper

surrounded by a sheer coral wall that starts at 40 ft and drops to 2,000 ft in some places. On shore are miles of sandy beaches. ☎ 1-800-338-8149 or 904-641-4468. Write to 11904 Hidden Hills Drive, Jacksonville FL 32225.

Expeditions

INTERNATIONAL EXPEDITIONS INC. offers custom guided trips for the naturalist to the Belize Barrier Reef. Tours are well organized to consider both skilled diver and novice snorkeler. ☎ 800-633-4734 or 205-870-5550; write to Suite 104, 1776 Independence Court, Birmingham AL 35216.

Belize Live-Aboards

CORAL BAY is a 58-ft motor yacht customized for divers featuring comfortable quarters for six passengers and three crew members. Two of the three passenger cabins have private

bath and showers. Bookings are predominantly charters. Air conditioning. ☎ 1-800-DIV-XPRT, 512-854-0247 or write to See & Sea at 50 Francisco St. Suite 205, San Francisco CA 94133.

BELIZE AGGRESSOR is a 100-ft luxury yacht expertly outfitted for diving Lighthouse Reef, yet offers all the amenities of a dive resort: air-conditioned private rooms, photo shop, E-6

Heliconia

film processing, mini movie theater, plus fast cruising speeds. ☎ 1-800-348-2628 or write See & Sea Travel, 50 Francisco St., Suite 205, San Francisco CA 94133. Telex 278036 Seas UR.

AQUANAUT EXPLORER is a new addition to the Sea & See live-aboard fleet. This 160-ft luxury yacht combines all the features of a small cruise ship and a dive boat for up to 40 passengers. Private cabins each have a private bath with hot shower. Beside 24-hr diving facilities the ship features a casino, jacuzzi, and casual dining salon. ☎ 1-800- DIV-XPERT or write See & Sea at 50 Francisco St. Suite 205, San Francisco CA 94133.

Sightseeing

Belize's best dive resorts are located on the offshore islands where sightseeing is limited to the beaches and lagoons and, of course, the reef. However day trips can easily be arranged to the Mayan ruins and the Belize Zoo. Visitors arriving in Belize City are best advised NOT to tour the inner city on foot as drugs are openly sold on the streets, and tourists sporting cameras, jewelry, or flashing money around may attract undesirable attention. By contrast the islands are lovely, sparsely populated and enjoyably safe.

Complete long and short expeditions into the rugged countryside, mountains, plateaus, and jungles of Belize can be arranged through Tropical Travel, 720 Worthshire, Houston, TX 77008, ☎ 1-800-451-8017 or International Expeditions, Suite 104, 1776 Independence Court, Birmingham AL 35216, ☎ 1-800-633-4734.

A complete listing of land tours and facilities can be found in *Belize, The Grand Tour*, available at the Belize City Book Store or by writing to Robert Nicolait & Associates Ltd., PO Box 785, Belize City, Belize ($10 U.S.).

Dining

Divers staying on Ambergris Caye, the main diver island, will find restaurants in the village of San Pedro offering fresh

Spotted trunk fish

seafood and local dishes. Chinese food is also extremely popular in Belize and can be enjoyed at The Jade Garden in the Barrier Reef Hotel on Ambergris Caye. Meals average about $10 U.S. per person.

FACTS

RECOMPRESSION CHAMBER. Nearest recompression chamber: Miami.

GETTING THERE. Fly Tan/Sasha, the Honduran airline; Taca, the El Salvadorian airline, from Miami or Continental Airlines from Houston to Belize. Interisland flights are available on Maya Airways to Caye Chapel and San Pedro.

TRANSPORTATION. Bus service around Belize City is readily available. Since there are few cars on the islands,transportation is usually arranged by the resort. On the mainland reservations can be made through National Car Rental. Reserve prior to trip. Jeeps and four wheel drive vehicles are mandatory on back roads. Avoid local car rental companies.

ENTRY REQUIREMENTS. Visitors arriving by air must hold a return or onward ticket and a valid passport and must have sufficient funds for the length of their stay. Vehicles entering Belize must have third party insurance, available at either border.

DEPARTURE TAX. U.S. $13.

CUSTOMS. Personal effects can be brought in without difficulty. Import allowances include 200 cigarettes or 1/2 lb tobacco, 20 fluid oz of spirits and one bottle of perfume for personal use. Note: removing and exporting coral or archaeological artifacts is prohibited. Picking orchids in forest reserves is illegal.

CURRENCY. Belize dollar = $.50 U.S.

CLIMATE. Belize has a sub-tropical, humid climate. Average temperature 79° F. The rainy season is from September to December. Hurricanes form during late summer. Best time to visit is February through May.

CLOTHING. Bring lightweight clothing with long sleeves to protect against sunburn and a light sweater for evening wear. The dive resorts are extremely casual. Leave dress wear at home.

For those who want to combine an expedition into the jungle with their diving vacation it is a good idea to check with the tour company. Bring mosquito repellent.

GEAR. Diver's rental equipment is limited in Belize so be sure to bring all of your own personal equipment. The resorts do supply weights and tanks, but little else.

ELECTRICITY. 110/220v 60 cycles. Most island resorts run on generators which are out of service for at least part of the day.

TIME. Central Standard Time.

LANGUAGE. English.

TAXES. 10 percent hotel service charge.

ADDITIONAL INFORMATION. Belize Tourist Board, P.O. Box 325, Belize City, Belize, Central America or Tropical Travel, 720 Worthshire, Houston TX 77008. ☎ 1-800-451-8017.

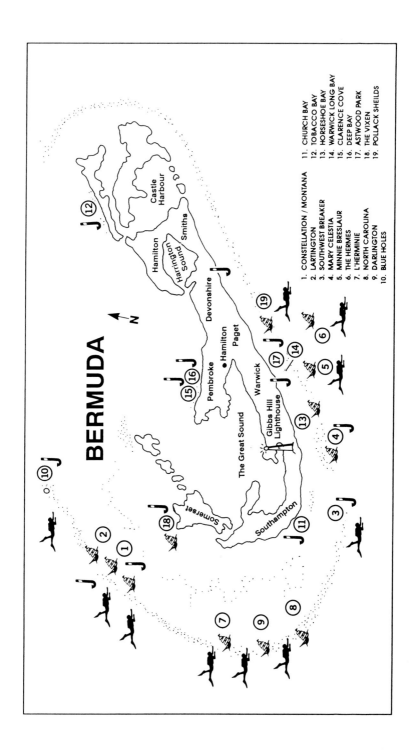

BERMUDA

1. CONSTELLATION / MONTANA
2. LARTINGTON
3. SOUTHWEST BREAKER
4. MARY CELESTIA
5. MINNIE BRESLAUR
6. THE HERMES
7. L'HERMINIE
8. NORTH CAROLINA
9. DARLINGTON
10. BLUE HOLES
11. CHURCH BAY
12. TOBACCO BAY
13. HORSESHOE BAY
14. WARWICK LONG BAY
15. CLARENCE COVE
16. DEEP BAY
17. ASTWOOD PARK
18. THE VIXEN
19. POLLACK SHEILDS

BERMUDA

Sitting hundreds of miles from anywhere, or more precisely 570 miles off the coast of North Carolina, Britain's oldest colony is known for its natural beauty. Everyone who's been to Bermuda understands why Mark Twain once wrote: "Americans on their way to heaven call at Bermuda and think they've arrived".

The expansive barrier reef system surrounding Bermuda is one of the largest fringing reef systems in the entire world. Three centuries of sunken ships lie at rest in Bermuda's briny deeps. The natural beauty of this tiny island, both above and below the sea is well guarded by preservation laws. Visitors are often surprised to find a noticeable lack of neon signs, parking meters, skyscrapers or fast-food strips. Many areas of the island have been kept exactly the same as when the first shipwrecked settlers arrived. The quality of life is high in Bermuda—no pollution, no unemployment and no illiteracy.

April through November is the season for divers to visit Bermuda. Most dive and snorkel cruise operators close up between November and April. In summer, the waters of the Gulf Stream's reach as high as 85°. During the winter the main flow of this warm water moves away from Bermuda, causing local temperatures to drop as low as 55°. This cold spell prohibits the growth of the more delicate corals and sponges seen

Area Contributor: Divemaster John J. Buckley (Skin Diving Adventures, Ltd & Blue Water Divers, Southampton) has researched and prepared the diving material and map of Bermuda.

Parasailing in Bermuda

elsewhere in the Caribbean, but Bermuda's reef system is populated with the heartier of the corals, such as brain, star, sea fans, soft corals and pillar corals and some long purple tube sponges.

The Shipwrecks of Bermuda

The Bermuda Government has a special department devoted strictly to shipwrecks, "The Receiver of Wrecks". This department is responsible for issuing licenses to individuals for the excavation of newly discovered shipwreck sites in Bermuda waters. Despite numerous safety precautions there are still occasional shipwrecks on Bermuda's reefs.

The Government officially acknowledges the existence of as many as 400 wrecks. These have been charted, more or less identified, properly worked, and most of them left alone. Some of the older and more historically important wrecks are protected sites, and divers are forbidden to visit these wrecks.

Best Dives of Bermuda

☆☆☆☆☆*CONSTELLATION/MONTANA.* Located a few miles off the northwestern coast of Bermuda, these two ships sank on exactly the same site, although 80 years apart. The *Montana* was an iron hulled ship; a great deal of her hull and boilers are remarkably intact and make for an excellent dive. Numerous reef fish and some rather large barracuda make the *Montana*, also known as the *Nola, Gloria* and *Paramount*, their home. Literally overlapping the *Montana* is the remains of the *Constellation*. This four masted, wooden hulled schooner carried 90,000 lbs of cement which, when washed with seawater, solidified into concrete and so remains to this very day. The *Constellation* is often referred to as the "Dime Store Wreck" because of the wide variety of artifacts that can be recovered. After a good healthy dig on the *Constellation*, a diver might think he had been diving at Woolworth's. She was carrying cut glass, china, Yo Yo's, 78 rpm records by RCA, radios, religious artifacts, and at least eight different types of drug ampules, which provided Peter Benchley with the premise for *The Deep*. This is a very enjoyable dive and all in 30 ft of water. The site is about five miles offshore. Areas of the reef are as shallow as 15 ft. The sea conditions vary with the wind direction and speed. Bottles and artifacts may be taken from the *Constellation*.

☆☆☆☆*LARTINGTON.* Listed for all time on the Bermuda wreck chart as an unidentified 19th-century wreck, the *Lartington* was often referred to as the *Nola*, until one of Skin Diving Adventures young divemasters discovered her name under the port side of her partially intact bow. The *Lartington's* saturation steam boilers are visible amidships and, at the stern, the drive shaft and propeller. The steering controls located on the fantail are now well encrusted with over 100 years of coral growth. The bow, partially destroyed, lies a few feet above the 30-ft-deep sand bottom. There is an air pocket inside the bow, but it is oxygen poor, so breathing in is definitely taboo.

☆☆☆**SOUTHWEST BREAKER.** This massive breaking reef, the cause of at least one wreck along Bermuda's south shore, rises from a 30-ft bottom and actually protrudes through the surface, casting up considerable white water even on the calmest days. Through the center of the breaker is a massive tunnel. often occupied by one or two black grouper and a resident barracuda. The surrounding reef is very colorful and appears quite lush with many smaller non-breaking heads. These are carved with numerous ledges and caves.

Wreck dive

☆☆☆*MARY CELESTIA*. After making at least five round trips to Wilmington, NC successfully, running the Northern blockade of Confederate ports, the *Mary Celestia* ran aground on the "Blind Breakers" and sank on September 6, 1864, only nine months after her sister ship, the *Montana* was wrecked on the Northern Reefs. The story, as reported in the *Royal Gazette* a week later, states that her captain, knowing the waters of Bermuda, warned the navigator of the breakers. The navigator remarked with a certain surety, "I know these waters like I know my own house!" He apparently hadn't spent much time at home, for within minutes the *Mary Celestia* struck bottom.

Today, the *Mary* sits quietly in just shy of 60 ft of water as if she were still steaming along. More than 120 years' accumulation of sand covers most of her hull, but her two rectangular steam boilers and engine machinery lie upright and perfectly visible. One of her twin paddle wheels stands upright, with the other lying on it's back next to the boilers. The entire wreck is surrounded by a high reef, honeycombed with caverns, canyons and cuts that open onto the sand bottom. The reef which starts at 15 ft and drops off to 60 ft is lush with hard and soft corals. Surface swells are common to this area.

☆☆*MINNIE BRESLAUR*. This was a British merchant ship that sank in the 1870's after striking Southwest Breaker. Her stern lies in a sand pocket in 70 ft of water with her bow pointing out to sea, totally collapsed on a flat coral reef at 40 ft. Her midships section, steam boilers and engine mechanism lie angled upward from the sand bottom at 70 ft to the flat reef top in 40 ft. Several old torpedo-shaped bottles, Belfast and marble bottles (made by pinching the neck around a clear marble) have been recovered from her hull, and several small black coral trees can be found on the site, with one growing right above the propeller on the stern of the wreck. Visiting the *Minnie Breslaur* requires some previous diving experience. Large surface swells are generally encountered at this location.

☆☆☆**THE *HERMES*** is the closest to a Walt Disney image of a shipwreck that can be found in Bermuda waters. She was intentionally sunk as a dive site in May, 1985, by the Bermuda Diving Association, with much of the work that had gone into her cleaning and final sinking performed by Ross Mensis, co-owner of one of Bermuda's diving operations. Her sinking was perfect and she presently sits on the bottom as if she were still steaming along. Her stern has been wedged into a gap between two large coral mounds, her bottom sitting at 80 ft, her deck at 50 ft and her mast structure still intact in less than 20 ft of water. The *Hermes* is 167 ft long. A surface swell is to be expected here, but generally does not affect underwater conditions. Some SCUBA experience recommended.

☆☆*L'HERMINIE* sank on a flat calm day in 1838. This huge French ship of the line was lumbering along in the doldrums with her crew of 500 returning to France after seeing action against Maxmillian in Mexico. She ground to a halt on the very shallow flats of Bermuda's western ledge. The reef in this area is rather bland, visibility is rarely in excess of 60 to 80 ft, and the water always has a slightly greenish tone, but it is a very exciting dive! Even though this site was thoroughly worked by three of Bermuda's finest wreck hunters, it still boasts over 30 cannon, easily visible atop the sand or reef. Divers occasionally discover very valuable artifacts from *L'Herminie*, such as a pair of matching black glass rum bottles, embossed across the bottom "H. Ricketts Bristol", a major bottle maker of that time. Another amazing find was a clear glass figural bottle in the form of a maiden with a water jug above her head.

☆☆☆*NORTH CAROLINA.* This late 19th-century wreck is still pretty much intact although broken into two distinct sections. The bow section is perhaps one of the eeriest pieces of

Snorkeling in Bermuda

wreckage ever dived. Her bowsprit looms rather menacingly, covered with algae and rustcicles; the sides of her hull hold the riggings for her sail fittings, called dead-eyes due to their resemblance to the death's head—two holes for the eye sockets and a third that represents the mouth. Given the silt and murkiness of the water in that area, the *North Carolina* can be considered a little spooky. But for a very photogenic wreck, the *North Carolina* ranks high on the list. Maximum depth 45 ft.

☆☆*DARLINGTON*. Located off the western end of Southampton, this ship too sank in the 1870's, running straight into one of the most shallow stretches of reef in Bermuda—Long Bar. The *Darlington* was a sailing steamer. Her huge cylindrical steam boilers lie amidships with the stern pulpit rising to within three ft of the surface and making for an impressive photo in late afternoon. The *Darlington* lies in no more than 25 ft of water and is often done as a second dive with the *North Carolina* on a two tank dive trip.

Other notable reef and wreck sites include The Caves, Kevin's Wreck (probably the *Lord Donegal*, 1822, and featured in a Jacques Cousteau special); The Catacombs (the reefs behind the *Virginia Merchant* site, 1620, located off Warwick Long Bay on the South Shores, Smuggler's Notch and Champagne Breaker.

Best Snorkeling Sites

Bermuda's most fabulous snorkeling sites are offshore and require a boat for access. Snorkeling excursion tours to the sea gardens shown on the map are available through the operators listed below. Those who prefer snorkeling from the beach might try Church Bay, Horseshoe Bay, Warwick Long Bay, Astwood Park on the south shore, Gravelly Bay and Castle Island on the east end; Tobacco Bay on the north side of St. George's Island; and Clarence Cove and Deep Bay on the north shores. (See locator snorkels on map).

☆☆☆**BLUE HOLES.** Not to be confused with the real blue holes of the Bahamas or Belize, these are deep sand pockets surrounded by exceptionally shallow reef—in some places as shallow as four ft—which drops straight down into an iridescent teal blue, reaching a maximum depth of nearly 60 ft. The reef here is incredibly lush with sea fans, soft corals and black coral bushes. There are two holes directly adjacent to each other which are joined at the bottom by a series of tunnels where one can often find a school of huge tarpon. An occasional enormous (150-200 lb) grouper can also be found on the reefs. There are many of the colorful reef fish that inhabit all of Bermuda's dive sites. Exceptional visibility. The Blue Holes dive site is also recommended for novice divers.

Dive Operators of Bermuda

SKIN DIVING ADVENTURES. Co-owner and divemaster John J. Buckley knows all the best reef and wreck spots for SCUBA and snorkeling around Bermuda. This operation, located on the west end of the island, caters to the serious diver and offers two-tank dives for groups and individuals on the outer reefs and wrecks. Dive guides assist visiting divers in uncovering artifacts and collectibles around the wrecks. Snorkelers welcome. All equipment supplied. Night dives arranged by request. Fast boats carry up to 20 divers. Located in Robinson's Charter Boat Marina at Somerset Bridge . Open from early March to January. Local ☎ 809-234-1034; 809-234-1787.

NAUTILUS DIVING LTD. Located at the Southampton Princess Hotel, Nautilus Diving offers one-tank reef dives in the morning and a shallow wreck dive in the afternoon. Snorkelers welcome. ☎ 238-2332 or 238-8000 ext. 6073.

SOUTH SIDE SCUBA offers a resort course in the hotel pool then a shallow dive on the reefs. Includes all dive equipment. Local ☎ 298-1833; 236-0394 after 5 PM.

GROTTO DIVING, a part of South Side Scuba, is located at the Grotto Bay Beach Hotel. Grotto diving visits the reefs on

Helmet diving

the east end and south shores of Bermuda. Snorkelers are welcome. All diving and snorkeling equipment is provided to visitors. Local ☎ 293-2915; 236- 0394 after 5 PM.

Snorkeling Cruises

BERMUDA CRUISES, P.O. Box HM1572, Hamilton No. 5. ☎ 295-3727. Passengers are picked up from Albuoy's Point in Hamilton, the Princess Hotel dock and Darrell's Wharf. All equipment provided. Refreshments on return trip. Operates from the end of April to mid November.

BERMUDA WATER SPORTS, Grotto Bay Hotel, Hamilton Parish. ☎ 293-2640 or 293-8333 ext. 1938. Three-and-one-half-hour snorkel cruises aboard the *Sun Deck II.* Snorkeling instruction and equipment. May to November.

HAYWARD'S EXPLORER SNORKELING. Bermuda Island Cruises Ltd., Albuoy's Point, Front Street, Hamilton 5-31. ☎ 292-8652. The 48-ft glass-bottom *Explorer* leaves the Ferry Terminal in Hamilton. Bring swim suit and towels. Snorkeling gear provided. Snorkeling instruction. May to November.

PITMAN BOAT TOURS. Located at the Somerset Bridge Hotel dock, Somerset Bridge. ☎ 234-0700. Snorkeling and glass-bottom boat trips. No children under 5 years.

SALT KETTLE BOAT RENTALS LTD. Salt Kettle, Paget. ☎ 236-4863 or 236-3612. Snorkeling cruises to the western barrier reef. Refreshments.

TOBACCO BAY BEACH HOUSE. Tobacco Bay, St. George's. ☎ 293- 9711. Snorkeling and underwater cameras for rent. Ideal for beginners.

HELMET DIVING. This is fun for non-diving companions of all ages. No lessons needed. Depth 10 to 14 ft. Does not get your hair wet. Available at Hartley's Helmet, Flatt's Village Smith's ☎ 292-4434 or Hartley's Under Sea Adventure, Village Inn dock, Somerset. ☎ 234-2861.

Accommodations

Visitor accommodations range from luxurious resorts to simple and tasteful housekeeping cottages.

THE REEFS, 56 South Road, Southampton 8-08, Bermuda. ☎ 809-298-0222. All rooms and cottages have ocean views.

SOMERSET BRIDGE HOTEL, P.O. Box SB 149, Sandys 9-20, Bermuda. Dive packages available. Features modern apartments.

SOUTHAMPTON PRINCESS. This luxury resort hotel sits on one of the highest points in Bermuda and is home to Nautilus Diving. P.O. Box HM 1379, Southampton, Bermuda. Dive packages.☎ 809-238-8000 or 800-223-1818.

SONESTA BEACH HOTEL. Located in Southampton Parish on the waterfront, this resort features a Solar Dome Pool, European health spa, beaches, shopping and a restaurant. SCUBA shop on premises. ☎ 800-343-7170 for reservations.

GROTTO BAY BEACH HOTEL & TENNIS CLUB. T h i s luxury resort is situated on 21 acres of beachfront gardens in Hamilton Parish. Dive shop on premises. P.O. Box HM 1291, Hamilton 5, Bermuda. ☎ 809-293-8333.

BERMUDA'S SMALL PROPERTIES offers a choice of housekeeping cottages, apartments and guest houses with rates as low as $25 a night. For a complete list of small inns call 800-541-7426.

Sightseeing

Taxis sporting blue flags are driven by qualified tour guides who know all about everywhere and usually throw in a few local anecdotes for good measure. Particularly interesting visits include Hamilton, the island's capital, Flatts Village for a tour of the Government Aquarium, Museum and Zoo with its superb collection of marine life, gaily-colored exotic birds and relics of Bermuda's history. Not to be missed are the Bermuda Perfum-

Bermuda sailing

ery in Bailey's Bay and the Blue Grotto with its troupe of bottlenose dolphins, performing in a natural habitat. St. George's, the historic former capital, is another must-see with the pillory and stocks in King's Square, as is St. Peter's Church with its glistening white facade and Bermuda-cedar-laden interior. It is the oldest Anglican church in the Western Hemisphere.

Dining and Entertainment

Bermuda menus cater to every taste and pocketbook. Prices for two range from $30 to $130 for dinner. Traditional dishes of Bermuda are mussel pie, fish chowder laced with black rum and sherry peppers, spiny Bermuda lobster (Sept. to Apr.), Hoppin' John (blackeyed peas and rice) and a Sunday morning breakfast of codfish and potatoes. The island drinks are a Rum Swizzle, a mixture of four colors of rum and fruit juices, and "dark and stormy," an interesting blend of black rum and ginger beer. The small eateries may offer delicacies such as conch stew, fritters, hashed shark and turtle steak. A 15 percent gratuity charge is added to the bill at most restaurants. Many places require that men wear jackets and ties after 6:00 pm.

In Southampton try Henry VIII where "wenches" in period dress serve such dishes as "Steak Anne Boleyn" (tenderloin subtly flavored with Armagnac, then flamed in cognac and served with a rich Madeira sauce) or hearty prime rib of beef with Yorkshire Pudding. Reservations for dinner. ☎ 238-1977. The Somerset Bridge Hotel offers excellent rockfish with a choice of indoor or terrace dining. For fast food stop in at the Flying Chef in Hamilton. German dishes and beer are a specialty especially for dinner. Dining indoors or outside in a closed-in garden area just off Washington Lane. No credit cards. ☎ 295-1595. The Lobster Pot is a fabulous seafood restaurant, famous for fish and conch chowders, stuffed and baked fish, oysters, clams and other succulent crustaceans, including lobsters from the in-house tank. The gamefish steaks, from yellowfin tuna to wahoo are delectable. Reservations ☎ 292-6898. The Pubs of Hamilton are popular for rehashing the day's dive and enjoying island dinner specialties. Try Hog Penny, Bermuda's oldest English style pub and restaurant or Longtail offering wiener schnitzel and curried fish crepes, or soup and sandwiches. ☎ 293-0207. Robin Hood on Richmond Road represents a transplanted bit of England, right down to the darts and pool room and "pub grub". No credit cards. ☎ 295-3315.

FACTS

RECOMPRESSION CHAMBER. Located at King Edward Memorial Hospital, Point Finger Road, Paget.

GETTING THERE. Daily direct flights leave from most U.S. East Coast gateway cities aboard American, Eastern, Delta, Air Canada, Pan Am, or British Airways. Cruise service is readily available through Bermuda Star Line, Royal Viking Lines, Chandris Fantasy Cruises, Cunard Lines, Ocean Cruise Lines, Royal Caribbean Cruise Lines and Sun Line Cruises.

ISLAND TRANSPORTATION. There are no rental cars available to visitors. Taxis, pink buses, bicycles or mopeds offer a variety of transportation methods. Traffic is on the left side of the roads at a speed limit of only 20 mph. Moped drivers must be at least 16 years of age and wear safety helmets securely fastened at all times. Ferries provide fine sights of the island.

DOCUMENTS. All travelers must carry proof of citizenship and personal identification relevant to the return to their own country or for re-entry through another foreign country. Visitors from the United States are required to have one of the following: a passport, birth certificate, U.S. re-entry permit, a voter's registration card, U.S. naturalization certificate, or U.S. alien registration card. Canadians need either a valid passport, a Canadian certificate of citizenship, proof of their landed immigrant status or a birth certificate.

CUSTOMS. U.S. citizens may take back up to $400 worth of merchandise after 48 hours, every 30 days, Canadians, $100 after 48 hours and once every three calendar months. U.K. citizens, 28 pounds worth.

CURRENCY. Legal tender is the Bermuda dollar which is equal to $1 U.S. Travelers' checks and major credit cards accepted in most establishments.

CLIMATE. Bermuda is a semi-tropical island. Rainfall is distributed evenly throughout the year. Average temperature during the period April to November is in the mid 70's to low 80's. Cool months: December-March, 65-70° F.

CLOTHING. As a rule of thumb, dress conservatively. Bathing suits, abbreviated tops and short shorts are not acceptable except at beaches and pools. In public, beach wear must be covered. Bare feet and hair curlers are not acceptable anywhere in public. Casual sportswear is acceptable in restaurants at lunch time but many restaurants require gentlemen to wear a jacket and tie in the evenings.

ELECTRICITY. 110 volts, 60 cycles A.C. throughout the island.

TELEPHONE. From the U.S. dial 1-809 plus the local number.

TIME. Atlantic Standard (Eastern Standard + 1 hr.).

GOVERNMENT. Self-governing colony of the United Kingdom.

LANGUAGE. English.

TAX. A 6 percent hotel occupancy tax is payable upon checkout.

TIPPING. Where the gratuity is not included in the bill, 15 percent is the generally accepted amount for most services.

FOR ADDITIONAL INFORMATION. See your local travel agent or write to the Bermuda Department of Tourism, Global House, 43 Church Street, Hamilton 5-24, Bermuda. U.S., ☎ 1-800-223-6106; NY ☎ 800-223-6107; Canada ☎ 416-923-9600 or in England ☎ 01-734-8813.

BONAIRE

Located 50 miles off the northern coast of Venezuela, Bonaire is an underwater explorer's paradise. The boomerang-shaped island is entirely surrounded by dense coral reefs that begin at the shoreline, terrace off at 30 feet and slope to a depth of 180 ft. Breathtaking underwater landscapes coupled with dependably dry weather and calm sea conditions make it a top choice for underwater photography.

The island, long inhabited by Arawak Indians, was discovered by Amerigo Vespucci in 1499. Vespucci named it after the Arawak word "bo-nah", or "low country".

Determined to preserve its natural beauty, Bonaire was the first of the Antilles to enact legislation that would protect land and sea, set aside a national park, and create a wildlife sanctuary to safeguard flamingos.

Bonaire's 24-mile-long, three- to seven-mile-wide landscape consists of various environments. The southern portion is relatively flat, except for mountains of salt at the Antilles International Salt Company's solar salt works. The salt pans, where the sea water is evaporated by the sun, serve as home and breeding ground for a majority of the island's 10,000 flamingos, the largest colony in the southern Caribbean.

The northern half of the island resembles Arizona, a blend of mountains and cactus-laden deserts.

Area Contributors: Harry M. Ward, former divemaster, Divi Flamingo Beach Resort; Bruce Bowker, divemaster, Carib Inn.

Sea turtle, Bonaire

This area contains Washington/Slagbaai National Park, a 15,000-acre wildlife sanctuary.

In 1979 the Bonaire Marine Park was established by local conservationists. The Marine Park encompasses all land and water in Bonaire and Klein Bonaire from high tidemark to a depth of 200 ft.

Most all recreational activity in the Marine Park takes place on the island's leeward side and the reefs surrounding Klein Bonaire, a small uninhabited islet. Visibility is always at a minimum of 100 ft on Bonaire's reefs. Because spearfishing and coral collecting have been outlawed, marine life has flourished and many fish rarely found elsewhere abound. Divers also flock to the reefs for moonlight dives. Reliably clear skies and the bright Caribbean starlight create a magnificent atmosphere for night diving; there is no need for artificial lights.

Iron Shore

Best Dives of Bonaire

☆☆☆☆☆**LA DANIA'S LEAP** is located at the northern end of Bonaire near the Karpata Ecological Center. La Dania's depth ranges from 10 to 120 ft and is excellent for snorkelers as well as novice to advanced divers. The first 40 feet of this dive site is a gentle slope. Between 40 and 120 ft the slope turns into a very steep wall covered with purple and orange sponges. Calm seas, visibility in excess of 150 ft, and abundant marine life, make this site a favorite spot for photography.

☆☆☆☆**KARPATA,** located just northwest of La Dania's Leap, may be reached from the beach. A channel through the dense walls of staghorn coral lining the shallows has been cleared all the way to the slope. Schools of small fish and sea urchins cover the bottom of the channel. Keep some air in your vest or stabilizer jacket to avoid hitting the sea urchins while swimming through

Knife Reef, off Klein Bonaire's north shore

the coral. Snorkelers should stay in the center of the channel to avoid being bruised or burned by the coral. At the end of the short swim through the channel divers will find lovely sea fans, tube sponges, small iridescent purple shrimp which come out to feed at sunset, clumps of brain coral and mushroom corals.

☆☆☆☆**FOREST REEF** is located on the southwest end of Klein Bonaire (see map) and ranges in depth from 15 to 100 ft. A macro photographer's dream come true, Forest's is alive with an abundance of shrimp, small critters and black corals. It is also heavily populated by schooling reef fish, morays which take food from divers' hands, filefish, trunkfish, puffers,and angels. Large colorful parrotfish, sting rays and two-ft queen triggerfish have been spotted at this site.

The reef here drops off gradually with typical slopes of 45° or less. Many shallow areas ranging between 10 and 30 ft in depth offer excellent snorkeling.

☆☆☆☆☆**TWIXT** is just north of Forest Reef, around the southwest bend of Klein Bonaire. It provides excellent opportunities for wide angle photography with large basket sponges in the foreground and sea whips, huge pastel fans, tube sponges and star corals in the background.

The depth of Twixt ranges between 15 to 100 ft. The coral wall slopes down to a sandy bottom. Seas are almost always calm and flat here.

☆☆☆☆**CARL'S HILL,** another Klein Bonaire location, is a favorite dive spot. The mini wall at Carl's Hill is very, very sheer and absolutely loaded with every imaginable type of marine life. They frequently venture out during the day. The wall is covered with clusters of tube sponges, sea fans, star coral, black coral, wire and mushroom corals. Small fish can be found in the tubes.

☆☆☆☆**EBO'S REEF** is located directly opposite the Sunset Beach Hotel on the northeast tip of Klein Bonaire. The depth ranges from 15 to 100 ft. A lovely shallow garden of elkhorn coral makes this an excellent location for snorkeling photographers. Black coral may be found here at a mere 35 ft. The coral slopes at Ebo's Reef are characterized by orange elephant ear sponges and black crinoids. The small tunnels and caves in the reef itself are packed with fish, anemones, sponges, shrimp, starfish and morays. The bottom is a sandy slope.

☆☆☆☆ **THE *HILMA HOOKER*,** a 250-ft freighter lies right off shore just north of Angel City Reef. This dive site may be reached from the beach or by boat. The ship was seized during a drug raid when a member of the Antillean Coast Guard discovered a false bulkhead. The crew abandoned the freighter and fled the island. Because of an unmanageable leak, Bonaire law enforcement agents were afraid that the ship would sink and damage the reefs, so they towed the ship out to where she now lies, creating an intriguing dive site. Bruce Bowker, owner of the Carib Inn, rates the wreck one of his favorites. Schools of yellowtail and other reef fish call the *Hilma Hooker* home. The wreck rests on a sandy bottom at 91 ft. Divers are warned to stay outside the wreck and to monitor bottom time. (There have been two cases of the bends already).

Best Snorkeling Sites

☆☆☆☆**LEONORA'S REEF,** on the north side of Klein Bonaire, is considered by many local divers to be the best snorkeling site in the area. Masses of fish greet you as soon as you enter the water. They are used to being handfed and will go right into your BC pocket looking for food if you've got some crumbs leaking out. Sometimes you can't see the reef through the fish.

☆☆☆☆☆**NUKOVE BEACH,** located at the northern end of the leeward side of the island, is a wonderful place for sunset snorkeling and a picnic on the beach. (Take bug repellent). The white sand beach here is secluded. The reef hugs the shore line and can be reached by swimming through a channel cut for divers.

☆☆**THE FRONT PORCH,** just off the beach in front of the Sunset Beach Hotel, is reached by swimming over a sand shelf.

It begins at about 30 ft and may be visible from the surface. Snorkelers who can make a shallow breath-holding dive may come upon an old anchor there.

Touch the Sea with Dee Scarr

Diving with author and naturalist Dee Scarr is an experience divers won't soon forget. "Touch the Sea" programs are personalized dives during which participants learn to pet moray eels, tickle anemones, get a manicure from a cleaner shrimp, massage the tummy of a "deadly" scorpion fish and befriend marine animals from which one normally keeps a safe distance. When asked how she approaches the unapproachable and touches the untouchable, Ms. Scarr casually mentions that many of these animals, such as the two scorpionfish at the town dock she calls the "Cookie Monsters" or the moray she has named "Crooked Jaw", are her personal friends. She recommends that divers not try these antics without first participating in her program but assures us that all divers can learn to make close friends with most marine creatures.

If underwater photography is your thing and you really don't want to kiss a frogfish you'll enjoy shooting these normally hard-to-get-close-to creatures as they pose for portraits or action shots with other divers.

"Touch the Sea" is a PADI Specialty Certification available to all certified divers. Dee Scarr is the author of a book titled *Touch the Sea,* a children's book, *Coral's Reef,* and a recent release, *The Gentle Sea,* a marine animal behavior book.

"Touch the Sea" is a five starfish dive. Arrangements to dive with Dee Scarr must be made prior to your trip to Bonaire by writing to her c/o Touch the Sea, P.O. Box 369, Bonaire, Netherlands Antilles, or calling 8529 on the island. From the U.S., ☎ 011-599-7-8529. A maximum of four divers may participate in one dive.

Boy with Iguanas

Moray eel off Kralendijk

Dive Operators

PETER HUGHES' DIVE BONAIRE is a top Caribbean dive facility. It has two shops and piers, a new on-site photo lab that provides instruction, rental equipment, still and video cameras, and 24-hour E-6 processing. Dive instructors will ask you to bring a C-card, a log book and join them on a warm up dive off the beach in front of the resort. ☎ 1-800-367-3484 or Write Divi Hotels, 54 Gunderman Road, Ithaca NY 14850.

CARIB INN owner Bruce Bowker, who's been diving Bonaire's reefs since the late 60's, can take you to his own private dive spots, never visited by clients of other dive shops because he keeps the locations secret. ☎ 800-223-9815, or local 599-7-8819. Write ITR, Four Park Ave., NY NY 10016.

BONAIRE

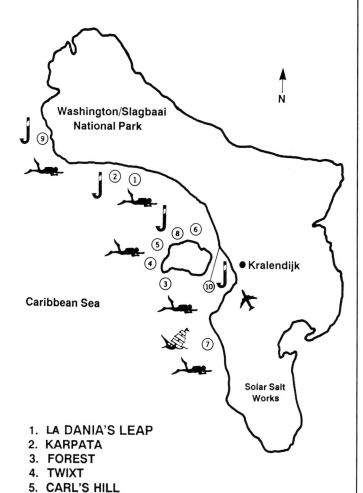

Washington/Slagbaai
National Park

Caribbean Sea

Kralendijk

Solar Salt
Works

1. LA DANIA'S LEAP
2. KARPATA
3. FOREST
4. TWIXT
5. CARL'S HILL
6. EBO'S REEF
7. HILMA HOOKER
8. LEONORA'S REEF
9. NUKOVE
10. CALABAS REEF

THE HABITAT DIVE SHOP offers 24-hour dive services. ☎ 1-800-327-6709, or 305-381-6390. Write 1080 Port Boulevard, Miami FL 33132.

BONAIRE SCUBA CENTER. Located at the Sunset Beach Hotel, the new Scuba Center operates large flat-top boats and offers complete packages for beach and boat diving and snorkeling. ☎ 1-800-526-2370 or write Bonaire SCUBA Center, P.O. Box 775, Morgan NJ 08879.

BUDDY WATERSPORTS is across from the Hotel Bonaire. Like Habitat, it offers 24-hour availability of tanks and air for beach diving. Guided trips, night dives and dive equipment rentals are available. ☎ 800-359-0747 or 212-662- 4858. In Bonaire, 8647.

SAND DOLLAR DIVE AND PHOTO is a new shop located at the Sand Dollar Beach Club just north of the Flamingo Beach Club complex. Run by Andre Nahr, a Bonaire native, the shop specializes in photography rentals, services, repairs, and processing. ☎ 8738 in Bonaire or 800-345-0805 or 609-298-3844. Write Travel Barn, 50 Georgetown Rd, Bordentown NJ 08505.

DIVE INN. Located on Kralendijk Bay adjacent to Sunset Inn. SCUBA packages, resort course, reef trips, picnic trips, sales and rentals. Happy Chappy motorbike rental. ☎ 8761.

Accommodations

Accommodations on Bonaire range from full-facility luxury resorts to small inns, guesthouses and villas. The entire island is oriented toward diving and all hotels offer dive packages. To telephone Bonaire directly you must dial 011- 599-7 + four digit number.

DIVI FLAMINGO BEACH RESORT is a premiere dive resort with 110 standard, superior and oceanfront deluxe guestrooms, 23 handicapped-accessible rooms plus 40 fully-equipped luxury studios, all air conditioned and each with its own patio or balconies (some right over the reef) and suites. For reservations ☎ 800-367-3484 or 607-277-3484. Or write Divi Hotels, 54 Gunderman Road, Ithaca NY 14850.

SUNSET BEACH HOTEL. This newly renovated hotel, located on Playa Leche Beach offers air-conditioned rooms with cable TV, baby sitting and laundry services. Dive shop on premises. ☎ 8448. No U.S. rep. Telex 1280 BTC NA. Write to P.O. Box 333, Bonaire, NA.

CARIB INN is located on the waterfront next to the Flamingo Beach Hotel. Reasonable prices. Comfortable air-conditioned apartments and suites available with pool, maid service and diving. ☎ 800-223-9815, local 8819 or write ITR, Four Park Ave., NY NY 10016.

SUNSET INN is on the waterfront in Kralendijk. All rooms are air conditioned with telephones and kitchenettes. Maid and baby-sitting services available. ☎ 8291 or 8314. Telex 1280 BTC NA. Write to P.O. Box 115, Bonaire, NA.

CAP'N DON'S HABITAT AND HAMLET is a community designed for divers. Accommodations range from single rooms to luxury oceanfront villas. ☎ 800-327-6709, local 8290. Write 1080 Port Blvd, Miami FL 33132.

SAND DOLLAR CONDOMINIUMS is located north of Kralendijk and offers you beachfront luxury and privacy; one-, two-, and three-bedroom oceanfront condos. Diving facilities on premises. ☎ 800-345-0805, 609-298-3844 or write 50 Georgetown Rd., Bordentown NJ 08505.

Sightseeing

A drive to the north end of the island will take you to Washington Slagbaai National Park, a 15,000 acre game preserve.

On the south end of Bonaire you'll see mountains of gleaming white salt at the Antilles International Salt Co. At the same location you'll find breeding grounds for over 10,000 flamingos. Continuing around the point you'll come to the Willemstoren Lighthouse, built in 1837.

Dining

DEN LAMAN AQUARIUM RESTAURANT, located between the Bonaire Beach Hotel and the Sand Dollar Condo-tel, specializes in turtle steak, conch, lobster and fresh fish. Diners enjoy viewing a 9,000 gallon aquarium containing sharks, moray eels and other exotic reef fish. ☎ 8955.

SUNSET BEACH HOTEL hosts a fabulous beach barbecue complete with steel band on Tuesday nights. The beach bar is open daily for lunch; the Neptune Dining Room, specializing in seafood and steaks, serves dinner nightly. There is a casino on the premises.

ZEEZICHT BAR AND RESTAURANT, a local favorite, specializes in Chinese cuisine and seafood. Open for breakfast at 8:30 AM ☎ 8434.

CAPTAIN DON'S RESTAURANT at the Habitat is the first and only place on Bonaire for fresh baked breakfast bagels seven days a week. ☎ 8290.

Slave huts at Salt Pans

FACTS

NEAREST RECOMPRESSION CHAMBER. San Francisco Hospital on the island.

GETTING THERE. American and Eastern offer flights from New York to Curacao with connecting service to Bonaire via ALM. Eastern and ALM offer service from New York and Miami to Curacao, with connecting service via ALM. ALM offers direct service from Miami to Bonaire weekly.

ISLAND TRANSPORTATION. Boncar Budget Rentals (at airport and large resorts); Bonaire sightseeing bus tours (☎ 8300 ext 225); Mini bikes (Happy Chappy Rentals, call 8761; U.S. driver's license accepted).

DRIVING. Foreign and international licenses accepted. Traffic moves on the right.

DOCUMENTS. U.S. and Canadian citizens may stay up to three months providing they show proof of citizenship in the form of a passport (preferably valid but not more than five years after expiration date), original birth certificate with raised seal or photocopy with notary seal, or voter's registration card.

CUSTOMS. U.S. citizens may bring home free of duty $400 worth of articles including 1 quart of liquor and 200 cigarettes. Canadian citizens may bring in C$300 of goods once each calendar year.

CURRENCY. Netherlands Antilles Florin or Guilder; $1 U.S.=FL 1.77; Traveler's checks $1 U.S. = FL 1.79.

CLIMATE. Mean temperature 82°F year round; 22 inches rainfall annually.

DEPARTURE TAX. US $10 per person over two years of age.

LANGUAGE. Dutch is the official language. The island dialect Papiamento, English and Spanish are widely spoken.

ELECTRICITY. 127 volts, 50 cycles.

CLOTHING. Lightweight, casual cottons; dressier for dining out, and visiting the casinos.

TIME ZONE. Atlantic Time (EST + 1 hr.).

TAX. 5 percent room tax on all hotel rates. A 10 percent service charge is added in lieu of tipping at most hotels. Restaurants generally add a service charge of 15 percent.

RELIGIOUS SERVICES. Roman Catholic, Adventist, Anglican, Jehovah's Witness.

FOR ADDITIONAL INFORMATION. The Bonaire Tourist Board, c/o Mallory Factor Inc.,Sontheimer Group, 275 Seventh Avenue, NY NY 10001-6708, ☎ 212-242-0000. Telex 11 710-581-2760,Cable MALLORYF.

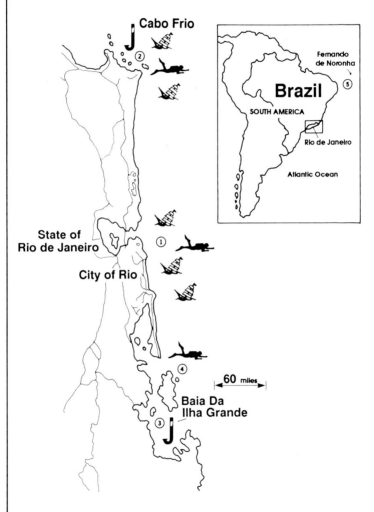

BRAZIL

Cabo Frio

Fernando
de Noronha
⑤

Brazil

SOUTH AMERICA

Rio de Janeiro

Atlantic Ocean

②

①

State of
Rio de Janeiro

City of Rio

④

60 miles

Baia Da
Ilha Grande

③

1. RIO'S ISLANDS
2. CABO FRIO ISLANDS
3. ANGRA DOS REIS
4. JORGE GREGO
5. BAY OF DOLPHINS

BRAZIL

Brazil is a country of marvelous contrasts in geography, people and diving experiences. Low lying wetlands, dominated by the Amazon River, rise to rugged pine forests and the magnificent Andes mountains. Stretching out over half of South America, Brazil shares boundaries with every South American country except Chile and Ecuador. Its coastline extends over 11,919 miles, much of it as white sandy beaches.

Within its geopolitical boundaries are the beautiful Atlantic islands of Trindade and Fernando de Noronha, home to the Bay of Dolphins.

Even as the average sport diver will be more than pleased with exploring established destinations, the naturalist, the rugged, and the adventurous will find Brazil a marvelous spot for wreck diving and treasure hunting.

The fascination of Brazil is the unknown, the mystical rocky reefs teeming with rare lavender urchins and giant starfish, some exceeding two ft in diameter, the remarkable Bay of Dolphins, and lastly Brazil's ancient ship wrecks. Today hundreds of centuries-old treasure ships rest silently on the sea floor, laden with chests of gold, silver, and jewels waiting to be found. Countless cargo ships crashed upon Brazil's rocky shoals during the past five centuries and many are just now being discovered. During 1988 a handful of sport divers in Rio began bringing up 17th century gold coins, and ancient artifacts.

Area Contributors: Lola Fritzsche, divemaster of Aqua Rio; Jean Tiedemann, The Diving Center.

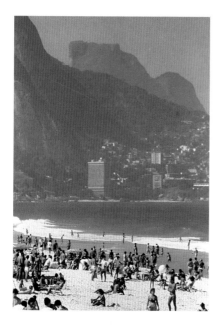

Ipanema Beach

Rio De Janiero

The heart of Brazil is Rio De Janiero. Frequently called the most beautiful city in the world, Rio is nestled between cloud-capped mountains and an endless emerald sea. Its shore line is indented with picturesque bays and coves, dotted with pastel fishing boats. Its coastline extends over 11,919 miles, much of it as white sandy beaches. Hotels range from modest to ultra luxurious.

Concluding a stopover in Rio De Janeiro, a returning U.S. sailor, in awe of the city's beauty, remarked, "If God is on earth, He must be in Rio."

Brazil's diving resorts are located in Cabo Frio on the northern coast of Rio, and off Angra Dos Reis, a swinging tropical resort area south of Rio. Special excursions visit the marine sanctuary at Fernando de Noronha, 200 miles off Brazil's northern coast.

Located just off shore of the city, Rio's islands offer a look at some 19th- and 20th-century wrecks. One is the "English Wreck" which dates back to 1912. Sitting in just 20 ft of water in a protected area, this wreck is ideal for snorkelers and novice divers.

Best Dives of Brazil

☆☆**THE** *BUENOS AIRES,* off Rio's Islands, went down in 1890, sits on a rocky bottom nearby at a depth of about 125 ft and is largely intact. Some brain corals and sponges grow around the wrecks, and both wrecks are home to huge angels, turtles, groupers, jew fish, and schools of reef fish. Though a stiff wind can stir up surface conditions, a protected area can always be found here. Water temperature averages 75°F requiring a wetsuit. Air temperature averages 85°F. Visibility is about 75 ft, greater when weather is calm.

ARRAIAL DO CABO/CABO FRIO. This rustic fishing village, located 150 mi northeast of Rio and a short drive south of the "Jet Set" retreat of Buzios Beach, is a jumping-off point for some of Rio's best treasure wreck dives and is noted for its abundant marine life. Arraial do Cabo dives are centered around several small islands that were formed when sand was pushed up by the meeting of the Brazilian and Falkland currents.

This meeting of currents, referred to as the *ressurgencia,* occurs mainly during the (southern hemisphere) summer. It brings cooler waters, full of plankton, which attract breeding mantas and other pelagics. The combination of thick fogs that occur during the sunrise and sunset hours and the absence of lighthouses in early Brazilian history were extremely hazardous to early navigation. Approximately 80 wrecks have been located and described by the Brazilian Navy at Cabo Frio's Massambaba beach and there are at least 10 more distributed among the islands of Cabo Frio.

Around the islands divers and snorkelers find shallow, protected waters and wrecks such as the *Carolina* at 20 ft, as well as deeper more challenging open-water dives. One such area is Dois Irmaos (Two Brothers) a small nearby island where divers find caves, walls, and a curious parade of fish. Mantas and other superb wild life are frequently encountered here. The reefs are predominantly rocky with hard corals. Visibility ranges from 50 to 75 ft. The best snorkeling off Arraial do Cabo is between Cabo Frio Island and Arraial do Cabo town where the water is warmer and protected from high wind and waves.

Novice and intermediate divers can explore an 1860 Portuguese wreck which sank between two small islands at Ilha do Frances in 50 ft of water. The wreck sits on a sandy bottom and offers a look at several iron cannons which lie on the sand. This is a good area for photography.

Divers as well as snorkelers will need a full wet suit in the Cabo Frio area as the water temperature is between 65 and 75° F. Visibility varies with sea conditions. Whether you visit a protected area good for snorkelers or an area with swells and fast currents depends on where your dive boat captain drops anchor. Specify exactly where you wish to be taken before boarding.

Best Cabo Frio Wreck Dives

☆☆☆*THE CAROLINA.* On September 29, 1913 the *Carolina* was anchored at the entrance to the Itajuru channel where a passing storm tossed her against the rocks. After the storm passed, the people of Cabo Frio recovered some of the imported fabrics, sewing machines and beautiful clothing which comprised her cargo.

This wreck sits in about 45 ft of water with the top at a depth of less than 10 ft, making it a favorite of both SCUBA divers and snorkelers. During 1988 a silver pitcher was uncovered from a few inches of sand close to the wreck.

☆☆THE *HMS THETIS* is a 46-gun frigate which carried a crew of 300. She was headed homeward from Rio, loaded with gold and silver worth then about $1 mil on December 6, 1830, when she sank after smashing into the base of the cliffs on Cabo Frio.

Buzios

The remains of the ship, including three cannons, a huge anchor and some cannon balls, are scattered along a slope ranging in depth from 25 to 90 ft. The boat trip to the wreck takes about one hour and 45 min.

☆☆**THE *DONA PAULA*** was an Imperial 50-gun frigate, named after the daughter of the emperor of Brazil, Dona Paula Mariana. She was built in 1795 and belonged to an East Indies Company, Surate Castle. In September of 1827, she left the Guanabara Bay in Rio de Janeiro, pursuing an Argentinian corsair ship and, for reasons still unknown, it sank on the dawn of October 2, between two islands that form the Ilhas dos Franceses archipelago. It is an impressive underwater sight. There are more than 50 cannons, a carpet of cannon balls and, mysteriously, two large anchors very close to each other—facing in opposite directions. In 1987, gold coins were found near the wreck in less than 30 ft of water. The wreck is sitting on a slope between 10 and 60 ft. Because of the steady current and recurring

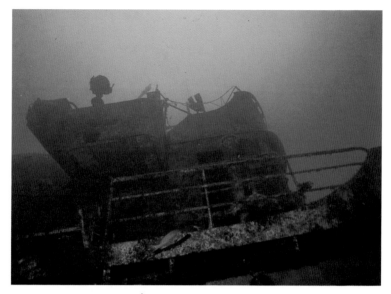

Wreck of freighter 60 feet down, off Fernando de Noronha, near the Bay of Dolphins

swells this dive is recommended for experienced divers. The boat trip to the wreck takes just over 1 1/2 hours. The bottom is sandy with some large rocks.

☆**THE *WAKAMA*** was a German ship carrying 6,000 tons of crystals, minerals and tungsten, On February 12, 1940, she was fired on by two British vessels and burst into flame. Sunk by her own crew, she now lies on the bottom between the islands of Ancora and Santana.

Best Snorkeling Wrecks

☆**THE *DOM AFONSO*,** the first war vessel of the Imperial Armada, put to sea in 1847 and sank on January 10, 1853 while patrolling the coast between Cabo Frio and Espirito Santo. A 187-ft, six- gun steamship, she was used to carry African slaves to the court in Rio. She went down at Massambaba beach about seven miles from the town of Cabo Frio. Depending on the sand movement, one can see the boiler, some cannons and part of the wooden hull. The top of the wreck can be seen in 10 ft of water with sections as shallow as three ft. This area is inhabited by lobster and mussels.

☆THE *PARANA* was a trans-Atlantic steamship that struck a sandbar and sank during the night of May 23, 1892. The captain and crew struggled to free her, but without success, and at daylight they began rescuing the passengers. By tying a dinghy to a cable that linked the boat to the beach, they safely recovered all the passengers and some cargo. Today, only the boiler and part of the huge hull are to be seen. The propeller and most of the stern are buried in the sand. The average depth is 12 ft. Sea conditions and visibility vary with the wind direction. The *Parana* is also reached from Massambaba beach.

Accommodations

POUSADA NAS ROCAS is a luxury sports resort located on its own private island (Ilha Rasa). Transportation for guests is provided from the Porto Buzios Marina which can be reached by driving two hours from Rio or by plane. Nas Rocas accommodations feature 40 bungalows with 80 rooms, all deluxe and designed to offer a maximum of privacy and contact with nature. All rooms overlook the ocean. A schooner takes guests on cruises around the islands and along the coast of Buzios. Dive-vacation packages here are offered through Brazilian SCUBA and Land Tours, 5254 Merrick Road, Suite 5, Massapequa NY 11758. ☎ 1-800-722-0205 or 516-797-2133.

A number of small inns (pousadas) located in Buzios charge $40 per night and up.

Cabo Frio Dive Operator

AQUA RIO is located in Cabo Frio. Divemaster Lola Fritsch offers dive tours to all the wrecks and reefs aboard a 40-ft wooden trawler. The modern, well equipped shop is open year round and has English speaking guides. A C-card and log book are required.

Angra dos Reis

Located about 100 miles south of Rio De Janiero, Angra dos Reis is a beautiful coastal resort town which serves as the jump-off point to the 300 palm-covered islands in the Ilha

Barracuda

Grande Bay. This is an underwater photographer's playground and a mecca for snorkelers where two-ft-long starfish nestle among bright blue anemones and lavender sea urchins. Huge rays glide gracefully by in the shallows, casting streamlined shadows on the sea floor. Ideal for couples where just one person dives, this natural harbor offers hundreds of protected coves for picnicking and swimming as well as snorkeling and diving on shallow boulders and walls. The water is warmer than Cabo Frio. The best dive and snorkeling area here is the wall at Angra Dos Reis. This steep, rocky slope starts at the surface and goes down to a sandy bottom at 40 ft. The big attraction here is the unusual marine life which includes friendly groupers, angels, crabs, gigantic star fish, octopi, marauding schools of yellow tail, red glass eye snappers and huge turtles.

Jorge Grego

Another area for diving is Jorge Grego, a tiny island off Ilha Grande, the largest island in the bay. This open- ocean area is recommended for very experienced divers only.

Here one finds rocky walls, canyons, ledges and overhangs frequented by a profusion of tropical fish.

Accommodations and Dive Operators (Angra dos Reis)

The Frade Hotel system operates two fabulous hotels in Angra dos Reis. The Hotel Portogalo is on the northern end of the bay (Baia da Ilha Grande) and features modern air-conditioned rooms overlooking the sea. Transportation from Rio is provided by the chain.For reservations ☎ 1-800-722-0205.

For dive tours of the bay conducted by English-speaking guides, contact Captain Yacht Charters, ☎ 021-252-1155.

Complete tour packages with meals, diving, accommodations, transfers and sightseeing are available through Brazilian SCUBA and Land Tours and may be booked through your travel agent; ☎ 1-800-722-0205.

Fernando de Noronha

☆☆☆☆☆**THE BAY OF DOLPHINS.** Fernando de Noronha is a small chain of rocky islands and out croppings located 200 mi off the coast of Brazil. This area is a natural sanctuary and breeding ground for spinner dolphins, green sea turtles, booby birds, and other wildlife. The islands are undeveloped, lush with tropical jungles sloping down to miles of pure white sandy beaches that are conspicuously void of human footprints. Snorkelers visiting the Bay of Dolphins on the northwest coast of the main island will see a centuries-old community of spinner dolphins. This sheltered bay serves as both congregation and breeding ground for hundreds of the charming mammals. Eighteenth century documents call this enchanted land the "Island of the Dolphins."

The bay is calm, the water is crystal clear with unlimited visibility during dry seasons. Though somewhat frightened by SCUBA gear, the shy dolphins are extremely gentle and trusting, allowing some snorkelers to get very close.

Accommodations and Dive Operators

Vacationers from the United States, Canada and Europe will find a visit to the Bay of Dolphins easier to arrange from home than in Brazil. As of this writing there is just one weekly flight to the islands from Recife, Brazil. Combining a mainland and island vacation would require at least a two-week stay.

Divers considering vacationing in Fernando de Noronha should note that it is essentially an unspoiled habitat and does not offer any resort amenities—no cities, no nightclubs, no tourist glitz. What it does offer, in addition to diving, is spectacular sunsets, a nightly festival of stars, a chance to unwind, and an opportunity to commune with nature.

The hotel here, Pousada Esmeralda, offers guests clean, comfortable rooms overlooking the sea. For dive-accommodation tours ☎ 1-800-722-0205, in NY ☎ 516-797-2133.

Spinner dolphins, Bay of Dolphins

Sightseeing in Rio

Tours around the city can easily be booked through your hotel. Be sure to specify what language you prefer the tour guide to speak. For tourist assistance in Rio ☎ call 221-8422.

BAY CRUISES. There are several tours of the beautiful Guanabara Bay, north of the city. These, which include lunch and dinner, can be taken from the Marina da Gloria within Flamengo Park or from a location adjacent to Rio de Janeiro's Yacht Club along Botafogo beach.

CORCOVADO. The statue of Christ the Redeemer standing on top of Corcovado peak (2,297 ft) provides one of the most breathtaking panoramas of sea and mountains in the world. You can get there by train from Corcovado Railway Station.

SUGAR LOAF. Located at the entry of Guanabara Bay this privileged location provides one of the best views of Rio's seashore and mountains. A cable-car will take you to Urca hill where cultural activities and entertainment are available.

Beaches

Among Rio's splendid natural assets are her 56 miles of gorgeous beaches. The Cariocas (natives) love them and consider them the prime social gathering place. Though all of Brazil's beaches are public, few have rest rooms or changing areas since most hotels are close to the beach.

FLAMENGO BEACH is within Flamengo Park, which also houses the Museum of Modern Art, historic monuments and the Carmen Miranda Museum.

COPACABANA has rightfully become the most famous beach in the world. Its 2.8 curving miles of white sand are bordered by Atlantic Avenue and its beautiful mosaic sidewalk. There are sidewalk fairs year round which are active until the wee hours of the morning. For people-watchers, Rio's cafes provide an interesting sidewalk show.

IPANEMA beach begins in Arpoador which is highly sought after by surfers who relish the high waves generated by its rocky coast. It ends at Leblon, where one finds many of the city's most exclusive restaurants, nightclubs and boutiques.

Dining and Nightlife

Rio's wide variety of nightclubs, bars, and restaurants ensure a lively and diversified nightlife sure to spark an all-night "fest". Local tradition dictates no place closes until the last guest leaves. In addition to Rio's highly refined and sophisticated international cuisine, you will also find the traditional and regional dishes of Brazil. Try *feijoada*, a dish of black beans and pork or beef, traditionally served with rice, kale and manioc meal and accompanied by a *caipirinha* a traditional cocktail made of sugarcane liqueur, lime and sugar. Another Brazilian specialty is the *churrasco*, in which large pieces of barbecued beef, pork and other meats are served with manioc meal and marinated onions. At *churrascarias* (barbecue restaurants), popular in Rio, waiters will bring skewers of choice meats to your table until you can eat no more. Sea food dishes include a variety of fish, lobster and shrimp. Prices vary from $3 to $5 for a simple meal to about $17 for a fancy dinner.

FACTS

RECOMPRESSION CHAMBER. Three chambers in Rio de Janiero. For medical emergencies ☎ 325-9300, 24 hrs.

GETTING THERE. Several airlines, including Varig, Avianca, TWA and Pan Am as well as cruises by Columbus Lines, Holland-America or Moore-McCormack Lines offer package tours to Rio De Janeiro. NY tour operator, Brazilian SCUBA and Land Tours, offers well-thought-out vacations especially for divers. Bill Smith and Jeannie Cameron, owners of the company, discovered the magic of diving Brazil in 1983 when they took their first open-water dive with Cau Pissurno, a commercial diver. Prior to finding Cau, the only English-speaking diver around, Bill and Jeannie spent several days trying to find the Portuguese words for SCUBA diving. For them *mergulhar* became the key to their new business. Brazilian SCUBA and Land Tours (☎ 1-800-722-0205) offer hassle-free planning as well as attractive dive/travel package rates to divers and snorkelers who wish to enjoy the sights of Rio in addition to Brazil's superb aquatic wildlife attractions.

DRIVING. Avis, National and Hertz rent Brazilian-made Volkswagen Beetles that rent for approximately $20 per day in Rio. Bookings may be made through your hotel. Taxis and bus tours are recommended for exploring the inner city.

DOCUMENTS. Visitors to Brazil must carry a passport valid for at least six months and a tourist visa . Be sure to keep a separate record of your passport number, place of issue and date with you in case you lose it. Obtaining a replacement passport is no easy task.

CUSTOMS. Diving and camera gear should be registered with customs before you depart. Carry receipts with you if you are taking new products. While in Brazil you may purchase up to $300 worth of duty-free products.

CURRENCY. The Brazilian currency is the cruzado (Cz$) divided into 100 centavos. The official rate of exchange is published daily in the main Brazilian newspapers. Foreign currencies of travelers checks can be exchanged for

Sting ray, Cabo Frio

cruzados at hotels, banks and tourist agencies. Travelers checks are recommended for currency here. Although international credit cards are accepted they may billed at a higher rate than in the United States.

AIRPORT. Aeroporto International do Galeao located on the island of Governador in Rio.

CAPITAL. Brasilia.

CLIMATE. Most of Brazil lies immediately to the south of the Equator. As a result, there is very little seasonal variation. The climate is comfortably temperate in most of the country, and refreshing sea breezes often blow along the coast all year round, the temperatures usually ranging from 65 to 85° F. The hottest months of the year are January to March. The coldest months are July and August when the thermometer dips into the low 70s. The best time to plan a dive-vacation to Brazil is from September to March. Frequent tropical rain storms occur during January and February, although they are usually short lived.

CLOTHING. Lightweight casual clothing is appropriate for the diving resorts. A sweater or light jacket is a good idea for cooler evenings. Dress wear is required for those wishing to sample the nightclubs and discos. A full wetsuit is needed in Cabo Frio and Fernando de Noronha, especially during the cooler months, July and August.

TIME ZONE. In most of the country and in the main cities, the time is three hours earlier than Greenwich (London) Mean Time. Because Brazil is within the same hemisphere, it is in the same time zone as North America and there is a maximum of two hours difference from New York's time. When New York is on daylight savings time there is only a one hour difference. **ELECTRICITY.** 110 or 120 V, AC, 60 cycles in Rio. Some hotels have European and American type outlets. Adapters are readily available in most hotels, if needed.

TAXES AND SERVICE CHARGES. Tipping is expected by taxi drivers. In restaurants, because a service charge is added to the bill, only a small tip is left if the service is outstanding. Brazil departure tax: approximately $9.00.

VACCINATIONS AND HEALTH PRECAUTIONS. Unless you are coming from an infected area vaccinations are not required to enter Brazil. If traveling to the interior check with your department of immigration and be sure to carry malaria prophylaxis pills. English speaking doctors may be found by calling The Rio Health Collective at 511-9040. Three recompression chambers are located in Rio. Drink only bottled water in Brazil and avoid unpasteurized milk.

RELIGIOUS SERVICES. Catholicism is the main religion in Brazil; however services for a wide variety of faiths can be found in Rio.

ADDITIONAL INFORMATION. Write to Brazilian Tourist Board, 551 Fifth Avenue, New York, NY 10176.

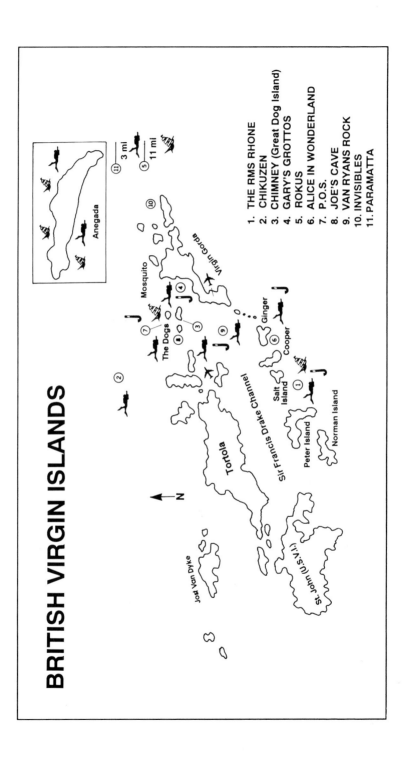

BRITISH VIRGIN ISLANDS

1. THE RMS RHONE
2. CHIKUZEN
3. CHIMNEY (Great Dog Island)
4. GARY'S GROTTOS
5. ROKUS
6. ALICE IN WONDERLAND
7. P.O.S.
8. JOE'S CAVE
9. VAN RYANS ROCK
10. INVISIBLES
11. PARAMATTA

BRITISH VIRGIN ISLANDS

World renowned as a sailing port, the British Virgin Islands (BVI) also play host to thousands of snorkelers and SCUBA divers each year.

Grouped around the Sir Francis Drake Channel the British Virgin Islands have long been a haven for sailing buffs, probably the ultimate combination of accessibility and remoteness. Hundreds of sheltered coves, white sand beaches and thousands of acres of protected marine parks make for superb snorkeling and diving. Divers find towering coral pinnacles, underwater caves, canyons, lava tunnels and almost 200 different wrecks. Most areas have little or no surge and only gentle currents. Visibility may reach anywhere from 50 to over 100 ft.

Great diving and snorkeling can also be found around the out islands—Norman, Cooper, Salt, and Peter; just south of Tortola (turtle dove); around North Sound, Virgin Gorda (the fat virgin) and Mosquito Island. The dense coral reef surrounding Anegada is the site of over 300 shipwrecks. The best time to visit the BVI is between October and June. Reduced rates at hotels and on charter boats are available during July to September, hurricane season.

The BVI reefs are protected by law, and no living thing may be taken. "Take only pictures, leave only bubbles."

Area Contributor: Gayla Kilbride, Kilbride Underwater Tours.

Best Dives of the BVI

☆☆☆☆☆ **THE *R.M.S. RHONE*.** Featured in the movie *The Deep*, the *Rhone* is by far the most popular wreck dive in the BVI. Struck by a ferocious hurricane in October 1867, this Royal Mail Steamer, was forced on the rocks at Salt Island as the captain Robert F. Wooley struggled desperately to reach open sea. The force with which the 310-ft vessel crashed upon the rocks broke the hull in two leaving two superb dive spots, a great snorkeling area at the stern, which lies in 30 ft of water amid rocks and boulders, and a good area for diving at the bow, which lies in 80 ft on a sandy bottom. The top of the rudder sits just 15 ft below the surface. Encrusted with corals, sponges, and sea fans, the superstructure provides a dramatic setting for underwater photography.

The *Rhone* is a boat-access dive. Sea conditions are usually calm; recommended for novices. Visibility is usually excellent, from 50 to over 100 ft. Also, the *Rhone* is a national park and off limits to coral collecting and spear fishing.

☆☆☆☆**THE *CHIKUZEN*.** This 268-ft steel-hulled refrigerator ship went down in 1981 and now lies in 75 ft of water about eight miles north of the east end of Tortola. The ship is lying on her port side allowing easy entry. The *Chikuzen* is fine for novice divers. Access by boat only.

☆☆☆**THE CHIMNEY.** Located at Great Dog Island off the west end of Virgin Gorda is a spectacular coral archway and canyon covered with a wide variety of soft corals, sponges and very rare white coral. Divers and snorkelers swim along the archway, followed by hundreds of fish, then ascend through a coral-encrusted tube-like formation resembling a huge chimney. Maximum depth of the Chimney is 45 ft. The many shallow

Virgin Gorda

areas and the protected cove location make this a "best snorkel dive" as well as a good selection for the SCUBA diver. Boat access only.

☆☆☆**GARY'S GROTTOS.** Located on the shore line four miles north of Spanish Town on Virgin Gorda, Gary's Grottos is a shallow reef characterized by three huge arches which give exploring divers a feeling of swimming through a tunnel. Divers are often greeted by a moray at the cave which is at the end of the three overpasses. This is a very rocky area teeming with shrimp, squid and sponges. The cove, protected from wind and waves, is also a choice spot for a night dive. The average depth is 30 ft.

☆☆**THE WRECK OF THE *ROKUS*.** On New Year's Eve, 1929, the Greek ship *Rokus* hit the reef on the southeast end of Anegada. She sank in 40 ft of water with much of her hull remaining above the surface until hurricane Frederick struck in 1979. Remains of her cargo of animal bones can be found scattered around the wreckage. The reef surrounding the hull is pretty, with large formations of elkhorn and staghorn as well as brain coral. During the winter months, February through March, the song of migrating humpback whales can be heard from this site.

☆☆☆☆**ALICE IN WONDERLAND.** This coral wall, located in the southwestern bay of Ginger Island, goes from 40 ft to a sandy bottom at 90 ft. Large mushroom corals, overhangs, and brain corals typify this reef. Long nose butterfly fish dart among the corals. Rays, conch and garden eels can be found on the bottom. Visibility is good and seas are usually calm.

☆☆☆☆**P.O.S.** Named after "Project Ocean Search", a Cousteau project which is operational once a year, this reef follows the shore line of Cockroach Island (one of the Dog Islands). This is a "must" for every underwater photographer. Beautiful formations of towering pillar corals, stag horn, and elkhorns in 35 ft of water are frequented by tarpon, fry, French angels, crabs, lobsters, and schooling fish. The "Keyhole", a hole in one of the coral walls just big enough for a diver to get through, is the perfect underwater photo-subject frame.

☆☆☆**JOE'S CAVE** is an underwater cavern located on the west side of West Dog Island. It can be explored by swimming from the entrance, at 20 ft, down to 75 ft where you'll find a magnificent opening to the sky. Outside the cave are many corals and rock formations. Eels abound. The bottom terrain is rough. Schools of gleaming copper sweepers live inside Joe's Cave. This is a protected area with no current or surges.

Basket sponge

☆☆**VAN RYAN'S ROCK.** This sea mount is located in the middle of Drake's Channel between Beef Island and Virgin Gorda. The top is at 16 ft and the bottom at 55 ft, with boulders and coral leading down to a sandy plain. Nurse sharks, eels, huge turtles, lobster, jacks, spade fish, and barracuda circle it. Divers and snorkelers should be careful of the abundance of fire coral here. A current is occasionally encountered here.

☆☆☆**INVISIBLES.** This sea mount, located off the northeast end of Tortola, is a haven for nurse shark, eels, turtles and all types of reef fish from the smallest to the largest. Gayla Kilbride describes this area as a "Symphony of Fish". Depths go from three down to 65 ft, a nice range for both snorkeling and diving.

Best Snorkeling Sites

☆☆☆☆**WRECK OF THE *PARAMATTA*** sits on a dense coral reef off the southeast end of Anegada in 30 ft of water. The shallows here make it a perfect place for snorkelers; if you stand on the ship's engine, you'll be shoulder deep. Enormous reef fish swim around the wreck, including a 200-pound jew fish, 30- pound groupers, butterfly fish, turtles, and rays. Still remaining are the stern and bow sections, long chain, port holes, and cleats of the wreck.

☆☆☆☆☆**THE BATHS.** At the southern tip of Virgin Gorda are partially submerged grottoes and caves formed by a jumble of enormous granite boulders. A favorite beach access area for snorkeling and one of the biggest tourist attractions in the BVI, the caves provide a home for a variety of tropical fish. This area can be found by taking the trail which starts at the end of the Baths Road. A small bar just off the beach rents snorkel equipment.

☆☆**CRAWL NATIONAL PARK.** Beginning   snorkelers should try Crawl National Park, also on Virgin Gorda, reached via a palm-lined trail from Tower Road. This is a bit north of the Baths. A boulder formation which has created a natural pond is good for children.

☆☆☆**DEVIL'S BAY BEACH.** Just south of The Baths, this bay was once a hiding place for smugglers. Good snorkeling is found at the south side of the bay among the boulders.

☆☆☆☆**THE CAVES.** Located at Norman Island, accessible only by boat, this snorkeling photo site is bright with sponges, corals and schools of small fish. The reef slopes down to 40 ft. Norman Island is rumored to have inspired Robert Louis Stevenson's *Treasure Island* and the Caves are reputed to be old hiding places for pirate treasure.

Dive Operators

KILBRIDE'S UNDERWATER TOURS. Bert Kilbride has been diving the British Virgin Islands since the 1950's—longer than anyone else. Well known for his treasure hunting he has found 138 wrecks on Anegada Reef alone. Together with his wife Gayla and 14 others of the Kilbride clan, Bert operates a 42-ft dive boat named *Shah* at Norman Island and the *Sea Trek,* also 42 ft, out of the Bitter End Yacht Club. Their boats take you to 50 different dive locations. You may be escorted by any one of sixteen diving Kilbrides. Tours can be booked by writing to Box 40, Saba Rock, Virgin Gorda, BVI. ☎ 809-49-42746. Mail may take as long as six weeks so write early.

DIVE BVI operates out of Leverick Bay and has several packages available. Two-tank dives on the 36-ft Seacat can accommodate up to 12 people. Resort courses through certification are available. Write: P.O. Box 1040, Virgin Gorda, BVI ☎ 809-49-55513.

UNDERWATER SAFARIS, owned by Gail and Bob Stafford at the MooringsMariner Inn on Tortola, is equipped with a 42-ft Mako and two 30-ft dive boats. Their shop is the largest retail dive shop in the BVI. Address: P.O. Box 139, Road Town, Tortola. ☎ (U.S.) 800-537-7032 or 809-49-43235.

BASKIN IN THE SUN, which operates out of the Prospect Reef Resort Marina, has two dive boats which can accommodate 10 and twenty divers comfortably. Divemasters will carry, rinse and store your gear and replace it on the boat for your next scheduled dive.

British Virgin Islands sunset

Package tours can be booked through Baskin in the Sun, P.O. Box 108, Road Town, Tortola, BVI. ☎ 809-494- 2858/9 or (U.S.) 800-233-7938.

BLUE WATER DIVERS, located at Nanny Cay on the south side of Tortola, serves divers staying at Sugar Mill or the Windjammer. Blue Water Divers operates a 47-ft Catamaran . Dive tours are to the eastern sites in the BVI, such as Jost Van Dyke, as well as all the sites in the channel. Write to: P.O. Box 437, Road Town, Tortola, BVI. ☎ 809-494-2847.

Sailing and SCUBA Live-Aboards

LAMMER LAW. Sailing fever attacks the heartiest of divers in the BVI. If you're looking for a luxury vacation combining the best of both diving and sailing, spend a week aboard the *Lammer Law.* One of the world's largest trimarans (95 ft x 42 ft), *Lammer Law* was specifically designed with the SCUBA diver in mind. As with most live-aboards, you are offered "all the diving you can stand. *Lammer Law* accommodates 18 passengers in nine large, airy, double cabins, each with private head and shower. Rates are commensurate with those charged for a week at any of the major resorts.

The *Cuan Law* is a new 105-ft-long addition to the fleet that offers the same features as the *Lammer Law.* These Sail/Dive cruises are booked up from three months to a year in advance. For booking or more information, ☎ 800-648-3393 or write Trimarine Boat Company, P.O. Box 1840, Portola, CA 96122.

TROPIC BIRD is a spacious 98-ft motor yacht with twelve double staterooms, full-sized bunks, five heads, hot/cold fresh water showers and baths. Air conditioned. Tropic Bird embarks from Road Town, Tortola.

Diving packages include a minimum of two dives per day and one night dive, three meals a day, free resort course for non-divers. Topless sunbathing permitted. To book, ☎ 800-433-DIVE or 805-654-8100 or write TLC Dive Vacations, 4572 Telephone Road, Suite 913, Ventura CA 93003.

Sailing: Bareboating

Private sailing yachts with diving guides and instructors are available from most of the charter operators listed below. You can arrange for your own personal live-aboard diving or snorkeling vacation. Be sure to specify your needs before going.

CSY, P.O. Box 491, Tenafly NJ 07670 ☎ 800-631-1593. CSY charters CSY 50, 51,42, and 44.5 boats. SCUBA gear may be rented from the local dive shop.

THE MOORINGS LTD., Tortola, has been operating for 18 years. Their charter boats include Moorings 35, 37, 51, 50, 432 (43 ft), 43, 39, and 37. A Moorings 51, Morgan 60 or Gulfstar 60 maybe chartered but with crew only. The Moorings' book "Virgin Anchorages" picture aerial photographs of the best anchorages in the BVI.

A three-day sailing vacation can be combined with a four-day resort/diving vacation at the Moorings Mariner Inn.

Write to The Moorings, Ltd., 1305 U.S. 19 South, Suite 402, Clearwater FL 34624. ☎ 800-535-7289 or 813- 535-1446.

STEVENS YACHTS, at Frenchmans Cay, West End, Tortola, has bareboat and crewed sailing charters available. For reservations ☎ 800-638- 7044 or 809-49-54740.

Accommodations

DRAKE'S ANCHORAGE on Mosquito Island, just north of North Sound off Virgin Gorda, is a hideaway with ten beachfront units and two deluxe villas. The island has four lovely beaches, with snorkeling off shore, moorings for cruising sailboats and gourmet cuisine. ☎ 800-624-6651 or write Drake's Anchorage Resort Inn, P.O. Box 2510 Virgin Gorda, BVI. Expensive.

THE BITTER END YACHT CLUB is located at John O'Point at North Sound. Rooms are in nicely furnished villas along the shore and hillside. ☎ 800-872-2392, or 809-49-42746 or write P.O. Box 46, Virgin Gorda, BVI. Moderate.

LEVERICK BAY RESORT, a five-acre resort on Virgin Gorda's North Sound, offers villas or apartments, all overlooking the ocean. ☎ 800-387-4964, 809-49-57421 or write BVI Villa & Resort Mgmt, c/o North Sound, Virgin Gorda Yacht Harbour, Virgin Gorda, BVI. Moderate.

THE MARINER INN, Tortola, is homeport to The Moorings charter boat operation. It has no beach. The poolside bar and restaurant are just a few steps from Underwater Safaris, the largest retail shop in the BVI. ☎ 800-535-7289, 809-49-42174 or write The Moorings Mariner Inn, 1305 US 19 S. Suite 402, Clearwater FL 34624. Moderate.

PROSPECT REEF RESORT is a sprawling 10-acre resort located on the west end of Road Town, Tortola, facing Sir Francis Drake Channel. The resort has over 130 rooms ranging from studios to standard rooms, full apartments, and luxury villas. SCUBA packages are arranged through Aquatic Centre. ☎ 800-223-0888, 809-49-43311. Write Box 104, Road Town, Tortola, BVI. Moderate to expensive.

SUGARMILL, on the northwest shore of Tortola, is a village of hillside cottages. An old sugar mill houses the restaurant where you may dine by candlelight on conch stew, grouper salad, grilled swordfish and salads with lettuce from the Sugar Mill garden. There is a small beach here. ☎ 809-495-4355. Write P.O. Box 425, Tortola, BVI. Moderate.

Dining

RHYMER'S BEACH BAR at Cane Garden Bay, Tortola, is a favorite among the locals.

MRS. SCATLIFFE'S RESTAURANT, another local favorite in Road Town, Tortola, specializes in local food such as fish soup made with coconut milk.

THE ANEGADA REEFS HOTEL, Anegada, serves lunch at their beach bar and specializes in local dishes.

In Roadtown

DRAKE'S ANCHORAGE, on Mosquito, has been written up in *Gourmet Magazine* for its fabulous Caribbean lobster and local fish dinners. Moorings are available for a low overnight charge.

SANDCASTLE at White Bay on Jost Van Dyke serves gourmet fish, lobster, fresh breads and desserts in an open air restaurant on the beach. No credit cards. Reservations may be made by marine VHF radio.

CARIB CASSEROLES, on Tortola, has a "Meals on Keels" service for bareboaters experienced with boil-a-bags, as well as sit-down service. Food is a combination of Caribbean, French, Greek and Creole. Peanut Creole Soup, curry and casseroles are featured here. Moderate.

PETER ISLAND HOTEL AND YACHT HARBOUR offers lunch at the Beach Restaurant from 12:30 to 2 PM. Dinners are somewhat formal: men must wear a jacket and women, "cocktail" attire. Expensive.

Mt. Sage, Tortola

FACTS

RECOMPRESSION CHAMBER. The nearest chamber is located on St. Thomas in the neighboring USVI.

GETTING THERE. San Juan, Puerto Rico is the airline hub for the Caribbean with frequent service to all parts of the United States, Canada and Europe. Beef Island is the major airport of Tortola and the BVI. Flights to San Juan with connections to the BVI can be booked from the United States on American, Eastern, Delta, TWA and American Trans Air. Air BVI or Eastern Metro can be taken from San Juan to Beef Island, Tortola, or Virgin Gorda. Inter-island water ferry service is also available including service to St. Thomas. Baggage can sometimes be delayed by a day on the small airlines. Divers carrying a lot of equipment should fly direct to St. Thomas and take a water ferry, to avoid having to change planes.

ISLAND TRANSPORTATION. Car rentals: (Tortola) Budget, Alphonso, Island Suzuki, International, Nibb's, Anytime, Avis; (Virgin Gorda) Bomba and National. Bicycles are also rentable from Hero's Bicycle in Tortola or Harrigan Rent-a-Cycle in Virgin Gorda.

TAXI SERVICE. Available from Beef Island Airport, Road Town Jetty, West End Jetty and from the dock on Virgin Gorda.

DRIVING. Valid BVI Driving License required. A temporary license may be obtained from the car rental agencies for $5.00. Driving is on the left-hand side of the road. Maximum speed is 30 mph. Bicycles must be registered at the Traffic Licensing Office in Road Town.

DOCUMENTS. A valid passport is required to enter the BVI. For U.S. and Canadian citizens an authenticated birth certificate or voter registration card will suffice.

CUSTOMS AND DUTIES. The United States allows each person an exemption of $400 (a 10 percent duty is charged over that amount). Also one carton of cigarettes and one liter of liquor are allowed per person over age 21. Unlimited allowance on anything that qualifies as craft. Products made from sea turtles are not allowed.

CURRENCY. U.S. Dollar. Personal checks not accepted.

CLOTHING. Casual, light clothing; some of the resorts require a jacket for dinner. Avoid exposed midriffs and bare chests in residential and commercial areas. Nudity is punishable by law.

TIME. Atlantic Standard (EST + 1 hr.).

LANGUAGE. English.

CLIMATE. The BVI are in the tradewind belt and have a subtropical climate. Average temperatures are 75 to 85° F in winter and 80 to 90° F in summer. Nights are cooler. The hurricane season extends from July through September.

TAXES. There is a departure tax and hotel accommodation tax of 7 percent.

NEWSPAPERS. *The Island Sun* and *BVI Beacon* are both printed weekly.

RELIGIOUS SERVICES. Methodist, Anglican, Roman Catholic, Seventh Day Adventist, Baptist, Jehovah's Witness, Pentecostal and Church of Christ.

NOTE: Possession of drugs is punishable by fines and jail sentences.

FOR ADDITIONAL INFORMATION and a list of all guesthouses, apartments, hotels, campgrounds, charter operators, and restaurants contact the British Virgin Islands Tourist Board. Note: reservations for many of the hotels may be made through the tourist board or your travel agent. In Tortola: P.O. Box 134, Road Town, Tortola, British Virgin Islands. In New York: BVI Tourist Board, 370 Lexington Avenue, NY NY 10017, ☎ 800-232-7770, 212-696-0400.

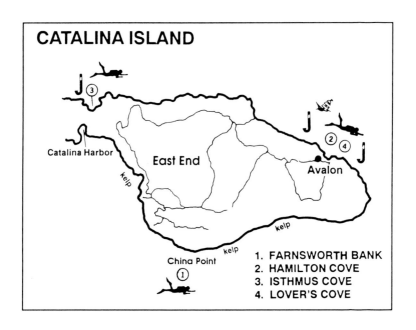

CATALINA ISLAND

Catalina Harbor

East End

Avalon

China Point

kelp

1. FARNSWORTH BANK
2. HAMILTON COVE
3. ISTHMUS COVE
4. LOVER'S COVE

CATALINA ISLAND

Of all the Southern Channel Islands (Catalina, Santa Barbara, San Clemente, and San Nicolas), Catalina, located 22 miles off the coast of Los Angeles, is the most popular. It offers the best diving and vacation facilities by far. Regular scheduled cross-channel boat and air service to Avalon, the island's only town, brings tourists from all over the world. Boat service is also available to Two Harbors. Note: Catalina Island is not a part of the Channel Islands National Park or Marine Sanctuary, covered elsewhere in this book.

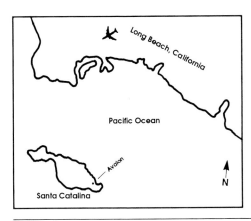

The water here is warmer and clearer than that around the Northern Channel Islands and it offers easier diving conditions. Beautiful kelp forests, abundant lobster and abalone holes abound. The underwater landscape has a rocky bottom and deep cav-

---

Area Contributors: BBD&O; Argo Diving; Bud Davis, Avalon, CA.

Avalon Bay

erns. A wide selection of accommodations, activities, great restaurants, and easy access from shore dive and snorkeling sites are available.

The Casino Building on Avalon Bay, which contains an art gallery, museum, theater and ballroom, is the island's most famous landmark. It was built in 1929 by The Santa Catalina Island Company.

Catalina Island is 21 miles long and ranges from one-half to eight miles wide. Mt. Orizaba (2,125 ft) and Mt. Black Jack (2,020 ft) are its highest elevations.

Avalon, the island's only city, is a picturesque array of story-book cottages, flower gardens, shops, boutiques, restaurants, and beautiful hotels.

Postcard-perfect palm-lined beaches and snorkeling coves fringe the island.

Best Dives of Catalina Island

Visibility is best during the winter months. Summer brings plankton blooms which cloud the water. The average water temperature is 65° F, (ranging from 57° to 71°), necessitating a full wet suit for diving.

☆☆☆☆**FARNSWORTH BANK** is Catalina's most exciting dive, though suitable only for very experienced ocean divers. It is located about three miles southwest of Ben Weston Point on Catalina's "Bach" or windward side. This rocky sea mount starts at 50 ft below the surface and drops off to over 150 ft. Some surge and a current, which can be heavy at times, is to be expected here. Visibility is usually outstanding. Sea urchins, anemones, pastel gorgonians, kelp, and rare lavender corals cover the mount. The coral is protected and should not be touched.

☆☆☆**SHIP ROCK.** Located off shore from the north side of Two Harbors, this outcrop is a favorite among SCUBA-equipped wildlife photographers. A 50-minute boat ride from Avalon brings you here. Depths range from 100 to 110 ft. The bottom is sandy. An exceptional amount of marine life can be viewed here, including sea lions who regularly swim with the divers, seals, moray eels, lobster, colorful urchins, small horn sharks, octopus, keyhole limpets (mollusks similar to abalone), sea hares and perch.

☆☆☆**ISTHMUS COVE.** This harbor marks the center point between the east and west ends of Catalina Island. A rocky reef is found at depths between 20 and 40 ft with a sharp drop-off to over 100 ft. The walls are carpeted with patches of towering kelp, lavender and red sea urchins, colorful anemones, starfish, and red gorgonians. Lobsters, moray eels and scallops can be found in the crevices. Halibut and kelp bass can be found on the reef. A nice spot for underwater photography. Currents are light, making this spot good for snorkelers and novice divers.

Best Snorkeling Sites of Catalina Island

☆☆**LOVER'S COVE.** Located just east of Avalon Bay, Lover's Cove is an easy entry from a small pebble beach adjacent to the ferry landing. This spot is reserved for snorkeling only and protected from spear fishing or collecting. The bottom is rocky with patches of kelp. A number of friendly fish will follow you around in hopes of being fed. Starfish, anemones, urchins, shrimp and some lobster can be found in the rocks and crevices. This area is calm with little or no current running. Water temperatures are consistently warmer here than on the windward side of the island.

☆☆☆**CASINO POINT UNDERWATER PARK.** Calm seas, good visibility, and easy access from a concrete walk to a roped-off preserve make this a divers' favorite. The park area, on the ocean side of the point, is roped off to protect divers from the boats that pass through the harbor. Divers can explore kelp patches and rocky reefs teeming with colorful invertebrates and other marine life. Several small wrecks are lying on the bottom. Seas are generally calm. Depth is 10 to 90 ft. Divers are prohibited from taking game in the park.

Dive Operators

ARGO DIVING SERVICE. Underwater tours, instruction, introductory dives, and boat dives. Write to Argo Diving Service, P.O. Box 1201, Avalon, CA 90704. ☎ 213-510-2208.

CATALINA DIVER'S SUPPLY. Dive gear rental, service, air fills and dive charters. Write to Catalina Diver's Supply, P.O. Box 126, Avalon, CA 90704. ☎ 213-510-0330.

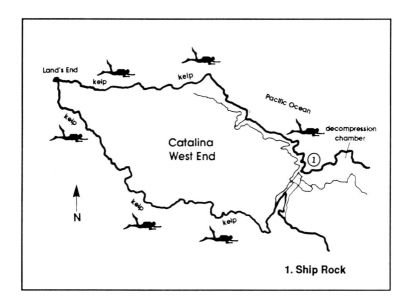

1. Ship Rock

Accommodations

Note: Two- and three-night minimums are sometimes required by the resorts for advance weekend reservations. From November to February one night advance reservations are accepted by most hotels

BAY VIEW HOTEL. Located one-half block from the beach on Whittley Avenue, this hotel welcomes dive groups and offers airy rooms and diving. ☎ 213-510-0600 or write Box 1017, Avalon, CA 90704.

HOTEL ATWATER is just a stroll away from the beach in the heart of Avalon. Catalina's shops and restaurants are also in walking distance. Features are private baths, color TV and cable; connecting rooms available. Bus tours are just across the street. ☎ 213-510-2000, in California ☎ 800-4-AVALON.

Sightseeing

Tours of the island include the Wrigley Memorial and Botanical Garden and the Inland Motor Tour, a 3¾-hour journey through

Anemone

the unspoiled interior and which includes a stop at El Rancho Escondido, and performances by Arabian horses. You may even see some of Catalina's free roaming buffalo and spot a soaring bald eagle.

DINING

A variety of fine eateries, both plain and fancy, can be found on Catalina.

CAFE PREGO. Considered one of the best restaurants in Southern California by *LA Magazine*, this fine restaurant located on Crescent Avenue offers seafood , steak and Italian foods, including soup, hot bread, salad and entree. Meals from $7.95. ☎ 510-1218.

DESCANSO BEACH SIDEWALK CAFE. A delicious variety of appetizers, salads, sandwiches and charbroiled burgers along with famous fresh fruit shakes are offered here. Open daily. ☎ 510-2780.

RISTORANTE VILLA PORTOFINO. Enjoy Mediterranean cuisine featuring seafoods, pastas, veal and fine wines in a casual oceanfront site. ☎ 510-0508.

AVALON SEAFOOD. Outdoors on the Green Pleasure Pier, it has a delicious variety of raw and cooked fresh fish. Open daily. ☎ 510-0197.

BAYSIDE BAKERY & DELI. This is the perfect apres-dive snack spot. ☎ 510-2632.

FACTS

RECOMPRESSION CHAMBER. A chamber is located on Catalina Island at the USA Marine Lab, ☎ 213-510-0811.

GETTING THERE. Catalina Cruises offers year-round service from Long Beach and Catalina Terminal, San Pedro. 700 passenger boats, comfortable seating, walking space on three decks, cocktail and snack bar. The cruise is less than two hours.Write to P.O. Box 1948, San Pedro CA 90733. ☎ 213-775-6111 or 714-527-7111. Groups should call 213-547-0802. Catalina Passenger Service from Orange County departs from historic Balboa Pavilion in Newport Beach. ☎ 714-673-5245. Allied Air Charter, Inc., offers flights from Montgomery Field. Reservations required. ☎ 619-456-1212. Catalina Express has fast boat service (90 minutes) from San Pedro, CA, ☎ 213-519-1212. Island Express has daily helicopter flights from Long Beach (by the Queen Mary) and San Pedro, at the Catalina Terminal ☎ 213-491-5550. Helitrans Air service offers helicopter connections from Los Angeles, ☎ 213-548-1314.

ISLAND TRANSPORTATION. Catalina Safari Bus offers daily scheduled service in summer and weekend bus service during winter around the island, ☎ 213-510-2800. Taxi service to all points and places on Catalina is available from Catalina Cab Co., ☎ 213-510-0025. Shore boat service from Avalon to White's Landing by Island Navigation 510-0409.

CLIMATE. Temperatures range between 50 and 68° F November through May.

CLOTHING. Lightweight during summer months with an extra sweater or jacket for cool evenings. Warmer fall clothing during winter months. A full quarter-inch wetsuit, with hood and booties, is needed for diving year-round.

FOR ADDITIONAL INFORMATION. Catalina Island Chamber of Commerce and Visitors Bureau, P.O. Box 217, Avalon CA 90704. ☎ 213-510-1520.

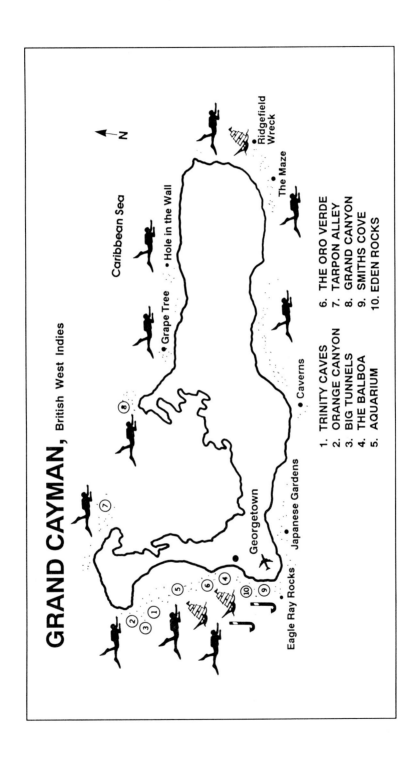

GRAND CAYMAN, British West Indies

Caribbean Sea

N

• Ridgefield Wreck

The Maze

• Hole in the Wall

• Grape Tree

• Caverns

Georgetown

Japanese Gardens

Eagle Ray Rocks

1. TRINITY CAVES
2. ORANGE CANYON
3. BIG TUNNELS
4. THE BALBOA
5. AQUARIUM

6. THE ORO VERDE
7. TARPON ALLEY
8. GRAND CANYON
9. SMITHS COVE
10. EDEN ROCKS

CAYMAN ISLANDS

The Cayman Islands—Grand Cayman, Cayman Brac and Little Cayman—are top Caribbean dive-vacation spots, each uniquely beautiful and all welcoming. Located just 480 miles, and one hour flying time, south of Miami, this Caribbean trio entertains over 100,000 divers each year.

Underwater Cayman is a submerged mountain range, the Sierra Maestra, complete with cliffs, drop-offs, gulleys, caverns, sink holes and forests of coral. The islands are the visible above-the-sea portions of the mountains. The Cayman Trench drops off to over 23,000 ft depths. The temperature averages 77°F and the climate is warm and inviting all year.

The atmosphere is casual and relaxing yet there is plenty of activity for the energetic. Whatever your preferred vacation style, you'll find it on one of the Cayman Islands. Grand Cayman offers chic resorts with a cosmopolitan flair and a diversified nightlife; Cayman Brac is less crowded, offering a rural tropical setting, but with two superb resorts, and many non-diving activities. Little Cayman, with a population of less than 20, offers nature lovers a picturesque wilderness with continual five-star diving.

Dubbed "The Islands that Time Forgot" by the *Saturday Evening Post,*The Cayman Islands today have become one of the fastest growing dive-travel destinations in the Western

Area Contributors: Mike Emmanuel, Mina Heuslein, Bill Heuslein, Kenneth Liggett, and Jim Spencer.

"Stingray City"

Hemisphere. Building construction has replaced fishing and agriculture as one of the mainstays of employment. Tourism now sustains 70 percent of the economy.

The Cayman Islands are one of the last dependent territories of Great Britain in the Caribbean Sea. This British background is strongly reflected in the people who, as loyal subjects of the crown, maintain a high respect for the law and fellow man. There is very little crime. The people are known for their warmth, friendliness and pleasure in welcoming visitors.

The Caymans have enjoyed freedom from tax "in perpetuity" since the late 1700's—in return, so the story goes, for heroic action of Caymanians in saving the lives of passengers and crews of 10 sailing ships. As a result Grand Cayman has attracted a great number of banks and corporations.

Like many other Caribbean islands, the discovery of the Caymans is attributed to Christopher Columbus who discovered the islands on his second voyage while en route from Panama to Cuba in 1503. Amazingly, his primitive ships were able to negotiate the coral reefs with little trouble. He named these islands "Las Tortugas" for the countless marine turtles who came to Cayman beaches to breed. The turtles, which lived in captivity for long periods, became a source of fresh meat for the sailors, and the Cayman Islands became a regular stop for exploring ships.

SCUBA diving and snorkeling in the Cayman Islands are special. The outstanding visibility, thriving dense coral forests and mammoth barrel sponges are merely a spectacular setting for the ever-performing marine animals. The marine animals are so friendly and tame one almost wonders if the antics of some are not orchestrated by Disney studios.

Flat-bottomed dive boats attest to the sea's dependable tranquility, making the area appealing to the rank novice as well as the experienced diver. Snorkeling is equally superb, and can be enjoyed by simply wading out from any one of the lovely sand beaches found on all three islands. Boat dives are all a few minutes from shore.

Best Dives of Grand Cayman

All three Caymans offer protecting barrier reefs. Shallow dives and snorkeling sites are best inside the reefs. Outside the fringe of the barrier reefs, spectacular wall dives drop off to unimaginable depths. Conditions are generally mild, although steady winds can kick up some chop. When this happens dive boats simply move to the leeward side of the island and calmer waters.

A tough Marine Protection Law prohibits taking corals, sponges, and living collector specimens, with penalties of $5,000. Also all spear fishing by visitors has recently been banned. The water sports operators have banned the use of gloves by divers. A brochure describing the regulations is available on the islands.

☆☆☆☆☆TRINITY CAVES, located off the northern end of West Bay, consists of a series of canyon trails at depths between 60 and 100 ft. Here divers find huge sponges, gorgonians, sea fans, hundreds of critters, black coral, turtles, angels and numerous crustaceans. Sea conditions are generally calm, with

Wreck of the Balboa

an occasional light current, and visibility is exceptional. Some experience is recommended. Three large cathedral-like caves give this site its name.

☆☆☆☆**ORANGE CANYON** is north of Trinity Caves. Named for clusters of vibrant orange basket and elephant ear sponges, this reef dive starts at 45 ft, the brink of a wall which drops off to an unknown depth. The reef is dense with staghorn and brain corals and lavender, red and pastel sponges. Feather dusters, sea fans, gorgonians and fire coral carpet the walls and provide cover for shrimp, sea cucumbers, brittle stars, arrow crabs, file fish, turtles and small octopi. A good spot for close-up photography.

☆☆☆☆☆BIG TUNNELS is north of the Seven Mile Beach area. The area's outstanding feature is a 50-ft coral archway linked to several tunnels and ledges. Eagle rays, grunts, puffer fish, jackknife-fish, morays, queen trigger fish and an occasional nurse shark inhabit the reef.

☆☆☆☆THE WRECK OF THE *BALBOA* is a favorite spot for a night dive. The remains of the *Balboa,* a 375-ft freighter, sit in just 30 ft of water. The twisted wreckage offers nice silhouettes for photography especially since the location is always calm with good visibility, although a number of divers visiting the wreck at one time can kick up a bit of silt.

☆☆☆AQUARIUM sits close to shore just off the center of Seven Mile Beach. Fish feeding is mandatory. Luring them with some crumbs or biscuits may bring more finned attention than you bargained for. They will crawl right into your vestpockets looking for more snacks or position themselves so close to your camera that you can't focus. Average depth is about 35 ft. Visibility is good and the surface is generally calm. Recommended for novices.

☆☆☆THE WRECK OF THE *ORO VERDE* is a short boat ride directly out from the Holiday Inn on Seven Mile Beach. This 180-ft freighter suffered extensive damage after running aground on the Cayman reefs in 1976. Local dive operators acquired salvage rights and purposely sank the ship creating an artificial reef and an exciting new dive spot. The wreck is intact, very photogenic and one of the favorite dives off the West End. Depths range from 30 to 50 ft. This area is calm and clear.

✩✩**TARPON ALLEY** is located off the north shore of Grand Cayman and as the name implies is home to a canyon filled with schools of giant silvery tarpon. The bottom is sandy, rising to thickets of coral. Beside the schooling tarpon, divers find large groupers and sting rays in this area. The average depth on top of the wall is about 60 ft with drop-offs to several thousand ft. Large pelagic fish are occasionally encountered here. Visibility is good but surface conditions are occasionally choppy.

✩✩**GRAND CANYON** is an enormous canyon enclosed by jagged perpendicular mountains of coral. The walls are lush with a dense cover of sponges, sea whips, sea fans, hard corals and plume worms. This is the favored north wall dive and is located off Rum Point. Diving starts at 60 ft and drops off to thousands of ft. Experienced divers only. Visibility is excellent.

Best Snorkeling Sites
of Grand Cayman

Good snorkeling can be found by wading out from many swimming beaches on Grand Cayman. Just a few yards off shore you will find a bevy of beautiful reef fish darting in and out of clumps of living coral. Clearer water and more dramatic coral formations are found farther off shore and may be reached by boat. Be sure to wear fins or coral shoes to avoid abrasion on the coral.

✩✩**SMITHS COVE,** south of George Town, contains a garden of beautiful elkhorn, brain and staghorn corals. The reef is shallow but drops off further from shore.

☆☆☆☆☆EDEN ROCKS is a favorite area for cruise ship groups. This area is less than 200 yds off shore and ranges in depth from five to 40 ft. In addition to the beautiful coral grottoes, walls, caves and tunnels you'll find fish eagerly awaiting snorkelers bearing gifts of aerosol cheese, crackers, and leftover toast from breakfast. Good visibility and light currents are the norm here.

Dive Operators and Accommodations on Grand Cayman

BOB SOTO'S DIVING LTD. This facility has locations all over Grand Cayman. The operation offers underwater photo and video services, open water PADI certifications, completion dives, and comfortable custom dive boats. Complete dive/accommodation packages can be arranged. ☎ 1-800-262-7686 or 1-809-949-8457. Write to P.O. Box 1801, Grand Cayman, BWI.

DON FOSTER'S DIVE GRAND CAYMAN, LTD. is based at the Royal Palms Beach. Dive packages are available in cooperation with Hospitality World Condominiums and The Grand Pavilion Hotel. ☎ 1-800- 526-1394 or 1-809-949-7025.

SUNSET HOUSE, a hotel that offers dive trips, is favored by discriminating divers who want a lot of island atmosphere in a relaxed setting. Write to P.O. Box 479, Grand Cayman, BWI. ☎ 800-854-4767 or 809-949-7111. Cable SUNSET.

SURFSIDE WATERSPORTS, LTD. has three locations on Grand Cayman, all offering complete dive and accommodation packages. ☎ 809-949-7330 or write P.O. Box 891, Grand Cayman, BWI.

For a complete listing of Grand Cayman resorts, rentals, and dive operators write the Cayman Islands Department of Tourism at 250 Catalonia Ave, Suite 401, Coral Gables FL 33134, ☎ 305-444-6551.

Sightseeing on Grand Cayman

The capital city, George Town, has a well scrubbed look not always found in the Caribbean. Renowned as a major banking and insurance center, George Town has over 450 banks in the four block section nicknamed "Little Switzerland". Visitors can tour the area by foot, bus, moped or rental car.

Heading north along the famed Seven Mile Beach you come to the largest congregation of hotels, condos, shopping malls and new construction sites. Each morning dive boats line up here and offer door-to-reef service to resort and condo guests.

A side trip to the Cayman Turtle Farm is always fun, as is a visit to Hell, the town where visitors delight in having mail postmarked to send back home.

Dining

Grand Cayman offers visitors an enormous variety of choices in dining. The new shopping centers along West Bay Road house several fast food eateries such as Burger King, Pizza Hut

Cayman Brac, Tiara Beach

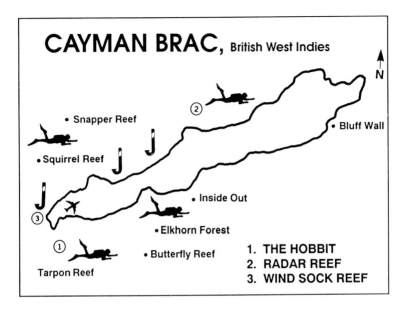

CAYMAN BRAC, British West Indies

N

• Snapper Reef

② Radar Reef

• Bluff Wall

• Squirrel Reef

• Inside Out

③ Wind Sock Reef

• Elkhorn Forest

① The Hobbit

• Butterfly Reef

Tarpon Reef

1. **THE HOBBIT**
2. **RADAR REEF**
3. **WIND SOCK REEF**

and Kentucky Fried Chicken and Triffles Ice Cream Emporium. For superb local specialties such as conch stew, curried chicken and native fish, try Turning Point in George Town (prices average $14). Conch lovers must stop in at Cracked Conch in the Selkirk Plaza or the Almond Tree near George Town. On Cayman Brac try dining alfresco at The Poseidon Room and the Grapetree Terrace and Lounge at the Divi Tiara Beach Hotel.

Best Dives of Cayman Brac

Often called the loveliest of the islands, this 12-mile strip of land is rumored to be the resting place of pirates' treasure. Lying some 87 miles east of Grand Cayman, Cayman Brac (brac is the Gaelic word for bluff) is named for an expanse of coral cliffs rising to 140 ft. which are shot through with caves. While some of these can be explored easily, some can be reached only by climbing vines and negotiating the face of the ironshore cliffs.

Wild green parrots, white herons and iguanas populate shrubs and trees. A visit to the Brac Museum in Stake Bay offers a look at the history of ship building on the island.

☆☆☆☆**THE HOBBIT** dive site puts you in a living fairy tale of giant barrel sponges, brilliantly colored walls of corals and tube sponges plus a flashing display of marine life, including schools of snapper, Bermuda chubs, turtles, queens and French angelfish, octopi, grunts and queen trigger fish. Average depth is 70 ft. Excellent visibility makes the Hobbit a good choice for video photography. Recommended for intermediate to advanced divers.

☆☆☆☆**RADAR REEF** is a series of coral pinnacles and canyons. Animal life comprises a lively community of turtles, sting rays, octopi, and a symphony of tropicals. Depths range from 30 to 60 ft. Surface conditions vary with the wind.

Best Snorkeling Sites
of Cayman Brac

Excellent snorkeling in calm, shallow water can be found all along the north shore. Several entry points are found at the boat launching areas where cuts through the dense coral have been blasted. Parking is available along side the north road.

On the south shore try Sea Feather Bay which is located at the Bluff Road crossing. Small coral heads and juvenile tropicals abound.

☆☆☆☆**WIND SOCK REEF**, which is off the now closed Buccaneer Inn, starts at about 25 ft, dropping to about 50 ft. This spur and groove reef offers a look at gardens of elkhorn, pillar corals, sea fans, orange sponges and gorgonians. Angels, barracuda, butterfly fish, file fish, trumpet fish and critters can be found hiding in the many crevices of the reef. Good visibility and usually calm seas make this a super spot for photography.

Dive Operators and Accommodations of Cayman Brac

DIVI TIARA BEACH HOTEL AND DIVE TIARA This operation is exceptional, with no effort spared to make every dive trip relaxing, safe and fun. Rooms are air-conditioned. Snorkeling and diving can be found right off the Tiara Beach Hotel's palm-lined beach. ☎ 1-800-367-3484.

BRAC REEF BEACH RESORT combined with Brac Aquatics offers comfortable, air-conditioned rooms with satellite TV, a great beach, fresh water pool, whirlpool, beach bar and restaurant. ☎ 1-800-327-3835 Write P.O. Box 235, Cayman Brac, BWI.

There are other facilities available such as "Soon Come," a charming two-bedroom house for rent located on the isolated south shore right at water's edge. (☎ 1-212-686-8333 for info.)

Best Dives of Little Cayman

Little Cayman is uncrowded and unhurried. This very rural eleven-mile-long island is populated by no more than three dozen people. One public telephone serves the community and the roads are yet unpaved. The runway is grass. Dive and fishing accommodations and services are plain and simple. For a true get-away vacation this is the place. Activities are limited to water sports and watching the iguanas.

☆☆☆☆☆**BLOODY BAY WALL** is considered by some to be the best dive in all the Caymans. Coral heads come within 15 ft of the surface. Bloody Bay Wall peaks as a shallow reef at 15 ft and drops off to an unfathomed bottom. Bright orange and lavender tube sponges, pastel gorgonians and soft corals form a dense floral garden. Conditions are usually calm although a stiff wind will churn the surface. Divers of all levels will find a good dive at Bloody Bay Wall.

Little Cayman

☆☆☆☆**LITTLE CAYMAN WALL** is a short boat trip off the west end of the island. This area is good for both snorkeling and diving. The bottom terrain is the characteristic shallow reef, starting at 15 ft then dropping off to unknown depths. Soft corals decorate the area, mixing with finger, brain and antler coral thickets.

Best Snorkeling Sites of Little Cayman

Little Cayman offers vacationers superb snorkeling spots with visibility often exceeding 100 ft. Ground transportation to beach access sites is easily arranged through the dive operators.

☆☆☆**POINT OF SAND,** located at the southeast end of Little Cayman, is a favorite spot of both experienced and beginning snorkelers. A gentle current flowing from west to east maintains dependably excellent visibility. The bottom is sandy with many coral heads scattered about. Marine life is fine and the site is accessible from the shore. Ground transportation can be arranged from the SCC.

☆☆☆**MARY'S BAY** stretches out for better than a mile inside the barrier reef just 50 yards from the beach. Recommended for beginner and experienced snorkelers. There is no current and visibility runs about 30 to 50 ft. At depths of three to eight ft, the bottom is turtle grass requiring booties or other submersible footwear. An old shack on an otherwise deserted shore marks the spot.

☆☆☆**JACKSON POINT** aka School Bus is for experienced snorkelers only. Swim out about 75 yards from the beach where you'll see a small wall towering from a sandy bottom at 40 ft to

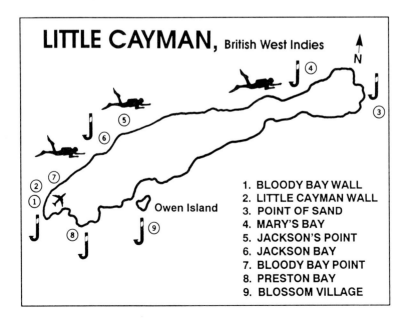

LITTLE CAYMAN, British West Indies

N

1. BLOODY BAY WALL
2. LITTLE CAYMAN WALL
3. POINT OF SAND
4. MARY'S BAY
5. JACKSON'S POINT
6. JACKSON BAY
7. BLOODY BAY POINT
8. PRESTON BAY
9. BLOSSOM VILLAGE

Owen Island

15 ft. Hundreds of fish, rays and turtles congregate in the shallows. Corals and sponges carpet the area. Swimming another 50 to 60 ft brings you to a much larger wall which drops off to extraordinary depths.

☆☆JACKSON BAY is similar to Jackson Point except the bottom of the mini-wall drops off to a depth of 50 to 60 ft.

☆☆☆☆BLOODY BAY POINT, recommended for seasoned snorkelers only, is well worth a visit. Beach access is difficult requiring a long swim out to the reef, located 100 yards from the shore. The bottom eases down to about 30 ft before the drop-off to The Great Wall begins. The main drop-off is shear and craggy. Mazes of tunnels, caves, and channels create an interesting undersea terrain. The shallow reefs on the ledge are abundant in exotic fish life. Overall, the coral and marine life are spectacular.

☆PRESTON BAY is the best choice for beginning snorkelers. Maximum depth is six ft; visibility 30 to 50 ft. Swarming schools of fish and a white sandy bottom offer endless photo opportunities.

☆☆BLOSSOM VILLAGE, reachable by boat, is another great choice for beginning snorkelers. A light current keeps the visibility between 50 and 100 ft. A wide variety of exotic marine life will entertain you in depths ranging between four and eight ft. Vase and tube sponges are numerous and provide refuge for many juvenile fish and critters.

Dive Operators and Accommodations of Little Cayman

Little Cayman dive operations are smaller than those on Cayman Brac and Grand Cayman. Accommodations are not air conditioned.

SOUTHERN CROSS CLUB is a 10-room fishing camp which warmly welcomes divers. Divemasters will take you to all the top dive and snorkel sites on the club's newest dive boat. ☎ 1-809-948-3255, in the U.S. ☎ 1-317-636-9501. Southern Cross Club, Little Cayman, Cayman Islands, BWI.

SAM McCOY'S DIVING AND FISHING LODGE, o f f e r s rustic accommodations for up to 14 divers (7 rooms). Twenty-ft fiberglass runabouts are used for reef trips. ☎ 203-438-5663 or write to Cayman Adventures, 14 Rochambeau Ave., Ridgefield, CT 06877.

PIRATE'S POINT features rustic guest cottages and a guest house. Owner Gladys Howard offers dive packages including

Seven Mile Beach

reef trips on comfortable inflatable run-abouts. BDWH divers rated Pirate's Point tops in friendly service and dive services. ☎ 809-948-4210.

Cayman Live-Aboards

See & Sea Travel Service has two floating dive resorts in the Cayman Islands, the *Cayman Aggressor II* and her sister yacht, *Cayman Aggressor III*. Based in George Town, both 110-ft cruisers feature seven double staterooms, one quad, air conditioning, TV, video equipment and hot showers. Write to Sea & Sea Travel Service, Inc. 50 Francisco St., Suite 205, San Francisco CA 94133. ☎ 1-800-DIV XPRT or 415-434-3400. Fax (415) 434-3409.

FACTS

RECOMPRESSION CHAMBER. George Town. This chamber is operated and staffed 24 hours a day by the British Sub-Aqua Club.

GETTING THERE. Cayman Airways provides scheduled flights from Miami, Houston, Atlanta, Tampa and New York to Grand Cayman with connecting flights to Cayman Brac and Little Cayman. Eastern, Northwest, and Air Jamaica fly nonstop from gateway cities into Grand Cayman. During peak season (Dec. 15 - April 15) charter flights direct from many major snowbelt cities to Grand Cayman are available from Cayman Airways. Flight time from Miami is 1 hour. Grand Cayman is a regular stop on many cruise lines as well.

ISLAND TRANSPORTATION. Rental cars, motorbikes, and bicycles are available on Grand Cayman and Cayman Brac. Friendly and informative taxi drivers are stationed at hotels and other convenient locations. On Grand Cayman, bus service is available from several hotels.

DRIVING. As in England, driving in the Cayman Islands is on the left. A temporary license is issued for a few dollars to persons holding U.S., Canadian or international licenses.

DOCUMENTS. Proof of citizenship (birth certificate, voter's registration certificate) is required from U.S., British, or Canadian citizens. No vaccinations are required unless you are coming from an endemic area.

CUSTOMS. The penalties for trying to bring drugs into the Cayman Islands are stiff fines and, frequently, prison terms.

CURRENCY. The Cayman Island Dollar is equal to $.80 U.S.

CLIMATE. Temperatures average about 77° F year round. The islands are outside of the hurricane belt and, although subject to some rainy periods, they are generally sunny and diveable.

CLOTHING. Casual, lightweight clothing. Some nightclubs require that men wear a jacket. Wetskins or shorty wetsuits are useful to avoid abrasions, as are light gloves for protection against the stinging corals. Snorkelers should wear reef gloves and protective clothing against sunburn.

ELECTRICITY. 110 V AC, 60 cycles. Same as U.S.

TIME. Eastern Standard Time.

TAX. There is a 6 percent government tax on accommodations. A service charge of 10 to 15 percent is often added to several restaurant bills. There is departure tax of $7.50 U.S.

RELIGIOUS SERVICES. Catholic, Protestant, Baptist, Mormon and non-denominational churches are found on Grand Cayman.

ADDITIONAL INFORMATION. The Cayman Islands Department of Tourism , 250 Catalonia Avenue, Coral Gables, FL 33134. ☎ 305-444-6551, or write P.O. Box 2066, Grand Cayman, Cayman Islands, BWI. ☎ 809- 94-97488.

CHANNEL ISLANDS
NATIONAL PARK & MARINE SANCTUARY

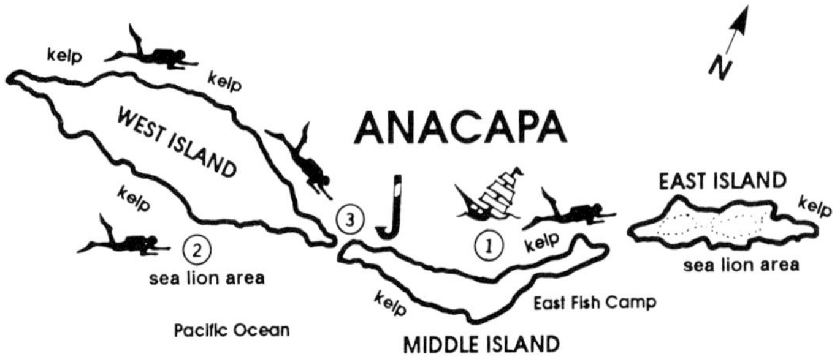

1. WINDFIELD SCOTT WRECK
2. CAT ROCK
3. FRENCHY'S COVE

CHANNEL ISLANDS NATIONAL MARINE SANCTUARY

Located off the coast of Southern California, the Channel Islands National Park includes San Miguel, Santa Cruz, Anacapa, Santa Rosa and Santa Barbara Island.

Accessible only by boat, these uninhabited islands present the diver with a panorama of windswept beauty filled with rugged volcanic cliffs, rolling hills, and rocky beaches occupied by brown pelicans, sea lions and elephant seals.

The Channel Islands National Marine Sanctuary was designated on September 22, 1980. The boundary of the sanctuary extends six nautical miles from the shores of Channel Islands National Park. This sanctuary is particularly valuable for recreation and research since it is located in a transition zone between the cold waters of the California Current and the warmer Southern California counter current. As a result, the Sanctuary hosts exceptionally diverse plant and animal life.

The waters of Channel Islands National Marine Sanctuary support a great variety of marine life from microscopic plankton to huge blue whales and basking sharks. Colorful tide pools,

Note: Sections reprinted with permission of the National Oceanic and Atmospheric Administration and Channel Islands National Marine Sanctuary. Area contributors: Nicholas Whelan, Park Ranger, Channel Islands National Park; Linda J. Kelly, U.S. Department of the Interior.

Anacapa

sandy beaches, wave beaten rocky cliffs and lush kelp forest surround the islands, which are actually the peaks of an extensive underwater ridge. A relatively shallow shelf with an average depth of 300 ft extends three to six miles around each island.

Underwater visibility runs between 40 and 60 ft, except during a plankton bloom when areas become soupy. Best visibility is found between August and December. Since water temperatures range from 55 to 70° F, divers must wear a full 1/4-inch or thicker wetsuit, complete with hood, gloves, and boots, year-round.

The islands are subject to storms and prolonged high winds, especially during winter months, which may prevent dive boats from crossing to the park.

The dense kelp forests surrounding the islands are named for the large brown seaweed, *Macrocystis pyrifera*. Anchored to the rocky bottom by root-like holdfasts, the kelp plants extend to the surface from depths as much as 200 ft. The species has been known to grow two ft a day. Sheltered by the canopy formed at the surface, hundreds of animals and other species of seaweed flourish. On the rocky reefs where the kelp is attached, urchins, crabs and abalone graze among encrusting sponges and plumed worms. Small colonial, filter-feeding organisms and multi colored snails are found on the leafy blades of the kelp. Many fish, like the rubber-lipped surf perch and the large, colorful sheephead, swim through the dense foliage. Fish and invertebrates also use the kelp for shelter and food.

A great variety of ocean creatures may be found in the rocky intertidal area of the sanctuary. Here tidepools are created when pockets of water are trapped between the cracks and hollows of rocks as the tide recedes.

In the deeper water of the sanctuary dolphins, porpoises and whales can often be seen, while other predators such as sharks and seal hunt the schools of fish found there. Of the more than 25 species of marine mammals known to inhabit the sanctuary, the seals and sea lions, known as pinnipeds, are among the most visible. At one time, pinnipeds roamed extensively along the southern California coast and hauled out on mainland beaches to breed.

ANACAPA ISLAND

Diving around the Channel Islands National Park area must be done from a boat. The best spots are around Anacapa Island and San Miguel Island.

Anacapa is the closest island to the mainland, just 11 miles southwest of Oxnard and 14 miles from Ventura. Anacapa is actually three small islands inaccessible from each other except by boat. January through March is whale-watch season. When the fog horn is blowing, don't approach the lighthouse on foot beyond the warning sign. Severe hearing damage may result. Diving activities on the east end of East Island are not affected by the foghorn. Vegetation on Anacapa is similar to that in a high-desert environment, due primarily to the year-round lack of rain. The most eye-catching plant is the giant coreopsis, a low, woody plant covered with green foliage and sunny yellow flowers in spring.

There are no land-dwelling mammals, except mice and black rats. However, seals and sea lions haul out on the island's rocky shores and there are birds of many species, including the brown pelican.

The waters surrounding the island are open to the public for fishing and diving. Day visits ashore and camping are permitted. However, the disturbance, damage or removal of any rock, plant or animal is prohibited within the park, except for fishing done in accordance with State of California regulations.

Best dives around Anacapa vary with the wind and sea conditions. Local charter dive boat captains are the best source of information. East Island has hiking trails, a campground, and a ranger station as well as the lighthouse.

Best Dives of Anacapa Island

☆☆**THE *WINFIELD SCOTT* WRECK.** This 225-ft paddle wheel steamer ran aground in dense fog and sank off Middle Anacapa in 1853. Remains of the wreck are scattered in 30 ft of water. Average visibility is 30 ft. The wreck is protected and nothing may be taken. Kelp beds are a short swim east of the wreck. Lobster, some abalone, sea urchins, starfish, and scallops may be found in this area. Check with local captains as to when you may take lobster and shell fish. Invertebrates may not be taken from waters less than 20 ft deep.

☆☆**CAT ROCK.** This area is off the south shore of West Anacapa Island. Diving is good when the southern swell is calm. The bottom is rocky and depths vary from 40 to 60 ft. A

Arch Point, Anacapa

variety of shellfish including lobster, abalone, starfish and scallops may be found here. Sea conditions vary with wind. Check for currents before entering the water.

Best Snorkeling Site of Anacapa

☆☆**FRENCHY'S COVE.** Located at West Anacapa, Frenchy's Cove has a beach and a good snorkeling area. Picnicking permitted. Depths range from 10 to 40 ft. Snorkelers will find colorful invertebrates including red starfish, sea urchins, sponges, and anemones, as well as some abalone . Some nice kelp forest. Seals sometimes visit the area as well as bass, octopi and an occasional ray.

SAN MIGUEL ISLAND

This westernmost of the northern islands boasts outstanding natural and cultural features. Some of the best examples of caliche, a mineral used in sandcasting, are found here. Enormous numbers of seals and sea lions haul out and breed on its isolated shores. An island fox can also be seen. Over 500 undisturbed archaeological sites , some dating back thousands of years, are located here. Juan Rodriquez Cabrillo, discoverer of California, is believed to have wintered and died at Cuyler Harbor in 1543. Although his grave has never been found, a monument overlooking the harbor was erected in 1937.

During World War II and the Korean War, the U.S. Navy used the island as a bombing range and later for missile testing. Staying on the trail is crucial since live ordnance is still occasionally uncovered by shifting sands. Visitors who wish to travel beyond the beach at Cuyler Harbor must be accompanied by a Park Ranger. Contact park headquarters for information and permit applications.

If you travel by private boat, you must obtain a permit in advance of your visit to land on San Miguel. The island is open for day use. Camping is available during the summer. Both the U.S. Navy and the National Park Service manage the island.

Kelp Forest diving around the island is excellent.

Best Dives of San Miguel Island

☆☆**WYCKOFF LEDGE.** Located off the south shore, Wyckoff Ledge offers divers a beautiful kelp forest and excellent visibility. Abalone, a variety of starfish, and sea anemones as well as some corals, and scallops can be found on the bottom. This is a good area for photography. The wall starts at 20 ft then drops off sharply to 90 ft. Sea conditions vary with wind and weather. A light current is always running.

☆☆☆**TYLER BIGHT.** This protected cove on the south side of the island offers a number of pretty rock formations and kelp gardens. Unusual starfish and flower-like anemones decorate

Point Bennett, San Miguel

the ledges and bottom. A number of scallops are found here. This is a nice spot for underwater photography. A light current is usually running.

Accommodations

There are no accommodations on these islands, but a wide selection of motels and hotels exist in and around Ventura County. Primitive camping is available on Anacapa, Santa Barbara, Santa Rosa and San Miguel, but is not recommended unless you like extremely rugged living conditions. Transportation to any of the islands can be arranged through Island Packers, authorized concessionaire to the Channel Islands National Park. Please note that weather can be a big problem for campers. Wind may blow for several days at a time and the only protection is what you have brought with you. Long periods of wet fog are not uncommon. Winter and spring rains turn the trails and campground into sticky mud. Sunscreen is a necessity. It is a harsh environment at best and a hostile and unforgiving one at its worst. Pets are not allowed on the islands at any time. For information, contact Island Packers, 1867

Spinnaker Drive, Ventura CA 93001. ☎ 805-642-7688, or Channel Islands National Park at 1901 Spinnaker Drive, Ventura CA 93001. ☎ 805-644-8262.

Ventura County Dive Operators

AQUA VENTURES, 1001 S. Harbor Blvd., Oxnard CA. ☎ 805-985-8861.

AQUATICS, 295 Channel Islands Blvd., Port Hueneme CA. ☎ 805-984-DIVE.

AMERICAN INSTITUTE OF DIVING, 1901 Pacific Coast Hwy., Lomita CA. ☎ 213-326-6663.

FAR WEST MARINE CENTER, Thousand Oaks, Simi Valley CA. ☎ 805-495-3600 or 805-252-6955.

GOLD COAST SCUBA, 955 E. Thompson Blvd., Ventura CA 93001.

OCEAN ANTICS, 2359 E. Thompson Blvd., Ventura CA 93001.

VENTURA SCUBA SCHOOLS, 1559 Spinnaker Drive, Ventura CA 93001.

Live-Aboards and Day Trips

Arrangements for day trips and overnight cruises can be made through the following operators:

ISLAND PACKERS, 1867 Spinnaker Drive, Ventura CA 93001. ☎ 805-642-1393 or 805-642-7688.

TRUTH AQUATICS, Sea Landing Breakwater, Santa Barbara CA 93109. ☎ 805-963-3564 or 805-962-1127.

CAPTAIN MIDNIGHT, Island Packers Landing, Ventura Marina, Ventura, CA. ☎ 818-954-8232.

CHANNEL ISLANDS
NATIONAL PARK & MARINE SANCTUARY

kelp
Castle Rock
Simonton Cove
Pacific Ocean
Prince Island
kelp
Caliche Forest
kelp
Adam's Cove
sea lion area
② kelp
kelp
kelp
kelp
SAN MIGUEL
kelp
kelp

1. WYCKOFF LEDGE ①
2. TYLER BIGHT

EXCALIBUR, Channel Islands Harbor, Oxnard CA. ☎ 805-529-4080.

AQUA-VENTURES, INC. Cisco Sportfishing, Oxnard CA. ☎ 805-484-1549.

PEACE, Ventura Marina, Ventura CA. ☎ 619- 292-0768.

SCUBA LUV DIVE SHOP, 704 Thousand Oaks Blvd., Thousand Oaks CA 91360.☎ 805-496-1014.

FACTS

RECOMPRESSION CHAMBER. ☎ 213-510-1053.

DIVERS ALERT NETWORK. ☎ 919-684-8111.

GETTING THERE. Golden West Airlines serves the Ventura County Airport in Oxnard with connecting flights from Los Angeles and other major cities. Train service aboard Amtrak is available to Oxnard and Santa Barbara. For details ☎ 800-USA RAIL. Greyhound Bus travels from Los Angeles to Oxnard as well. Travel to the northern Channel Islands can be arranged through any of the dive shops listed above or Island Packers. ☎ 805-642-1393.

CLIMATE. Temperate; daytime temperatures vary from 80 down to 50° F. Frosts are very rare, but night and morning fog often blanket the islands. Average yearly rainfall is 10 to 12 inches, falling mostly during the winter months.

CLOTHING. Keep weather extremes in mind. Pack a jacket or extra sweater for evenings. The rainy season is from November to March. A full wetsuit is needed to dive the Northern Channel Islands, including gloves, boots and a hood.

TAKING GAME. A California Ocean Fishing license is required for taking shell fish or fish from the Channel Islands. A one-day license costs $4.25. Scallops, abalone, lobster, chiones, clams, cockles, sea urchins and shrimp may be taken in specified areas. Scallops may taken year-round while lobster season runs from early October through mid March. Abalone season is from mid-March to mid-January. Spearfishing is also permitted in those areas outlined in the California Fish and Game Rules. Ecological reserve regulations and a map of closed areas are available from park headquarters.

TIME. Pacific Standard Time.

USING YOUR OWN BOAT. If you plan to take your own boat refer to National Ocean Survey Charts 18720, 18729 and 18756. The Santa Barbara Channel is subject to sudden changes in sea and wind conditions especially in afternoons. Be familiar with local conditions. Cruising guides may be purchased at the park's Visitor Center. For assistance, contact the U.S. Coast Guard on Channel 16 of your marine band radio.

LANDING PERMITS. To visit San Miguel Island and Santa Rosa Island you need a permit from park headquarters. Sea conditions around both islands are often rough; only experienced boaters with sturdy vessels should attempt the trip. Landing on privately-owned Santa Cruz is by permit only. No landing is permitted on the eastern side. To land on the west side contact Santa Cruz Island Preserve, P.O. Box 23259, Santa Barbara CA 93121. ☎ 805-964-7839.

ADDITIONAL INFORMATION. Write to Channel Islands National Park, 1901 Spinnaker Drive, Ventura CA 93001. ☎ 805-644-8262. The Visitor Center is located at the end of Spinnaker Drive in Ventura. Here you can view a 25-minute film, purchase publications, maps and nautical charts, and arrange for boat service to the islands.

COZUMEL

Mexico is often called the country with everything for vacationers, and that includes island resorts in the Caribbean Sea.

Cozumel and Isla Mujeres are just off the eastern coast of
the Yucatan Peninsula near Cancun, the famous resort, about
800 miles northeast of Mexico City.

Cozumel, the divers' island, is 30 miles long and 10 miles
wide at its broadest spot. Its cultural and commercial center,
with many hotels, restaurants, cantinas and shops, is San
Miguel, a city of 25,000.

A well-known archaeological dig, San Gervasio, is located on
Cozumel, but the island's major attraction is its many reefs, all
of which offer excellent diving and snorkeling.

Along the west side of the island are superb shallow snorkeling reefs and a deep barrier reef. For the adventurous SCUBA
diver and snorkeler there are miles of virgin reef to explore.

Warm, fast-moving Yucatan currents (a part of the Gulf
Stream) sweep through the deep channel which separate the
west side of the island from the mainland. These currents bring
a constant wash of plankton and other nutrients that support
thousands of exotic fish. Visibility remains a constant 100 to
150 ft year-round, often exceeding 200 ft.

A 20-mile section of Cozumel's most beautiful coral gardens
has been designated a marine sanctuary. It begins at the cruise
ship dock in San Miguel and parallels the southwestern tip of

---

Area Contributors: Scott Sunshine, Jim Spencer.

Blue tang & crab

the island. To commemorate the first Catholic Mass said on the island, a 12-ft bronze statue of Christ created by sculptor Enrique Miralda has been placed in the sanctuary on Palancar Reef.

NOTE: To telephone any of the Mexican listings from the U.S., dial 01152 + 987 + the five digit number.

Best Dives of Cozumel

Most SCUBA diving tours include a drift dive along the outer wall of the reef and a second shallow dive on the inner reef. In drift diving, the dive boat drops you off at one end of the reef then follows your bubbles as you drift with the current to a predetermined point where you surface to rendezvous with the boat.

Cozumel native hut

☆☆☆☆☆**PALANCAR REEF.** Located one mile off the southwestern tip of the island, Palancar Reef stretches over three miles, shot through with winding tunnels and canyons of coral. A 12-ft bronze statue of Christ adorns the shallow north end of the reef (Big Horseshoe). Depths range from 30 to 60 ft. Visibility is always superb here, in excess of 100 ft— allowing snorkelers to view the statue, which sits in 40 ft of water, from the surface.

☆☆☆☆**SAN FRANCISCO REEF.** This area is a favorite of underwater photographers. A ledge of coral arches, caves and

tunnels at depths of 20 to 70 ft are teeming with huge angels, rays, groupers and sea turtles. Beautiful lavender sea fans, yellow and orange vase sponges, barrel sponges, sea whips and towering corals create a kaleidoscope of seascapes. The ledge drops off to channel depths. The wall is usually a drift dive. Visibility is excellent—usually 150 ft.

☆☆☆**PARAISO REEF NORTH.** This popular shallow dive is just north of the cruise ship pier in San Miguel. The reef is accessible by swimming straight out 200 yds from the beach at the Hotel Sol Caribe or by dive boat. The remains of a twin engine airplane, sunk intentionally as part of a movie set, rests at 30 ft creating a home for a vast array of fish life. The reef is a good choice for novice divers.

Best Snorkeling Sites

Good snorkeling may be found all along the east coast beaches on Cozumel. The reefs off the beaches at Galapago Inn and Casa Del Mar have some nice stands of elkhorn.

☆☆☆**CHANCANAB LAGOON.** South of the cruise ship pier at Laguna Beach is Chancanab Lagoon. Protected from wind and waves it is ideal for snorkeling. Depths range from very shallow to about 30 ft. Schools of grunts, angel fish, damsel fish, trumpet fish, turtles, and snapper dart between the clumps of coral. Seafans and soft corals adorn the reef. Visibility runs about 75 ft, sometimes better.

Snorkeling gear may be rented from shops on the beach. Changing rooms, freshwater showers and lockers are available.

Small admission fee. A botanical garden and restaurant are on the premises.

Palancar Reef

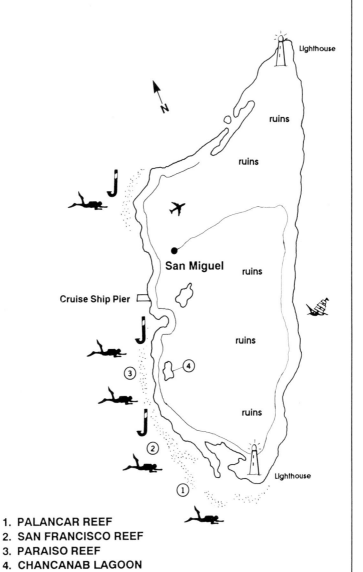

COZUMEL, Mexico

Lighthouse

ruins

N

ruins

San Miguel

ruins

Cruise Ship Pier

ruins

③

④

ruins

②

ruins

①

Lighthouse

1. PALANCAR REEF
2. SAN FRANCISCO REEF
3. PARAISO REEF
4. CHANCANAB LAGOON

Dive Operators

AQUA SAFARI. Located on the ocean at 5th St. South, Aqua Safari offers drift dives, rentals and repairs. ☎ 2-0661 or 2-0101. In the U.S. 800-854-9334.

CARIBBEAN DIVERS. This full-service operation with five locations on Cozumel, offers reef trips, rentals, resort and certification courses. Locations: 1) Ave Melgar 38 in San Miguel. ☎ 2-0180. 2) Mayan Plaza Hotel. 2-0072. 3) Cabanas del Caribe Hotel at Santa Pilar Beach. 2-0017 or 2-0072. 4) Cantarell Hotel on Playa Turquesa. 2- 0144. 5) Chancanab Underwater Park.

DISCOVER COZUMEL DIVE SHOP. Located at the Hotel Barracuda and at Ave Melgar 22 in San Miguel, Discover Cozumel offers SCUBA and snorkeling tours on Palancar Reef and Paradise Reef. Equipment sales and rentals, some repairs and resort courses are available. In town, ☎ 2-0280. At the Hotel Barracuda, 2-0002. In the U.S. 503-726-8879.

DIVE COZUMEL. SCUBA and snorkeling trips aboard three large fast boats can be arranged in town at Ave Melgar 499; ☎ 2-0146 or at the Diver's Inn call 209145.

Accommodations

HOTEL EL PRESIDENTE. Located on San Francisco Beach at the south end of the island, El Presidente is a deluxe resort featuring a large pool, tennis, restaurants, entertainment and dive packages. Reservations through your travel agent.

CASA DEL MAR. This luxury resort offers 98 air-conditioned rooms with on-site dive shop, snorkeling reef, shopping, pool, and restaurant. Write to Casa del Mar, 8117 Preston Rd., Suite 170, Lockbox No 4, Dallas TX 75225. ☎ 800-621-6830, in Texas 214-692-5277. Telex 792475.

LA CEIBA, located just south of town, is a modern professional dive resort offering fast access to the reefs, beach diving,

Playa San Francisco

air-conditioned rooms, all with cable TV and a convenience bar. Write to Two Worlds Travel, 1307 First Street, Humble TX 77338. ☎ 800-446-2166 or 713-446-2166.

GALAPAGO INN. Designed for divers, this 34-room hotel is both casual and elegant, with thatch-roofed huts lining the beach. Write to Aqua-Sub Tours, P.O. Box 810306, Houston TX 77281. ☎ 800-847-5708 or 713-783-3305.

Sightseeing

To explore the windward east coast of Cozumel, rent a jeep. You'll find pounding surf along stretches of uninhabited beaches lined with mangroves and coconut palms. It may be wise to avoid swimming here because of the dangerous currents and strong undertow.

Remains of Mayan temples and pyramids can be found at the northern end of the island. Guided tours to explore San Gervasio (once the Mayan capital), also on the north end, may

Cozumel sunset

be booked through most large hotels. Ferry trips to the larger, more impressive Mayan ruins on the mainland can be booked in town at the International Pier. Be sure to pay a visit to the botanical gardens at Chankanaab Lagoon. Sightseeing flights around Cozumel, to neighboring islands, or the mainland can be arranged at the airport.

Dining

Local lobster, native grilled fish and a variety of Mexican dishes such as tacos, enchiladas or caracol (a giant conch) predominate at Cozumel's restaurants and road side stands.

PEPE'S GRILL on Ave. Rafael Melgar features savory steaks, lobster and seafood. ☎ 2-02-13.

CAFE DEL PUERTO. At the plaza. One of Cozumel's best spots for lobster and crab. You'll be entertained with live guitar music. ☎ 2-03-16.

EL PORTAL offers fabulous Mexican style spicy breakfasts.

CARLOS' N CHARLIE'S AND JIMMY'S on Ave. Rafael Melgar 11 is a divers' favorite for Mexican steaks and seafood. ☎ 2-01-91.

LA LAGUNA, the beach restaurant at Chankanab National Park, serves up tasty shrimp, crabs and fish. ☎ 2-05-84.

PIZZA ROLANDI on Ave. Melgar 22 specializes in Italian favorites.

FACTS

RECOMPRESSION CHAMBER. Located at the Cozumel Hospital.

GETTING THERE. From Miami: Mexicana, Continental. From Dallas-Fort Worth: American. From Cancun: Aero Cozumel. There are additional domestic flights from Acapulco, Cancun, Guadalajara, Mexico City, Merida, Monterey, and Veracruz. Cruise ships from Miami: Norwegian Caribbean Lines, Holland

America, Carnival. The island also can be reached by bus ferry, car ferry and hydrofoil from Cancun. Isla Mujeres is reached by bus ferry, car ferry and air taxi from Cancun.

ISLAND TRANSPORTATION. Taxi service is inexpensive and readily available. Mopeds, cars and Jeeps may be rented in town or at the airport. Book rental cars in advance of your trip.

DRIVING. On the right.

DOCUMENTS. U.S. and Canadian citizens need a tourist card. To obtain one, you must show a valid passport or birth certificate. Citizens of other countries should contact their nearest Mexican consulate for regulations. The tourist card is necessary to leave the country as well and may be obtained from the Mexican consulate or your airline prior to departure.

CUSTOMS. Plants, flowers and fruits may not be brought into Cozumel. Persons carrying illegal drugs will be jailed. You may bring three bottles of liquor and one carton of cigarettes. Dogs and cats should have a current vaccination certificate. Divers carrying a lot of electronic or camera gear, especially video equipment, should register it with U.S. Customs in advance of the trip.

WATER. Drink only bottled or filtered water to avoid diarrheal intestinal ailment. Also avoid raw vegetables and the skin of fruit and foods that sit out for any length of time.

CURRENCY. The exchange rate of the Mexican peso fluctuates a great deal. At this writing $1 U.S. = 2270 pesos. Banks are open weekday mornings. Major credit cards and traveler's checks are widely accepted in Cozumel.

CLIMATE. Temperatures range from the low 70's in winter to the high 90's in summer with an average of about 80° F. Winter months bring cooler weather and periods of heavy rain and gray skies.

CLOTHING. Lightweight, casual. Wetsuits are not needed, but lightweight (1/8") short suits or wetskins are comfortable on the deeper wall dives.

ELECTRICITY. 110 volts; 60 cycles (same as U.S.).

TIME. Central Standard Time.

LANGUAGE. Spanish; English widely spoken.

FOR ADDITIONAL INFORMATION. The Mexican Government Tourist Office, 405 Park Avenue, Suite 1002, New York, NY 10012. ☎ 212-755-7261. Or Mexican National Tourist Council, 10100 Santa Monica Blvd., Los Angeles, CA 90067. ☎ 213-203-8151.

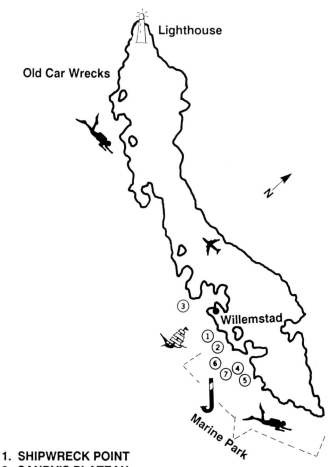

CURACAO, Netherlands Antilles

Lighthouse

Old Car Wrecks

Willemstad

Marine Park

1. SHIPWRECK POINT
2. SANDY'S PLATEAU
3. SUPERIOUR PRODUCER
4. DIRECTOR'S BAY
5. EEL VALLEY
6. DIVER'S LEAP
7. TOW BOAT

CURACAO

First-time visitors to Curacao are enchanted by the contrasts between its old-world European and West Indian cultures, its rural charms and cosmopolitan sophistication, and its stately mansions and action-packed nightlife. Divers are struck by its secluded beaches and superb diving and snorkeling.

Although Curacao is less than 40 miles from the coast of Venezuela, the primary influence on its culture is Dutch colonial. Willemstad, the capital, looks strikingly like Amsterdam and gives one cause to wonder whether a portion of that city has broken away from the Netherlands and floated to the Caribbean.

Curacao is the largest of five islands that make up the Netherlands Antilles, the others being Bonaire, Saba, St. Maarten and St. Eustatius. It covers 173 square miles and has a population of 160,000. Although the official language is Dutch, the local dialect is Papiamento, a mixture of Dutch, English, Spanish, Portuguese, Indian and African. However, most Curacaoans speak English.

Daily reminders of its maritime background are the arriving cruise ships which, while entering the harbor through St. Anna Bay, appear to be sailing through the streets of Willemstad.

Like her sister Bonaire, Curacao is a desert island with dozens of secluded coves, beautiful soft white sandy beaches and dependably dry weather.

Area Contributor: Chris Richards, Manager, Curacao Seascape Dive & Water Sports.

Snorkeling in Curacao

Curacao is just now being discovered as a Caribbean dive-travel destination. A National Underwater Park encircles a good portion of the southern part of the island and new reef conservation laws have opened up many diving areas while insuring a healthy future for the superb coral walls and drop-offs fringing the shore line. Special marked trails for snorkelers have been created and sixteen concrete moorings have been set to protect the reefs from anchors.

Best Dives of Curacao

☆☆☆☆☆**SHIPWRECK POINT.** Located off shore in front of the Curacao Seaquarium, this dive site (aka Bopor Kibra) contains a reef, wreck, and wall set in an exposed rocky cape. The reef slopes off gradually from the shallows to 50 ft where the wall drops over 200 ft. This reef is very pretty with many sea fans, club finger coral, pillar corals, and thickets of elkhorn coral.

☆☆☆☆**SANDY'S PLATEAU.** This is a terrific dive for beginners and snorkelers. The reef starts at 15 ft and drops off to a fabulous ledge at 30 ft, turning into a wall down to 120 ft. Lush elkhorn corals growing in 10 ft of water, pastel gorgonians, sea fans, nice brain coral formations and black corals (at depth) are found on the reef. Signs naming the various corals have been anchored on the reef making an excellent snorkeling/diving trail. Beware of the "Do-not- touch-me sponge" which can inflict a painful skin burn on divers swimming too close.

☆☆☆*SUPERIOUR PRODUCER.* This wreck sits upright in 100 ft of water. She sank in 1977 and is already covered by a blanket of sponges and black corals. Because of the depth and surges this dive is recommended for experienced divers only. Schools of manta rays and porpoises are frequently sighted here. The sea is usually choppy with a light current running.

☆☆☆☆**DIRECTORS BAY.** This wall and reef dive runs perpendicular to the shore line and is characterized by enormous gorgonians, some of which are 10 ft tall. The reef is about 1000 ft off shore starting in 30 ft of water and descending to 150 ft. Fields of pencil corals, star corals and sea fans along sand channels slope down to walls of black coral and huge orange sponges.

☆☆☆**EEL VALLEY.** This is a fairly shallow terrace which begins at the surface and slopes off to 120 ft. Numerous morays make their home here. Beautiful formations of large brain, star and staghorn corals create interesting photo subjects.

If you don't mind a bit of a rough boat ride, you can visit other reef/wall dives at **CATHY'S PARADISE,** and **SMOKY REEF.**

Huge staghorn coral in Curacao's Marine Sanctuary

Best Snorkeling Sites

☆☆☆**DIVER'S LEAP.** Located just east of Jan Theil Bay, this drop-off is great for shallow diving and snorkeling. Divers encounter a lush dense reef beginning at 20 ft. Marine animals are abundant including sea turtles, barracuda, trumpet fish, blue chromis and octopus.

☆☆☆☆☆**TOW BOAT.** Calm, protected waters and an intact small wreck make this the best snorkeling and shallow water dive in the marine park. The hull is covered with brightly colored corals and is great for photographic seascapes. Adjacent to the Tow Boat, which is situated on a wide, shallow ledge, is a nice coral reef which drops off to about 100 ft. A lot of black corals grow on the slopes here. Residents include spotted morays, parrot fish, wrasses, and numerous French angels. Visibility is excellent.

Dive Operators

CURACAO SEASCAPE DIVE & WATERSPORTS. A full-service shop located at the Caribbean Hotel. Manager Chris Richards is expert on Curacao marine habitats and diving. Custom dive tours. Affordable packages may be combined with Bonaire vacations. ☎ 800-345- 0805 (US), 609-298-3844 (NJ) or 800-265-1692 (Canada).

UNDERWATER CURACAO. Located at the Curacao Seaquarium, this dive operation maintains two large fast dive boats and a fully- equipped retail and rental shop. Write to P.O. Box 3102, Curacao, Netherlands Antilles. ☎ 5999-616666 or 616670.

DIVE PISCADERA WATER SPORTS. Operating out of the Curacao Caribbean Hotel and Casino in Willemstad, this shop has four dive boats which carry between six and 12 divers. Write to Curacao Caribbean Hotel, Willemstad, Curacao, Netherland Antilles.

DIVE CURACAO. Located at the Curacao Plaza Hotel, Dive Curacao offers complete dive-vacation packages. ☎ 25000.

MASTER DIVE, INC. Dive trips, rentals, and sales may be arranged through Master Dive, Inc. Write to Fokkerweg 13, Curacao, Netherlands Antilles. ☎ 5999-54312.

Live-Aboard

AQUANAUT EXPLORER. Style and atmosphere make this live-aboard special. Each cabin is air conditioned. All have a private bathroom and shower, and either a picture window, porthole or balcony. Week-long tours visit dive sites around Curacao and Bonaire. Captains Gerry Hytha and Erich Heindl bring many years of safe, comfortable diving and cruise ship experience to this operation. Certification courses are available. ☎ 1-800-327-8223 (U.S.), 800-432-8894 (FL).

Tugboat wreck off Curacao

Accommodations

CURACAO CARIBBEAN HOTEL CASINO. This large waterfront hotel, which features a small beach, a pool, casino and a shopping arcade, offers dive packages. Reservations may be made through your travel agent.

PRINCESS BEACH HOTEL. Just southeast of Willemstad, this hotel is adjacent to the Curacao Underwater Park and Seaquarium and features a weekly barbecue, casino gambling, and nearby snorkeling. ☎ 800-223-9815 or write Princess Beach Hotel, Dr. Martin Luther King Blvd 8, Willemstad, Curacao, N.A.

LAS PALMAS HOTEL AND VACATION VILLAGE. T h i s resort features an Olympic pool, tennis courts, restaurant, casino and shopping mart. Fully-equipped villas are available as well as dive packages. ☎ 800-622-7836.

AVILA BEACH HOTEL. If you're seeking a hotel with character, try this former governor's mansion in Willemstad. Near town. ☎ 1-800-223-9868 or write PO Box 791, Willemstad, Curacao, NA.

Other Activities

Hotels offer most of the water sports activities, such as sunfish sailing, use of windsurfers, water scooters and fishing tackle. Non-diving companions can now take an underwater safari through rainbow-colored coral to see a technicolor array of more than 400 species of fish... without getting their feet wet. The Curacao Seaquarium, which opened in 1985, is the world's most natural sea life habitat outside of the ocean itself. This unique Seaquarium, housing a representation of the sea life from Curacao's surrounding ocean, is situated on a tiny peninsula just east of Willemstad. The exhibition area consists of 75 aquariums, ranging in capacity from 750 to 2,500 gallons, each a realistic home for Curacao's exotic tropical fish, giant lobsters and anemones and more than 150 different kinds of colorful coral...among them fire, pillar, flower and lettuce.

The Curacao Seaquarium is open daily, from 10 AM to 10 PM. Admission is $5 for adults, $2.50 for children, with a 30-day admission pass available for $8 per person. For more information, call the Curacao Seaquarium at ☎ 61-6670.

Sightseeing

The best place to start a tour of Curacao is the enchanting capital of Willemstad, noted for its unusual architecture, good shopping and fine cuisine. The St. Anna Bay cuts through the city like an Amsterdam canal, dividing the Punda from the Otrabanda, which literally means "other side" in Portuguese. A pontoon bridge, which opens several times a day to allow cruise ships to enter, connects the two sides of the city.

Almost everything is located within a six-block radius in the Punda section, making it easy to explore the city on foot.

Turn right on Breedestraat and you'll pass Spritzer and Fuhrman, the Tiffany's of the Caribbean. Along the street, there are a number of other tempting shops in handsomely restored Dutch Colonial buildings.

Turn left at Columbustraat and visit the Mikve Israel Synagogue, the oldest synagogue in continual use (255 years) in the Western Hemisphere. ☎ 662-664.

Willemstad waterfront

Dining

PRINCESS BEACH HOTEL AND CASINO. Next to the Underwater Park and Aquarium, this resort offers weeknight specials: Tuesday, barbecue, steel band and limbo show; Friday, Curacao Night with local food and indigenous entertainment; Sunday, a great buffet. ☎ 614944.

WINE CELLAR RESTAURANT. Gourmet dining is offered in intimate surroundings. This restaurant won the International Gastronomic Award Europe for 1984. Lunch and dinner. Small. ☎ 612178.

GOLDEN STAR. Located on Socratesstraat 2, this informal restaurant offers Curacao native dishes such as goat stew, conch stew, fish and funchi (a cornmeal dish) or traditional steaks and chops. Bar. Lunch and Dinner. ☎ 54795/54865.

PIZZA HUT. Curacao's most popular eatery, the Pizza Hut offers home-made desserts and an award-winning native pizza. Two locations: Salina, ☎ 616161, and Santa Maria, 88276.

FACTS

RECOMPRESSION CHAMBER. St. Elisabeth Hospital.

GETTING THERE. From New York take American Airlines; from Miami, ALM and Eastern. There are six flights weekly from Puerto Rico via ALM. Curacao is a popular cruise ship port. Some hotel-air packages are available through your travel agent.

DRIVING. Foreign and international licenses accepted. Traffic moves on the right.

DOCUMENTS. U.S. and Canadian citizens must show proof of citizenship and return ticket.

CUSTOMS. For U.S. citizens—$400 duty free, 10 percent up to $1,000 every 30 days. An unlimited number of gifts costing no more than $25 each may be mailed home. Duty-free cigarettes, one carton per person. Duty-free liquor, one quart per person, both within the $400 limit. Canadians: $100C after 48 hours. Up to $300C, once a year.

CURRENCY. Guilder (NAf). 1.77 = $1 U.S. Credit cards widely accepted.

CLIMATE. Temperature averages 80° F.

CLOTHING. Lightweight, casual. Wetsuits are not needed for warmth, but a lightweight shortie or lycra wetskin is useful to avoid coral abrasions.

ELECTRICITY. 110-130 V-AC. 50 cycles.

TIME. Atlantic Standard.

LANGUAGE. Papiamento and Dutch. English widely spoken.

TAX. $10.00 U.S. per person at departure.

RELIGIOUS SERVICES. Catholic, Jewish, Protestant, Episcopal, Seventh Day Adventist.

FOR ADDITIONAL INFORMATION. Curacao Tourist Board, 400 Madison Ave, Suite 322, NY NY 10017. ☎ 212-751-8266. In Curacao, Plaza Piar, 613397.

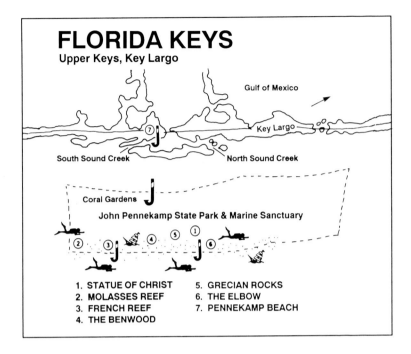

FLORIDA KEYS
Upper Keys, Key Largo

Gulf of Mexico

Key Largo

South Sound Creek

North Sound Creek

Coral Gardens

John Pennekamp State Park & Marine Sanctuary

1. STATUE OF CHRIST
2. MOLASSES REEF
3. FRENCH REEF
4. THE BENWOOD

5. GRECIAN ROCKS
6. THE ELBOW
7. PENNEKAMP BEACH

FLORIDA KEYS

Once a favorite hunting ground of ruthless pirates like Black Caesar and Blackbeard, the spectacular coral reefs fringing the Florida Keys now attract SCUBA divers and snorkelers from all points of the globe.

The heart of diving in the Florida Keys is John Pennekamp Coral Reef State Park and the adjacent National Marine Sanctuary. Over half a million diving and snorkeling vacationers visit John Pennekamp annually. The park consists of 178 square miles of undersea reefs and 75 land acres as a haven not only for divers and snorkelers, but also campers, bird watchers, fishermen and sunbathers. Visitors of all ages and physical capabilities can tour the undersea gardens by glass-bottomed boat or by donning a mask and snorkel.

Diving in the Florida Keys is weather-dependent. You can go out to the reefs in the morning after a storm and find visibility as low as 25 ft and return in the afternoon to calm seas and visibility in excess of 100 ft. The best months are usually October through June. Because the reefs are fairly shallow (45 ft or less) winds that churn up the seas may cause lowered visibility.

When the occasional storms rule out trips to the outer reefs, some divers visit locations on the Gulf side of the Keys, which is almost always calm.

Area Contributors: Jim Spencer, The *Divemaster*; Carl Nielsen and Scott Robinson, John Pennekamp State Park; Ginna Thomas, Key Largo Chamber of Commerce; Anita Liggett, BDWH.

Mural on Key Largo

Best Dives of John Pennekamp Coral Reef Park

☆☆☆☆☆**THE STATUE.** The statue of Christ in John Pennekamp Park is the most popular SCUBA and snorkeling site in the Florida Keys. Given to the Underwater Society of America in 1961 by industrialist Egidi Cressi, the 9-ft bronze statue, "Christ of the Abyss," is a duplicate of the original cast by sculptor Guido Galletti for placement in the Mediterranean Sea.

The top of the Florida statue is in 10 ft of water and can be seen easily by snorkelers hovering on the surface. The base rests on a sandy bottom 20 ft down and is surrounded by huge brain corals and elkhorn formations. Dramatic underwater photo opportunities are created by sunlight splashing down over the out-stretched arms of the statue.

Christ of the Abyss

☆☆☆☆**MOLASSES REEF,** located at the southwest end of the park, is perhaps the most popular reef dive. Named after a ship carrying molasses that ran aground here, the reef actually provides several dives, depending on where your boat is moored. Moorings M21 through 23 are for diving. M13 through

20 for snorkeling. Molasses consists of a series of coral ridges and grooves, overhangs, ledges and swim-through tunnels. Depths vary from very shallow to approximately 40 ft.

☆☆☆**FRENCH REEF,** also in the park, is slightly northeast of Molasses Reef. French is noted for its beautiful caves, ledges and swim-throughs. You may find enormous groupers, schools of copper sweepers, sergeant majors, grunts, rays, barracudas and morays. Depths vary from five to 45 ft.

☆☆☆**THE WRECK OF THE *BENWOOD*** is located just north of French Reef. A World War II freighter that was hit by a German submarine, she was sunk as a navigational hazard by the Coast Guard and now sits on a sandy bottom in 45 ft of water.

Wreck of the Benwood, *Key Largo*

The 300-ft wreck is a fun night dive as well as a good site for photography and fish watching during the day.

Diving On Your Own

Reef dives in the Florida Keys are reachable only by boat. Rentals are widely available and dock space is plentiful for those towing their own boat both at John Pennekamp State Park docks and private marinas. Anchoring on the reefs in the park is illegal and subject to a hefty fine so be sure to send for a copy of the Mooring Buoy System brochure produced by the National Oceanic and Atmospheric Administration. Write to: Key Largo National Marine Sanctuary, MM 102.5, Key Largo, FL 33037. Many divers choose the large fast boats operated by the dive shops or the park concessions rather than the smaller rentals. Before venturing out on your own be sure to get a chart of the area.

Best Snorkeling Sites

☆☆☆**GRECIAN ROCKS** is located southwest of the Statue of Christ and is marked by a spar buoy and mooring buoys G1 through G5. The in-shore side of the reef is always calm. The depths at Grecian Rocks vary, with coral growing right up to the surface and down to 25 ft. Good visibility.

☆☆☆**THE ELBOW,** located northeast of Grecian Rocks and about eight miles out, is marked by a 36-ft steel tower. Mooring buoy E-1 marks the shallow area of the reef. The Elbow is a beautiful example of a spur and groove coral system. Wrecked cargo vessels, anchors and cannons are scattered on the bottom. This area attracts large fish and turtles. As some of the barracudas here have been hand fed, you may be surprised to find a six-footer swimming up to peer into your mask. Don't be alarmed; he's just looking for a familiar face. Average depths 10 to 40 ft.

☆**PENNEKAMP BEACH,** on the land portion of the park, is a good area in which to try out new gear. An artificial reef made of old cars is much like the real thing and has attracted many reef fish. Snorkelers enjoy the clear calm water. There are some small coral heads scattered about, fish swimming in the grassy bottom of the shallow areas and a few old cannons. This area is a nice stop for a day-trip to Key Largo.

Upper Keys Dive Operators and Services

WEEKEND PHOTO SEMINARS for groups and individuals are offered by naturalist Jim Spencer. His extensive knowledge of Pennekamp Park and underwater photography assures you the best of friendly fish, outstanding coral grottoes, and spectacular underwater portraits. His sessions include instruction and use of a Nikonos camera. Successful participants receive a PADI underwater photo certificate upon completion. Write P.O. Box 726, Key Largo, FL 33037. ☎ 305-451-2662.

CORAL REEF PARK CO. is the land concession for John Pennekamp State Park. The concession books SCUBA trips on the *Divemaster*, a 32 ft Prowler which has been customized for easy diving. Skipper and owner John O'Connor visits the south end of the park from Grecian Rocks to Molasses Reef and takes groups to his own secret spots. The *El Capitan* and *Infante* carry groups of up to 60 snorkelers to the best dive locations.

Fourteen different SCUBA and dive rescue courses are taught by Coral Reef Park Co. including Ecology, Ocean Reef, Search and Recovery, SCUBA lifesaving and Accident Management.

SEA DWELLERS SPORT CENTER, located at Mile Marker 100 on Ocean Highway, operates tours throughout the marine park. Resort and certification courses are offered. Snorkel trips available. ☎ 305-451-3640 or write 99850 Route 1, MM 100, Key Largo FL 33037.

ATLANTIS DIVE CENTER is off the main highway on Garden Cove Drive. Owners Amy and Captain Spencer Slate offer personalized dive tours. Dive trips daily, resort courses, rentals. ☎ 800-331- DIVE or 305-451-1325.

ADMIRAL #1, MM 100 Marina, P.O. Box 0113, Key Largo FL 33037. ☎ 800-346-DIVE or 305-451-1114.

AMERICAN DIVING HEADQUARTERS INC., P.O. Box 1250, Key Largo FL 33037. ☎ 800-634-8464 or 305-451-0039.

BUDDY'S DIVE SHOP, P.O. Box 409, Islamorada FL 33036. ☎ 800-882-DIVE or 305-664-2200.

CONCH REPUBLIC DIVERS, INC., 90311 Overseas Hwy, Tavernier FL 33070. ☎ 800-274-DIVE or 305-852-1655.

DIVERS DEN OF KEY LARGO, 110 Ocean Dr., MM 100, Key Largo FL 33037. ☎ 800-526-DIVE.

DIVER'S PARADISE, Tavernier Creek Marina at MM 90.5, Tavernier FL 33037. ☎ 305-852-4800. Boat rentals.

DIVER'S WORLD OF KEY LARGO, P.O. Box 1663, MM 99.5, Key Largo FL 33037. ☎ 800-445-8231 or 305-451-3200.

HOLIDAY ISLE DIVE SHOP, P.O. Box 482, Islamorada FL 33036. ☎ 800-327-7070 or 305-664-4145.

LADY CYANA DIVERS, P.O. Box 1157, MM 85.9, Islamorada FL 33036. ☎ 800-221-8717 or 305-664-8717.

OCEAN DIVERS, INC., 522 Caribbean Drive, Key Largo FL 33037. ☎ 305-451-1113, 800-451-1113.

QUIESCENCE DIVING SERVICE, P.O. Box N-13, MM 103.5, Key Largo FL 33037. ☎ 305-451-2440.

REEF SHOP DIVE CENTER, Rte 2, P.O. Box 7, Islamorada FL 33036. ☎ 305-664-4385.

SCUBA DO DIVE CHARTERS, P.O. Box 2237, Key Largo FL 33037. ☎ 305-451-3446.

SEA QUEST OF THE FLORIDA KEYS, Garden Cove Marina, P.O. Box 571, Key Largo FL 33037. ☎ 305-451-4941.

STEPHEN FRINK PHOTOGRAPHIC, P.O. Box 19-A, MM 102.5, Key Largo FL 33037. ☎ 305-451-3737.

SUNDIVER, PO Box 963, Key Largo FL 33037. ☎ 305-451-2220

TAVERNIER DIVE CENTER, P.O. Box 465, MM 90.5, Tavernier FL 33070. ☎ 305-852-8799.

TREASURE DIVERS, Rte 2, P.O. Box 11, MM 85.5, Islamorada FL 33036. ☎ 305-664-5111.

WORLD DOWN UNDER SCUBA ACADEMY, 81586   US Rte 1, MM 81.5, Islamorada FL 33036. ☎ 305-664-9312.

ADDITIONAL INFORMATION on diving services in John Pennekamp Coral Reef Park contact: **KEYS ASSOCIATION OF DIVE OPERATORS,** P.O. Box 1717, Key Largo FL 33037.

Jules' Undersea Lodge

"To live beneath the sea was once just the dream of science fiction writers. Now it is a reality," says Dr. Neil Monney, co-developer and president of Jules' Habitat, Inc.

On November 15th, 1987, the debut of a new technology occurred. For the first time ever, people could live, dine and dream at five fathoms (30 ft) under the surface of the ocean.

"Waking up to view a pair of angelfish looking in your bedroom suite window is a moment you'll never forget", says vice-president and co-developer, Ian Koblick, a world-renowned ocean pioneer. Jules' Undersea Lodge is a 50-ft-long, 20-foot-wide tribute to man's quest for adventure. Less than an hour's drive from Miami, and about a mile from John Pennekamp State Park, the lodge is a futuristic showplace of undersea comfort and advanced marine technology.

The living space includes two private suites each with private bath, and a large entertainment complex—living room area, complete with a galley set up for gourmet dining. In each suite there is a 42-inch picture window offering a panoramic view of the many varieties of sea life in the lagoon.

"We can even offer guests an underwater video camera to record their adventures," notes Koblick. And, upon returning to the surface, guests receive an "Aquanaut" Certificate.

The land-based Mission Control Center is connected to the lodge by an umbilical cable which delivers fresh air, water, power and communications. The entire facility is monitored constantly.

Guests must be qualified in the basic skills of SCUBA diving to stay in the lodge. ☎ 305-451-3388 or write to Jules' Undersea Lodge, 51 Shoreland Drive, Key Largo FL 33037.

Future Jules' Habitats are on the drawing boards.

Accommodations Upper Keys

MARINA DEL MAR is adjacent to Pennekamp Park on the ocean. This luxury resort offers guests a variety of single rooms, suites and two-bedroom, two- bath apartments with full kitchens. ☎ 800-451-DIVE, or 305-451-4107. Write: P.O. Box 1050, Key Largo FL 33037.

SHERATON KEY LARGO RESORT is located north of Pennekamp Park on Rte 1. The 200- room hotel overlooks Florida Bay and features a lagoon pool and patio area with two fresh water pools, ☎ 800-325- 3535 or ☎ 305-852-5553.

HOWARD JOHNSONS of Key Largo is opposite the entrance to the park. It features deluxe rooms, restaurant, a bar, and laundry facilities. Dive Packages. ☎ 800-654-2000 or write P.O. Box 1024, Key Largo FL 33037.

BEST WESTERN OF KEY LARGO offers luxury accommodations overlooking the water. Dive packages are arranged through Captain Corky. ☎ 800-445-8231 or write to 201 Ocean Drive, Key Largo FL 33037.

TROPICAL REEF RESORT is a bit off the beaten path at mile marker 85 in Islamorada. Features include three fresh water pools, Cablevision, a large marina with two boat ramps, and a lovely picnic area. ☎ 800-654-9748; or 800-843-9810.

Camping

JOHN PENNEKAMP STATE PARK offers   ocean-front campsites, both primitive and with electricity and water. Write P.O. Box 487, Key Largo FL 33037. ☎ 305-451-1202.

KEY LARGO KAMPGROUND offers waterfront sites, laundry and bath house. Write MM 101.5 , Key Largo FL 33037. ☎ 305-451-1431.

Apartments & Homes for Vacation Rentals

For a complete list of realtors and rentals contact The Key Largo Chamber of Commerce, 103400 Overseas Hwy, Key Largo FL 33037. ☎ 305-451-1414.

Dining

The Florida Keys restaurants are known for their fresh seafood dinners, conch chowder and key lime pie. Both fast food and traditional restaurants are found all along Rte 1.

MARKER 88 is on the Gulf of Mexico side at Highway Mile Marker #88. It is one of the finest gourmet restaurants in the Florida Keys featuring local seafood dishes. ☎ 852-9315 or 852-5503 for reservations. Expensive.

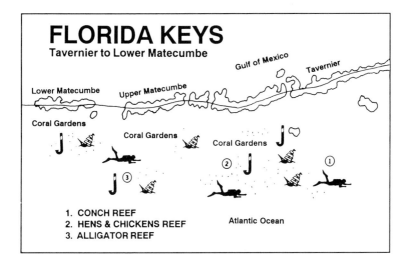

FLORIDA KEYS
Tavernier to Lower Matecumbe

1. CONCH REEF
2. HENS & CHICKENS REEF
3. ALLIGATOR REEF

SNOOKS BAYSIDE CLUB at Mile Marker 99.7 offers the ultimate in tropical atmosphere and superb gourmet cuisine. Seating is *al fresco* on a huge, palm-lined bayside terrace or in air-conditioned dining rooms. Pastel linens accent the glorious sunset displays. ☎ 305-451-3857.

THE WHALE HARBOR INN is located oceanside on Islamorada at Mile Marker 84. The restaurant is built around the old lighthouse which saved lives during hurricane Donna in 1960. Diners at the Whale Harbor Inn have a nice view of the ocean and adjacent fishing boat docks. The fare is an all-you-can-eat seafood buffet. Moderate prices.

BASKIN ROBBINS/MR. SUBMARINE at Mile Marker 100 has fabulous gyros, sandwiches and snack food.

Other Activities

Fishing and diving are the most popular activities in the Florida Keys. Ocean swimming must be done from a boat in most areas. Deep sea fishing is considered the best in the world by some. Fishing boat skippers proudly hang up photos of Don Johnson, Paul Newman and other celebrities who choose Islamorada to fish for marlin, tuna and swordfish.

Best Dives of the Middle Keys
(Marathon - Big Pine Key)

Marathon, the second largest community in the Keys is also the center of diving and vacation activity in the Middle Keys.

☆☆☆**SOMBRERO REEF** is marked by a 135-ft steel tower. The reef here begins at the surface in some spots and slopes down to 30 ft. Divers swim through beautiful elkhorn and pillar corals.

A rare spotted drum

Dolphin trainer, Grassy Key

☆☆*THUNDERBOLT* is a fairly new wreck dive. The 190-ft cable-laying ship was intentionally sunk off Marathon in 110 ft of water to create an artificial reef. Schools of sergeant majors, squirrel fish, angels, parrotfish, and grunts inhabit the wreck. The top is at 70 ft. Visibility is usually good.

☆☆☆ **LOOE KEY** is a National Marine Sanctuary named for the *HMS Looe,* a frigate which ran aground here in the mid 1700's. With a range in depth from two to 35 ft and gin clear

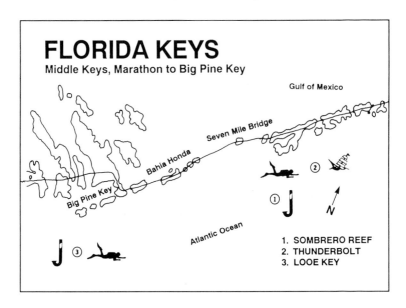

FLORIDA KEYS

Middle Keys, Marathon to Big Pine Key

Gulf of Mexico

Seven Mile Bridge

Bahia Honda

Big Pine Key

Atlantic Ocean

N

1. SOMBRERO REEF
2. THUNDERBOLT
3. LOOE KEY

water when seas are calm, Looe Key is a superb spot for both snorkelers and SCUBA divers. The sanctuary is located offshore from Big Pine Key.

Middle Keys Dive Shops (Marathon through Big Pine Key)

CUDJOE GARDENS MARINA AND DIVE CENTER, MM 21, Cudjoe Key FL 33050. ☎ 305-745-2357.

DIVING SITE/CORAL LAGOON RESORT, 12399 Overseas Hwy., MM 53.5, Marathon FL 33050. ☎ 800-634-3935.

HALL'S DIVING CENTER AND RESORT offers complete dive and accommodation packages with a written guarantee that you will go diving unless a hurricane or similar "act of God" interferes. Write to Hall's, 1994 Overseas Hwy, Marathon FL 33050. ☎ 800-331-HALL or 305-743-5929.

HAWK'S CAY DIVERS, HAWK'S CAY RESORT, MM 61, Marathon FL 33050. ☎ 800-327-7775.

TILDEN'S PRO DIVE SHOP, 4650 Overseas Highway, Marathon FL 33050. ☎ 800-223-4563 or 305-743-5422.

LOOE KEY DIVE CENTER, Looe Key Reef Resort, P.O. Box 509, MM 27.5, Ramrod Key FL 33042. ☎ 800-942-KEYS or 305-872-2215.

UNDERSEAS INC. U.S. Rte 1, P.O. Box 319, Big Pine Key FL 33043. ☎ 305-872-2700.

Accommodations On the Middle Keys

HAWK'S CAY RESORT AND MARINA, located on a 60-acre island in Marathon, is a fairly new dive resort. It features a dive shop, restaurants, a saltwater lagoon, tennis, golf, charter fishing and sailing. Adjacent to a dolphin training facility. ☎ 800-327-7775. Florida: 800-432-2242.

VACATION RENTALS. For apartment or home rentals, contact the Greater Marathon Chamber of Commerce, 3330 Overseas Hwy, Marathon FL 33050. ☎ 305-743-5417.

Other Activities

Deep sea fishing trips can be arranged at the Ocean Sports Center, MM 50.5 (☎ 305-743-5246) or with Captain Randy Rode (☎ 305-743-3424). Miniature golf, movies, shopping. The Marathon Community Theatre features jugglers, mimes, magicians, arts and crafts and more. The theatre is at Knights Key Campground at the south end of Marathon (☎ 305-743-4386). Marathon has miles of bike trails. For rentals, KCB Bike Shop at MM 53. ☎ 305-289-1670.

Dining

In Marathon, dining can range from a quick meal at the golden arches to candlelight elegance at The Caribbean Room on Hawk's Cay.

CHEF'S, located at the Sombrero Resort and Lighthouse Marina, is a favorite of the locals. Chef's is at 19 Sombrero Blvd., Marathon FL 33050, ☎ 305-743-4108.

CASTAWAY HOUSE OF SEAFOOD specializes in shrimp steamed in beer and other local seafood favorites. Located at the foot of 15th Street in Marathon. ☎ 305-743-6247.

KEY COLONY GROCERY AND DELI. This is probably the only place in the Florida Keys where you can find a New-York-style corned beef or pastrami sandwich. Delivery available. Key Colony Beach Shopping Center, Causeway, Key Colony Beach. ☎ 305-743-6676.

Best Dives of the Lower Keys and Key West

Most of the dive sites visited by operators of Key West shops are either on very shallow reefs surrounding the small offshore islands, such as Sand Key or Cottrell Key or deep wreck dives

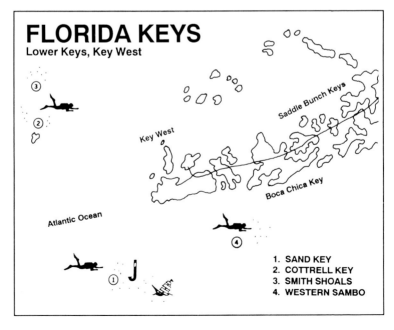

FLORIDA KEYS
Lower Keys, Key West

Saddle Bunch Keys

Key West

Boca Chica Key

Atlantic Ocean

1. SAND KEY
2. COTTRELL KEY
3. SMITH SHOALS
4. WESTERN SAMBO

Seaplane and submarine, Grassy Key

which are recommended only for advanced divers. The shallow reefs are beautiful and on a calm day offer excellent visibility. Day trips to the outer islands are fun for snorkeling and picnics or camping overnight at Fort Jefferson on the Dry Tortugas. Transportation can be arranged through the dive shops or Key West Seaplane Service. ☎ 305-294-6978.

☆**SAND KEY** is approximately five miles south of Key West and is marked by a 110-ft lighthouse. It is good for snorkeling and SCUBA since one side of the island is always sheltered from winds and waves. The reef grows to the surface at some spots and slopes down to 90 ft on the south side.

Take a Half Day Out-Island Trip

DRY TORTUGAS are located 65 miles south of Key West and can be reached only by seaplane or boat. This area consists of eight uninhabited islands with over 100 square miles of virgin reef. Campers must bring in their own fresh water and supplies. Visibility over these reefs is almost unlimited since the Gulf Stream flows over them year round. The snorkeler will enjoy miles and miles of shallow reefs teeming with thousands of fish, rays, turtles and corals surrounding the islands. Those with SCUBA gear can explore shallow wrecks, and spectacular walls, ledges, caves and sea mounts at depths from 30 to 90 ft. Key West Seaplane Service runs half-day snorkeling trips to Fort Jefferson in the Dry Tortugas and will also drop off campers wishing to spend some time on the islands. Dive shops and marinas can arrange for boat transportation.

Dive Shops of the Lower Keys

CAPTAIN BILLY'S KEY WEST DIVER, INC. MM 4.5, U.S. 1, Stock Island, Key West FL 33040. ☎ 800-87-DIVER.

SEASPORTS DIVING CENTER, 101 Margaret St. Key West FL 33040. ☎ 305-294-6224.

REEF RAIDERS DIVE SHOP, 109 Duval St., Key West FL 33040. ☎ 305-294-3635.

OCEANSIDE DIVE CENTER, 5950 Maloney Ave., Key West FL 33040. ☎ 800-331-5999 or 305-294-4676.

KEY WEST PRO DIVE SHOP, INC., 1605 Roosevelt Blvd., Key West FL 33040. ☎ 305-296-3823.

Accommodations

Key West has a number of guest houses, resorts, and private home rentals. Some of the guest houses are restricted to men or women only and some specify no children. Check before making reservations.

PIER HOUSE is located in the center of Old Key West at One Duval St. This resort has three restaurants, four bars, a pool and a beach and is in walking distance of dive shops and entertainment. ☎ 800-327-8340 or reserve through your travel agent. Moderate to expensive.

SOUTH BEACH OCEAN FRONT MOTEL has 47 units on the ocean and its own fishing pier. Moderate rates. Close proximity to dive shops. ☎ 305-296-5611 or write 508 South St., Key West FL 33040. Moderate.

OCEAN KEY HOUSE offers luxury accommodations in the heart of Key West. One- and two-bedroom suites with in-room Jacuzzi, kitchens and private balconies. Moderate to expensive. ☎ 800-328-9815 or write Zero Duval St., Key West FL 33040.

ADDITIONAL INFORMATION. For complete listings of hotels, guest houses, trailer courts, apartment and house rentals throughout the Florida Keys ☎ 1-800-FLA-KEYS.

Other Activities

Historic tours, para sailing, sailing charters, seaplane rides, golf are available. Visit Mel Fisher's Treasure Museum, Key West Aquarium, Ernest Hemingway's House, The Audubon House and Gardens.

Dining

No trip to Key West is complete without a visit to **SLOPPY JOE'S** at 201 Duval St. This bar and eatery was Hemingway's favorite hangout. Entertainment.

OCEAN KEY HOUSE has a nice dockside bar overlooking the harbor at Zero Duval St. ☎ 305-296-7701.

A & B LOBSTER HOUSE is a landmark restaurant with panoramic views of historic Key West Harbor. Seafood specialties. Located at 700 Front Street. ☎ 305-294-2536.

THE BUTTERY at 1208 Simonton St offers a gourmet menu for the discriminating diner. Reservations. ☎ 294-0717.

Getting There

All major airlines serve Miami International Airport. Key Largo is about a two-hour drive from Miami. Jet service is available to and from Key West. Smaller charter lines operate regularly between Miami and Marathon. Car rentals are available at Miami International Airport. If you drive from Miami, take LeJeune Road south to 836 (west), go west to Tollway (821), then south to U.S. Rte 1 and the Keys.

If you come from the north on the Florida Turnpike, you'll see Exit No. 4 announcing Homestead, Key West and the West Dade Tollway (821), which connects with U.S. 1 at Florida City and goes to Key Largo. From Key Largo take Rte 1 south to all points in the Keys.

GUADELOUPE

Touted by Jacques Cousteau as "one of the world's ten best diving spots," Guadeloupe combines the cultural and cosmopolitan charm of a European vacation with fabulous diving on reefs untouched by all but a minimal group of discriminating dive-travelers. Guadeloupe is actually two main islands connected by a bridge across the River Salee and several out islands. From the air it resembles the wings of a butterfly. Basse-Terre, the western wing, is mountainous, highlighted by the still-active volcano, Mt. Soufriere. Travelers touring this portion of the islands will find tropical rain forests, bamboo trees, hot springs, postcard waterfalls, and a profusion of tropical flowers, fruits, almond and palm trees. Grande-Terre, the eastern wing of Guadeloupe, is flat, dry, and home to modern resorts, beautiful swimming beaches, fields of sugar cane and unlimited topside tourist attractions.

The prime dive-vacation attraction is Pigeon Island, located just off the central western coast of Basse-Terre. Pigeon Island is a mountain in the sea whose base is surrounded by miles of dense coral reefs. It is the site of the film,*The Silent World*.

Non-French-speaking divers visiting Guadeloupe should pick up a French phrase book and familiarize themselves with

Area Contributors: Richard Ockelmann and Beth Ann Molino, BDWH; Myron Clement, French West Indies Department of Tourism; Guy Genin of Chez Guy Diving; Raphael Legrand, Directeur, Auberge de la Distillerie Hotel; Florence Marie, Relais du Moulin Hotel.

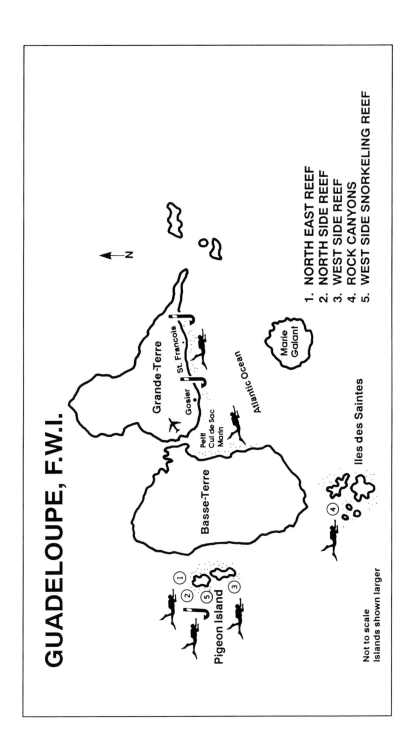

GUADELOUPE, F.W.I.

N

Grande-Terre

St. Francois

Gosier

Atlantic Ocean

Petit
Cul de Sac
Marin

Basse-Terre

Marie
Galant

Iles des Saintes

④

Pigeon Island

①
② ⑤
③

Not to scale
Islands shown larger

1. NORTH EAST REEF
2. NORTH SIDE REEF
3. WEST SIDE REEF
4. ROCK CANYONS
5. WEST SIDE SNORKELING REEF

Pigeon Island

the language. English is NOT widely spoken; even the grunts grunt with a French accent. Topless sunbathing, snorkeling, SCUBA and swimming is *de rigueur* on Guadeloupe.

Best Dives of Guadeloupe

Pigeon Island, composed of volcanic stone and scrub trees, lies off the western coast of Basse-Terre, the western wing of Guadeloupe. The area consists of two land masses, North Pigeon and South Pigeon. The waters surrounding it come under French Government protection as an Underwater Natural Park—the Cousteau Marine Sanctuary.

Underwater landscape off Pigeon Island

☆☆☆☆☆**NORTH EAST REEF.** The northeast side of North Pigeon Island is a superb wall dive. Beginning at the surface, the wall drops 40 ft to a shelf then slopes down to 70 ft and finally plunges steeply to 140 ft. The wall is carpeted with multi-hued soft corals, sponges, plate corals, and large pillar coral formations. Recommended for both novice and experienced divers.

☆☆☆☆☆**NORTH SIDE REEF.** You'll find superb sea-scapes for photography on the north side of North Pigeon Island. Huge clusters of tube sponges, some six feet tall, and enormous green and purple sea fans grow on the ledges and outcrops of the wall. The reef begins in the shallows and drops off to a maze of small canyons and outcrops. North Side Reef is a super dive for novices as well as experienced divers. Average sea conditions are calm and visibility is often more than 100 feet.

☆☆☆☆**WEST SIDE REEF.** This side of North Pigeon Island is everyone's favorite. The wall begins at the surface and drops to a shelf at 25 ft and slopes down to 40 ft, where it drops off sharply to the bottom at 140 ft. Fish life is abundant. Inhabitants of the reef include large hog snappers, trumpet fish, and parrotfish. Calm seas and superb visibility invite divers of all levels of experience to West Side Reef.

☆☆☆**ROCK CANYONS.** Located off the southern tip of Basse-Terre is Iles Des Saintes, a small group of islands surrounded by coral reefs. They are the site of Rock Canyons, a dive recommended for experienced divers since the current and surface surges can be tricky. The entrance to the canyons is at about 10 ft and the bottom drops to about 45 ft. The canyon walls, encrusted with corals, go off in many directions. Carved into them are hundreds of small caves populated by myriads of critters and fish. Huge formations of rare pink corals are also found here.

Best Snorkeling of Guadeloupe

☆☆☆☆☆**WEST SIDE REEF** is the best snorkeling area in the Cousteau Marine Sanctuary. Shallow walls are painted with enormous feather dusters; barrel-sized basket sponges thrive amidst soft corals of many colors.

Additional snorkeling and diving sites are found among the lagoons and bays of Les Saintes, the east coast of Basse- Terre, and off-shore Gosier (the south coast of Grande Terre). Check out Mouton Vert, Mouchoir Carre, and Cay Ismini. They are close by the hotels in the bay of Petit Cul de Sac Marin, near Riviere Salee, the river separating the two halves of Guade-

Iles des Saintes

loupe. North of Salee is another bay, Grand Cul de Sac Marin, where the small islets of Fajou and Caret also offer decent diving. St. Francois Reef on the eastern end of the south shore of Grande-Terre is a good snorkeling reef as is Ilet de Gosier, off Gosier. Diving is a young sport on Guadeloupe and every dive-explorer has a unique opportunity to find a new "best dive" of his/her own. New sites are discovered every day.

Dive Operators

CHEZ GUY has two locations, one directly opposite Pigeon Island on Malendure Beach in Bouillante on Basse-Terre, and another on Les Saintes. Operator and master diver Guy Genin has three fast comfortable boats for daily dive and snorkeling excursions to Pigeon Island. ☎ Pigeon, 98-81-72; at Les Saintes, 99-52-19.

THE NAUTILUS CLUB, which faces Pigeon Island from the beach at Malendure, specializes in diving excursions here. ☎ 98-85-69.

LES HEURES SAINES is a modern dive center facing Pigeon from Rocher de Malendure. Daniel Mell, Dominique Derame and Florence Beaufere, a trio of NAUI instructors, offer daily dives and night dives once a week. ☎ 98-86-63.

AQUA-FARI CLUB is based at La Creole Beach Hotel in Gosier, a bustling resort area 15 miles east of Point-a-Pitre, Guadeloupe's largest city. Divemaster Alain Verdonck offers guided wreck dives and excursions to nearby coral reefs and Pigeon Island. Prices range from $30 to $55 dollars depending on dive site. A 10-dive package is available; it includes airport-to-hotel transfer, welcome cocktail, bus trip to Pigeon, two dives a day and one night dive, and cocktail party. Price $458 plus hotel. ☎ 84-26-26.

KARUKERA PLONGEE is located at the Hotel PLM Azur Callinago in Gosier. Karukera runs full-day dive trips to Les Saintes twice a week and offers local half-day dives.

PLM AZUR LOS SANTOS HOTEL on Les Saintes island has recently opened a watersports club under the direction of Lionel Maury who works with La Colline. Over 20 dive sites are visited around Les Saintes. Packages available through your travel agent.

Live-Aboards

Groups of up to eight people can arrange for a sail-dive vacation aboard a luxury 45-ft custom catamaran, *Privilege*, through Jacques and Florence Playonst. Write to them at Marina Bas du Fort 97110, Pointe a Pitre, Guadeloupe, FWI.

Accommodations

If your tongue doesn't curl comfortably around conversational French, head for one of the bigger hotels where English is spoken. Or if getting to know people is one of the reasons you travel, stay at a Relais Creole, a small family-owned inn. Most of the hotels are situated on Grande-Terre. Among the small hotels close to Pigeon Island on Basse-Terre are Raphael Legrand's charming 12-room **AUBERGE DE LA DIS-TILLERIE** at Tabanon near Petit-Bourg. This fully air- conditioned inn is a short ride from Pigeon Island dive operators. The adjacent restaurant, Le Bitaco is popular with the locals and noted for Creole dishes. Freshwater pool.

Rock Canyons, Iles des Saintes

Relais du Moulin, Grande-Terre

RELAIS DU MOULIN, near Sainte Anne on Grande-Terre, is marked by a sugar-mill tower which serves as the office. This small resort features 20 air-conditioned bungalows. Relais du Moulin is about an hour's drive from Pigeon Island. Reservations through your travel agent.

LA CREOLE BEACH HOTEL is located on the beach at Gosier. It was once a Holiday Inn and the rooms are large and well appointed. The Aqua-Fari Dive shop on premises offers tours to the coral reef surrounding Gosier Island as well as excursions to Pigeon Island. Contact your travel agent for reservations.

MERIDIEN GUADELOUPE is just east of Gosier at St. Francois. This is a four-star deluxe beachfront resort with 272 rooms. On the road east of it are any number of beachside bistros serving lobster and seafood. Dive shops here offer daily trips to the off shore reefs of Grande-Terre and Pigeon Island.

Other Activities

Sailboats, crewed or bareboat, are plentiful. For rentals or tours try Vacances Yachting Antilles at Marina Bas-du-Fort, Pointe-A-Pitre. ☎ 90-82-95. Full-day picnic sails on the trimaran, *La Grande Voile*, or catamaran, *Papyrus*, can be arranged through your hotel. ☎ 82-87-26.

Sightseeing

Hiking through Basse-Terre's Parc Naturel takes you along well-marked trails through tropical rain forests to waterfalls, mountain pools, and La Soufriere, a 4,813-ft volcano and the park's most famous site. Horseback riding along the beaches can be arranged at Le Relais du Moulin (☎ 88-23-96).

Dining

Guadeloupe is a gourmet's delight. Top restaurants and hotel dining rooms offer classic French and Caribbean cuisine. Though the island is French it is also decidedly Creole, and Creole eateries are gaining enormously in popularity. Some are beachside cafes, some are in-town bistros, and several are little more than the front porch of the cook's home.

On Malendure Beach, Basse-Terre check out **CHEZ LOULOUSE** , noted for Chef Loulouse's crayfish sauce Amer-

Catamaran, Privilege, *off Guadeloupe*

icaine. This is a small native seafood eatery in a simple setting. ☎ 98-70-34. In Gosier, try **LE BASSIGNAC** on the Beach Road (Route de la Plage).

FACTS

RECOMPRESSION CHAMBER. Located in Pointe-a-Pitre, Grande-Terre.

GETTING THERE. Connections from Miami on Air France and Eastern Airlines. From San Juan, take American Eagle Airlines or Eastern. Inter-island flights can be arranged at Le Raizet Airport aboard Air Guadeloupe or Safari Tours. Water ferries to Iles Des Saintes are available from the city of Basse- Terre or Trois Rivieres on the south coast.

Six-foot sponge, Pigeon Island

ISLAND TRANSPORTATION. All major car rental agencies are at the airport. Reservations should be made before arriving in Guadeloupe to insure getting a car. Bus service in Mercedes vans is available between cities. The cities are clearly marked on the outside.

DRIVING. Right side of the road. The main roads between major cities are clearly marked. A wonderful tourist map is available from the tourist office in Pointe-a-Pitre.

DOCUMENTS. For stays of up to three months Canadian and U.S. citizens require a return ticket and two forms of I.D.— either a passport or proof of citizenship such as a birth certificate or voter's registration card with some type of photo. A passport is recommended. British citizens require a passport.

CURRENCY. French franc. 6.5FF = $1.00 U.S.

CLIMATE. Temperatures range from 75 to 85° F. Water temperatures are warm year round so you won't need a wetsuit, although a wetskin or 1/8 inch shortie wetsuit is comfortable in mid- winter.

CLOTHING. Casual light clothing. Most beaches are topless.

EQUIPMENT REQUIRED. Bring all of your own SCUBA gear except for tanks and weights. Most operators have Scubapro tanks which do not require any special regulator adaptor.

ELECTRICITY. European adaptors required.

TIME. Atlantic Standard (EST + 1 hr).

LANGUAGE. French, local Creole dialect.

TAX. A service charge of 10 to 15 percent is included on most hotel and restaurant tabs.

PHOTOGRAPHY. Fast, reliable film processing is not yet available on Guadeloupe. Take your own film and have it processed after returning home.

RELIGIOUS SERVICES. Catholic, Protestant, Jewish.

FOR ADDITIONAL INFORMATION. French West Indies Tourist Board, 610 Fifth Avenue, NY NY 10020. ☎ 212-757-1125.

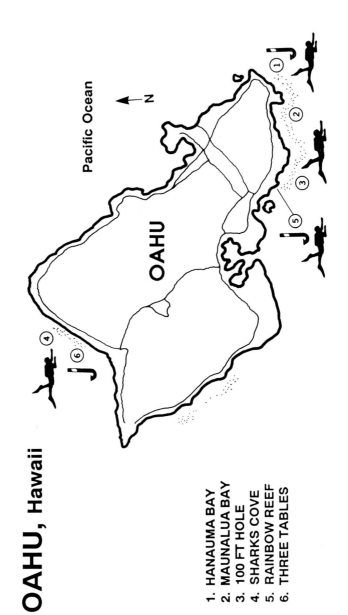

OAHU, Hawaii

OAHU

Pacific Ocean

N

1. HANAUMA BAY
2. MAUNALUA BAY
3. 100 FT HOLE
4. SHARKS COVE
5. RAINBOW REEF
6. THREE TABLES

HAWAII

Hawaii has become one of the world's top dive vacation spots. Topside, Hawaii is a tropical paradise, lush with swaying palms, wild orchids, and exotic plants. Glistening mountains slope down to endless white sand beaches and inland there are miles of sugar cane and pineapple fields.

Underwater Hawaii is a magical world of lava tubes, tunnels, archways, cathedrals, and caves carpeted with multi-hued corals and sponges. Marine life is abundant with more than 100 species of fish (some not found anywhere else). Turtles, squid, dolphins, whales, crustaceans, octopus, and tame morays frolic in the crystal waters. Sunken tanks and Jeeps, abandoned after World War II, lie motionless on the ocean floor camouflaged now with a layer of coral and barnacles.

Oahu is the gathering place for vacationers and Waikiki Beach, with miles of high-rise hotels creating a luminescent skyline, is the undisputed capital. Honolulu is the cultural center, bright with concerts, dance performances, and live theater. The Nuuanu Pali Lookout provides a panoramic view of the windward side of the island. At the uncrowded beaches, expert body surfers test their skills. At Makapuu Point daring hang-gliders soar from towering cliffs. On the leeward side of

Area Contributors: Leslie Sternberg of Dive Maui; Ed and Susan Robinson of Hawaiian Watercolors; Steve Mahaney of Sea Paradise Scuba; James Robinson of Kona Coast Divers/Kona Coast Scuba Schools; and Barbara Brundage of Pacific Stock. Credit: Portions of this chapter are reproduced from *Dive Hawaii* with permission.

Waianae Range, small towns and wide beaches line the coastline. Most of the diving at Oahu is done on the south and west shores where a 165-ft minesweeper and a 200-ft sunken barge lie silently on the bottom. North shore diving is excellent during the summer when the seas are calm.

Best Dives of Oahu

✮✮✮✮✮**HANAUMA BAY** on the southeast shore of Oahu is the most popular diving and snorkeling site in all of Hawaii. It is a state marine preserve hosting over a million visitors each year. Formed from an ancient volcanic crater, the bay is lined with a shallow inner reef which starts at 10 ft and slopes down to an outer reef at a depth of 70 ft.

✮✮✮✮**MAUNALUA BAY,** which is just west of Hanauma, offers a variety of dives. Turtle Canyon at the east end is alive with green sea turtles of all sizes. The bottom is varied, with lava flow ridges and sandy canyons. Big Eel Reef is home to many types of moray eels and eagle rays. Fantasy Reef, located on the western end of Maunalua Bay, is made up of dramatic lava ledges and archways. Kahala Barge, lying in 80 ft of water, is a 200-ft barge that was sunk to create an artificial reef. The top of the wreck is at 50 ft.

✮✮✮**100-FT HOLE** is an oasis-like lava formation located a mile off-shore. Marine life includes an eight-ft moray eel, lobsters, crabs, white-tip shark, and tropicals. Depths range between 65 and 85 ft.

View from Nauuanu Pali, Oahu

☆☆☆☆**SHARK COVE,** on the northwest shore of Oahu, is the most popular cavern dive on Oahu. Light shimmering through openings in the tops of the caves resembles a stained-glass window. Depths range from 15 to 45 ft. Only experienced divers accompanied by a professional guide should attempt Shark Cove.

Best Snorkeling Sites of Oahu

☆☆☆**RAINBOW REEF,** just west of Waikiki Beach, is a favorite dive and snorkeling site for beginners. The reef, also known as Magic Island, begins at 10 ft and slopes to 30 ft.

☆☆☆**THREE TABLES** on the northwest shore of the island is named for a trio of flat rocks which break the surface close to the beach. Starting at a depth of 15 ft, snorkelers can explore large rock formations, caverns, and ledges. Beach access is easy. (Diveable only during summer months.)

Oahu Dive Operators

AARON'S DIVE SHOP , 602 Kailua Road, Kailua HI 96734. ☎ 808-262-2333. Owner, Jack Aaron.

ALOHA DIVE SHOP , Koko Marina Shopping Center, Honolulu HI 96825, offers dive packages, SCUBA and snorkeling tours, instruction, and rentals. Owner Jackie James.

LEEWARD DIVE CENTER, 87-066 Farrington Hwy, Maili HI 96792, ☎ 808-696-3414. Owner, Gene Clark.

Hanauma Bay, Oahu

SOUTH SEAS AQUATICS offers special tours for beginners as well as seasoned divers aboard a custom-built 44-ft dive vessel. Located at 1050 Ala Moana Blvd., Honolulu HI 96814. ☎ 808-538-3854. Owner, Masao Nakana. South Seas Aquatics second location is 870 Kapahulu Avenue, No. 109, Honolulu HI 96816. ☎ 800-252-MAHI or 808-526-9550.

STEVE'S DIVING ADVENTURES, 1860 Ala Moana Blvd., Honolulu HI 96815. ☎ 808-947-8900. Owner, Steve Holmes.

Accommodations on Oahu

There are over 100 hotels on Oahu. Average price per room is $60. Many of the dive shops offer diving packages which may include accommodations in either luxury condominiums or resorts.

REAL HAWAII VACATIONS feature oceanfront suites with fully equipped kitchens, cable TV, one or two bedrooms, one or two baths, swimming pools, Jacuzzi, and tennis courts. Dive vacation packages include round trip airfare from Los Angeles,

San Francisco, or Seattle, car rental, diving, and condominium. Prices are $799 per week. Write to 1341 Pacific Avenue, Santa Cruz CA 95060. ☎ 800-367-5108.

Dining

Oahu offers an endless choice of fast-food eateries, Chinese, Japanese, American and seafood restaurants, and commercial luaus, the feast in which a pig is roasted slowly in an underground oven.

EL CRAB CATCHER & SEASIDE CAFE. The cafe menu features fresh shrimp, crab, clam and oyster dishes. Located at Ala Wai Harbor, Ilika, Hilton Hawaiian Village, Sheraton Waikiki, Reef Hotel, Royal Hawaiian, Moana, and Hyatt resorts. ☎ 808- 955-4911

PARADISE COVE LUAU is on the West Coast of Oahu at Campbell Estates, West Beach. It is one of the best spots in which to enjoy a luau. Moderate prices. ☎ 808-945-3571.

Waikiki at night

NICK'S FISHMARKET, located at the Waikiki Gateway Hotel in the heart of Waikiki, is known for outstanding seafood. ☎ 808-945-3571.

JAMESON'S BY THE SEA is on the northeast side of Oahu overlooking the north shore. Seafood specialties. Expensive.

MAUI, THE VALLEY ISLE

Two mountain ranges, the West Maui mountains and Haleakala, cover most of Maui. Haleakala rises to 10,000 ft. Hiking here, especially at sunrise, is more of an "encounter" than a sport. Visitors enjoy wandering along the "road to Hana," a remote town on the windward side of Haleakala, which passes bamboo forests, waterfalls and gardens of wild fruits and flowers. On the northwest side of Maui you can explore Lahaina, an old whaling village. Lahaina Harbor is a bustling sailing port where you can see yachts from all over the world.

Maui County offers divers an endless variety of diving and snorkeling sites. It is also a jumping-off point for dive tours to the islands of Lanai, Molokai, Molokini and Kahoolawe. At these out-island dive sites, you'll see strange creatures rarely seen elsewhere, docile 50-foot whale sharks and, during the winter months, humpback whales. Side trips to Molokini and other nearby sites take 15 to 30 minutes; trips across the channel to Lanai and Molokai can take 1 1/2 hours.

Best Dives of Maui

☆☆☆☆☆**KAHOOLAWE ISLAND CAVERN.** Kahoolawe is located just off the southwest tip of Maui. The Cavern is a roomy underwater cave, tucked into the cliffs. Fronting the cave is a sheltered bowl. With the bottom at 40 ft, it is spooky but not dangerous; average visibility is 100 ft. A lush coral reef has built up on the outer shell of the cave.

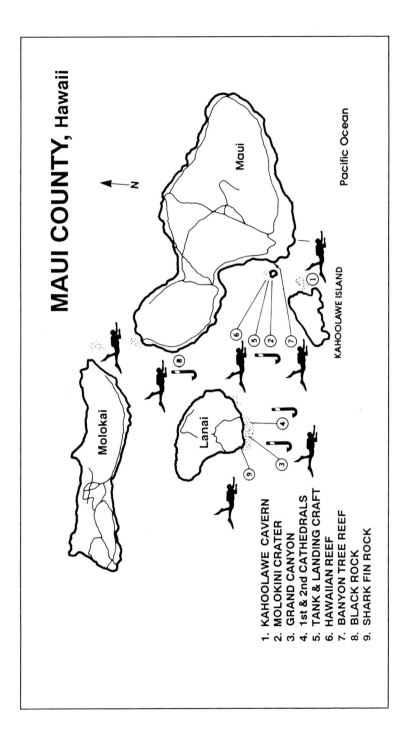

MAUI COUNTY, Hawaii

Maui

Pacific Ocean

Molokai

Lanai

KAHOOLAWE ISLAND

N

1. KAHOOLAWE CAVERN
2. MOLOKINI CRATER
3. GRAND CANYON
4. 1st & 2nd CATHEDRALS
5. TANK & LANDING CRAFT
6. HAWAIIAN REEF
7. BANYON TREE REEF
8. BLACK ROCK
9. SHARK FIN ROCK

Molokini Crater

☆☆☆☆☆**MOLOKINI CRATER** is a crescent-shaped is-land two miles from Maui island. It is by far Maui's most popular dive site and you will often see 30 or 40 dive boats anchored here at one time. Formed by the top of an old volcanic crater, this area is unique because it combines many ecosystems within a small area: deep water, shallow reef, flowing and still waters, with their natural complements of marine animals. Good visibility. Whales, porpoises and unusual marine animals are common at Molokini Crater. Over the years Ed Robinson of Hawaiian Watercolors has tamed many moray eels on the ridge, some of whom (Garbonzo, Hazel, Brew and Frisky) may be safely handled. They make patient photo subjects. Depths range from 10 ft near the shore to about 80 ft. Dropoffs go as deep as 200 ft. A wonderful video film by Ed Robinson featuring Molokini can be rented or purchased from Hawaiian Watercolors (see listing for address). Divers should plan trips to the crater for morning since stronger currents are encountered in the afternoon.

☆☆☆**GRAND CANYON,** off the southern end of Lanai, is an enormous underwater canyon with walls of lava where huge turtles and rays glide along the bottom. Depths: 20 to 100 ft.

☆☆☆☆**FIRST & SECOND CATHEDRALS.** At this dive site, also off Lanai, divers and snorkelers find pinnacles rising from 60 ft to just below the surface. Far below in spacious

The Molokai Channel, between Oahu and Maui

Haleakala, Maui

caverns that loom like cathedrals, there are lobsters, ghost shrimp, spotted moray eels, and eagle rays. Do not attempt to dive these caverns unless you're accompanied by a very experienced local guide. Morning is recommended since afternoon currents are sometimes treacherous. Visibility is excellent during periods of calm water and weather.

☆☆☆**TANK AND LANDING CRAFT** was created by the sinking of two U.S. Army vehicles in 60 ft of water off the Southwest Mehena coastline of Maui. It is done as a drift dive starting at the tank and drifting to the landing craft. Around the wrecks are Army relics and schools of tropical fish that can be handfed. You may be startled by a large trumpet fish who will dangle in front of your mask.

☆☆☆☆☆**HAWAIIAN REEF** is located between Maui and Molokini crater. Depth is 85 ft with a number of lava formations that rise 20 ft above a sandy bottom. Many large antler coral trees line the base of the reef, and big schools of blue lined snappers, large shells and eagle rays are common residents.

☆☆☆BANYON TREE REEF is just off the S.W. Makena shore of Maui. A number of reefs here rise off the bottom about 15 ft. Depth is 65 ft. This area has several very large antler coral trees and lots of fish.

Best Snorkeling Sites of Maui

☆☆BLACK ROCK is located on the northwest shore of Maui off Kaanapali beach. Snorkelers enjoy exploring the cove created by a peninsula. Visibility is good. Depths shallow. Maximum 20 ft.

☆☆☆☆SHARKFIN ROCK, off the south shore of Lanai, is a large rock formation that protrudes from the water like a shark's fin. A vertical wall drops from the surface to 90 ft. This is a popular site.

Dive Operators of Maui

HAWAIIAN WATERCOLORS is operated by Susan and Ed Robinson and Roger Pannier. Ed Robinson has been diving and photographing the reefs off Maui since 1971. His photographs have appeared in over a hundred publications including *National Geographic, Oceans* and *Islands* magazine.

Hawaiian Watercolors is a good choice for naturalist tours, personalized videos with music and still underwater portraits.

Ed's beautifully orchestrated underwater video of Molokini Crater and Lanai dive sights is available for $20. P.O. Box 616, Kihei HI 96753. ☎ 808-879-3584.

CENTRAL PACIFIC DIVERS operates a roomy 43-ft boat. Dive packages available. 780 Front Street, Lahaina HI 96761. ☎ 800-551-6767 or 808-661-8781. Owner: Jane Cambouris.

DIVE MAUI, INC. Lahaina Marketplace, Lahainaluna Road, Lahaina HI 96761. ☎ 808-667-2080 or 808-661-4363.

Dive instructor and owner Leslie Sternberg knows of many dive spots right off the beach where guests can join huge turtles and hundreds of different reef fish.

HAWAIIAN REEF DIVERS , 129 Lahainaluna Road, Lahaina HI 96761. ☎ 808-667-7647.

OCEAN ACTIVITIES CENTER is Maui's largest ocean sport center. It operates a 37-ft twin diesel dive boat that takes up to 12 snorkelers on half-day trips to Molokini Crater and Lanai, with a continental breakfast and deli-style lunch served aboard. They are located at Wailea Shopping Center, 3750 Wailea Alanui D-2, Wailea HI 96753. ☎ 800-367- 8047, ext 448, or 808-879-4485.

THE DIVE SHOP OF KIHEI, 1975 S. Kihei Road, Kihei HI 96753 ☎ 808-879-5172.

Diving on Your Own

Most of the dive shops rent equipment and can suggest the best and safest locations for beach dives. Some of the beaches have strong currents and riptides. Diving caverns or open-ocean locations without an experienced guide can be extremely dangerous because sudden storms can drastically change sea conditions in minutes, reducing visibility from excellent to zero. Most boat dive trips are scheduled for mornings.

Other Activities

Sailing trips around Maui and the out islands are available from Captain Nemo's at 700 Front Street. Helicopter rides are offered from Maui Helicopters, ☎ 800- 367-8003. Horseback riding arranged through Pony Expresss, ☎ 808-667-2202. Train ride tours, through Pacific Railroad, ☎ 808-661-0089. A hiking permit must be obtained from the park concession for hikes around the volcano in Haleahala National Park. Wind surfing is popular; Sailboards Maui ☎ 808-871-7954 for rentals and recommended locations.

Accommodations on Maui

All of the major hotels arrange diving trips. Your travel agent can suggest hotels or other accommodations to suit any pocketbook. Package tours can be arranged by dive shops or Real Hawaii Condominium Vacations. ☎ 800-367-5108.

PLANTATION INN on Maui's west coast is the island's only dive resort. Vacationing divers staying here will enjoy a casual yet elegant country inn atmosphere. The inn offers air conditioning, and pool, plus a restaurant. ☎ 800-433-6815 or 808-667-9225.

STOUFFER'S WAILEA BEACH is located on the southwest coast. This resort features five beaches, restaurants, and golf. Reserve through your travel agent or write Wailea, Maui HI 96753. ☎ 808-879-4900. Expensive.

SHERATON MAUI HOTEL in Lahaina is near Black Rock, a favorite reef and wall dive. ☎ 800-325-3535 or see your travel agent. Expensive.

MAUI LU RESORT HOTEL is located on the beach at 575 S. Kihei Rd, Kihei Maui, HI 96753. The resort has air-conditioned rooms, TV, restaurant, and pool. ☎ 800-367-5124, in Canada 800-423-8733. Moderate.

Dining

KIMO'S at 845 Front Street in Lahaina is popular for Polynesian dishes and desserts. Moderate. ☎ 808-661-4811.

GERARD'S at the Plantation Inn offers elegant French cuisine. Expensive. ☎ 808-661-8939.

COOK'S AT THE BEACH is against a backdrop of streams and footbridges. Breakfast, lunch and dinner. Inexpensive. Westin Maui, 2365 Kaanapali Parkway. ☎ 808-667-2525.

CHOPSTICKS at the Royal Lahaina Resort has an "all appetizer" dinner menu. ☎ 808-661-3611.

HAWAII, THE BIG ISLAND

Located 120 miles southeast of Oahu (40 minutes by air), Hawaii is the largest island of the Hawaiian archipelago. The birthplace of King Kamehameha, the best known ruler of the islands, it is also the location of the islands' only active volcanoes. Molten lava still flows to the sea. Over 20,000 varieties of orchids are grown.

Over 50 miles of the shoreline are protected from high winds and swells, and many snorkeling areas can be reached easily from the beach. The most spectacular diving is just offshore.

Best Dives of the Kona Coast, Hawaii

☆☆☆☆☆**RED HILL** is located 10 miles off South Kailua. This area has four different dive sites which range from 15 to 70 ft in depth. Visibility ranges from 75 to 100 ft. Divers explore lava tubes, finger and leather coral formations. The fish population is enormous.

☆☆☆☆☆**THE AQUARIUM AT KEALAKEKUA BAY,** an underwater state park, is a beautiful reef inhabited by thousands of tame fish who enjoy following divers and snorkelers. The shallows can be reached from the beach, but the deeper reefs and drop-offs require a boat. The bottom is hard coral—lobe, finger, plate, cauliflower, octocorals—and patches of sand. Visibility is best on the outer reef. This is where Captain Cook was killed.

☆☆☆☆☆**KAIWI** is two miles from Kailua Bay—a five minute boat ride. Depths range from 15 to 50 ft. Divers can swim through caves, around pinnacles and over coral encrusted lava arches. Eagle rays, large turtles and conch shells are found on the reef as well as 7-11 crabs. Visibility is excellent and the seas are calm.

☆☆☆☆**THE PINE TREES,** just 13 minutes by boat from shore, is a sensational lava flow area with many caves and arches. During the winter, whales are frequently sighted. Turtles, eels, manta rays, and porpoises reside here.

Best Snorkeling Sites

Snorkelers are advised to consult with local dive operators about best areas when weather is questionable. They should wear gloves and kneepads where there are sea urchins.

☆☆☆**KEALAKEKUA BAY** near the Captain Cook Monument is a super snorkeling area. You'll see many kinds of tame reef fish and corals. Ideal for photography. Restrooms are within walking distance. Nice pebble beach.

☆☆**ANAEHO'OMALU BAY BEACH PARK** is north of Kealakekua Bay just past Mile Marker 77. The sand beach is lovely. Snorkelers will find pretty corals and a lot of fish. Visibility decreases with high winds and heavy surf.

☆☆☆**PALEMANO POINT** is the southern end of Kealakekua Bay. The coral is particularly colorful here and snorkelers

Black sand at Kaimu Beach, Hawaii

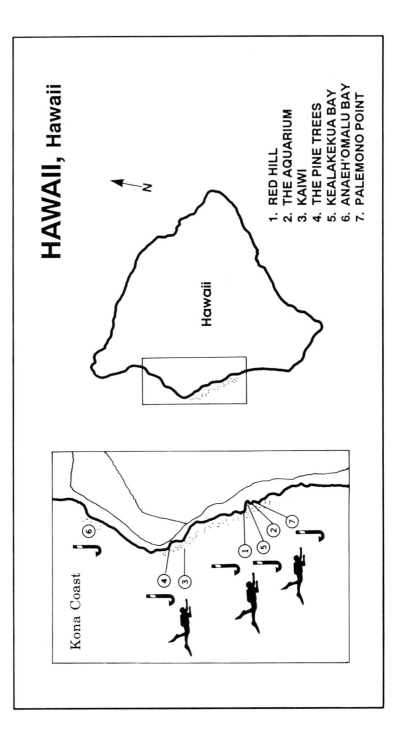

HAWAII, Hawaii

N

Hawaii

Kona Coast

1. RED HILL
2. THE AQUARIUM
3. KAIWI
4. THE PINE TREES
5. KEALAKEKUA BAY
6. ANAEH'OMALU BAY
7. PALEMONO POINT

will enjoy photographing rudderfish, yellow tangs, and trumpetfish. Visibility is good, water usually calm. No facilities. Rocky shoreline.

Dive Operators of Kona Coast, Hawaii

KONA COAST DIVERS offers complete dive vacation packages. Owners Julie and Jim Robinson operate a full-service dive shop with a well-equipped underwater photography center. 75-5614 Palani Road, Kailua-Kona HI, 96740. ☎ 800-329-8802 or 808-329-8802.

JACK'S DIVING LOCKER offers NAUI and PADI certifications and resort courses with equipment provided at no charge. P.O. Box 5306, Kona Inn Shopping Village, Kailua-Kona HI 96740. ☎ 808-329-7585.

KOHALA DIVERS, LTD. is located at the north end of Kona Coast. P.O. Box 4935, Kawaihae HI 96743. ☎ 808-882-7774.

SEA PARADISE SCUBA, 78-7128 Kaleopapa Road, P.O. Box 5655, Kailua- Kona HI 96745. ☎ 808-322-2500/4775.

Live-Aboards

KONA AGGRESSOR takes you to offbeat, undiscovered reefs with unlimited diving and personalized service. Luxury style and comfort. Write to Mike Nakachi, P.O. Box 2097, Kailua-Kona HI 96745. ☎ 800-344-KONA or 808-329-8182.

Other Activities

Be sure to see Hawaii Volcanoes National Park. Active volcanoes make a fascinating show as you stand on the rim of Halemaumau Firepit in the Kilauea Caldera. On the south coast there are black sand beaches where all types of outdoor sports can be found, even skiing. Deep sea fishing can be arranged through the Kona Activity Center ☎ 329-3171. Horses may be rented for riding the trails of Kohala through

Waipio Ranch, ☎ 775-0373 or 775-7425. Skiing? Yes you can ski on snow atop Mauna Kea if enough snow falls. Only for the daring. Try Ski Shop Hawaii in Waimea, ☎ 885-4188. All skiing is above 10,000 ft.

Accommodations on Hawaii

THE KONA MAKAI, a deluxe oceanfront condominium, offers hotel-dive packages with Kona Coast Divers. It is located 1 1/2 miles from Kailua-Kona and is convenient to everything. $799 for seven nights includes air transportation from California, condo, and diving. ☎ 800-367-5108.

KONA VILLAGE RESORT offers a luxurious retreat from TV, radio, and telephones. Guests stay in thatched-roof houses. ☎ 800-367-5290. Expensive.

KONA BY THE SEA is a nice oceanfront condominium complex. ☎ 800-367-5124. Moderate.

Dining

VERANDA RESTAURANT is ideal for a light snack, breakfast or lunch. Located at the Hotel King Kamehameha, Kailua-Kona. Inexpensive. ☎ 808-329-2911.

TESHIMA'S RESTAURANT on Highway 11 in Honalo, Kona, offers great Japanese dining. Credit cards not accepted. ☎ 322-9140. Inexpensive.

KONA GALLEY RESTAURANT overlooks scenic Kailua Bay. Open for lunch and dinner, specializing in local seafood. ☎ 329-3777. Inexpensive.

SPINDRIFTER RESTAURANT overlooks the ocean. Specialties include Hawaiian steaks. ☎ 329-1344. Moderate.

Waipio Valley, on the northern Hamakua Coast of Hawaii

KAUAI, THE GARDEN ISLE

Kauai is a tropical oasis with postcard waterfalls, beautiful beaches and swimming lagoons (featured as the dream world of Bali H'ai in the movie South Pacific and in the TV series Fantasy Island), exotic birds, rain forests, botanic gardens, deep canyons, and lush valleys, it is also the oldest Hawaiian island and richest in folklore and history.

Because Kauai is so old, its marine life may be more unusual and varied than the marine life anywhere else in the state. South shore dive sites are accessible year-round and offer divers an underwater fantasyland teeming with every kind of fish and coral imaginable.

Dive shops are clustered in the Wailua and Koloa/Poipu areas. They have a choice of four launch areas, all minutes from local dive sites.

Best Dives of Kauai

☆☆☆☆**BRENNEKE'S DROP** is a lava shelf shot through with overhangs and holes that drop from 60 to 95 ft. Huge turtles sleep under the ledges and schools of taape cloud the area.

☆☆☆☆☆**SHERATON CAVERNS.** Three immense lava tubes parallel one another to create Kauai's most popular cavern dive. Turtles regularly swim through caverns and there's a lobster nursery in one of them. Depth range is from 35 to 60 ft.

☆☆☆☆**GENERAL STORE** is a horseshoe-shaped ledge with two caverns. General Store is also the site of a 19th-century shipwreck, five large anchors and a chain. Green moray eels peek out from under the ledges. Black coral grows on the bottom. Depth range: 65 to 80 ft.

☆☆☆☆☆**OCEANARIUM** off the north shore is a spectacular dive presenting tall pinnacles and sheer drop-offs to 140 ft (experts only). Many manta, eagle rays, and ulua. Depth: 60 to 140 ft.

☆☆☆☆☆**NIIHAU (the Forbidden Island)** is located 18 miles from Kauai. The island is privately owned and is populated almost entirely by Hawaiians. It is a cultural preserve dedicated to the traditions and culture of old Hawaii. Residents

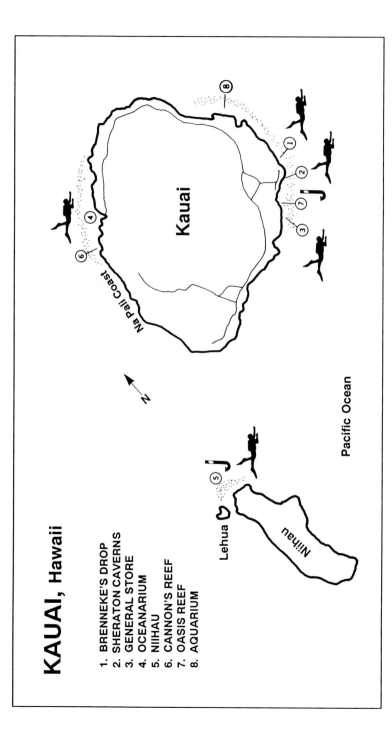

lead a primitive life style without benefit of electricity, medical facilities or paved roads. Outsiders are forbidden to step on shore.

The island is surrounded by virgin reefs with spectacular formations, huge caverns, and large fish such as rays and sharks.

Best Snorkeling Sites of Kauai

☆☆☆**CANNON'S REEF** drops quickly from the shoreline on the north side of Kauai, forming a long ledge permeated with lava tubes. Diveable in summer only.

☆☆☆☆**OASIS REEF** on the south shore is protected and diveable all year. A lone pinnacle surrounded by sand rises from 35 ft to just below the ocean surface. This is a gathering place for thousands of fish including false moorish idols, triggerfish, butterfly fish and porcupine puffers. Depths from four to 35 ft.

☆☆☆☆☆**AQUARIUM** is on the southeast side of Kauai and is named for the variety of colorful tropicals that reside here. The site is a shallow reef with lava ledges and small valleys. You'll see several cannons from an 18th-century wreck. Depths from 25 to 40 ft.

Dive Operators of Kauai

AQUATICS KAUAI, LTD. offers custom dive-vacation packages, 38-ft custom dive boat, videos, rentals. 433 Kuhio Hwy, Kapaa, HI 96746. ☎ 800-822-9422 or 808-822-9213.

Boat basin, Ala Wai Canal, Honolulu

FATHOM FIVE ADVENTURES. Dive packages, night diving, reef walks, snorkeling tips, certification and resort courses. P.O. Box 907, Koloa HI 96756. ☎ 800-422-DIVE.

SEA SAGE DIVING CENTER, 4-1378 Kuhio Hwy, Kapaa HI 96746.

Other Activities

Sail the south shore by catamaran with South Shore Sailing (☎ 245-9141) or try your luck at deep sea fishing with Sea Fever Charters (☎ 826-6815). Golf fanatics will love Kukuiolono Park and Golf Course (☎ 332-9151). Hiking through Kokee State Park is a scenic pleasure. The park has over 40 miles of trails. If you enjoy horseback riding along the beach contact Po'oku Stables (☎ 826-6777).

Dining

BALI HAI at the Hanalei Bay Resort on the north coast has a spectacular setting overlooking the bay. Continental breakfast, lunch and dinner. ☎ 826-6522. Moderate.

TAHITI NUI RESTAURANT in the heart of Hanalei town offers luaus and American cuisine. ☎ 826-6277. Moderate.

BRENNECKE'S BEACH BROILER at 2100 Hoone Road, Poipu Beach, features casual ocean-front dining. ☎ 742-7588.

FAST FOODS

BRICK OVEN PIZZA, Kalaheo, DAIRY QUEEN, Eleele Shopping Center, MC DONALD'S, Waipouli, WENDY'S, Lihue. KEOKI'S in Lihue serves fast island-type food.

Accommodations on Kauai

REAL HAWAII. Dive packages booked through Real Hawaii offer diving and accommodations. ☎ 800-367-5108.

SHERATON KAUAI HOTEL is on the beach at Poipu. All rooms are air conditioned and have TV. ☎ 800-325-3535, or write Sheraton Hotels in Hawaii, P.O. Box 8559, Honolulu HI 96815.

PLANNING YOUR TRIP

ADDITIONAL TRAVEL INFORMATION. See your travel agent or write to Hawaii Visitors Bureau 2270 Kalakaua Avenue, Honolulu HI 96815.

ADDITIONAL SCUBA AND SNORKELING INFORMATION is available from Dive Hawaii, a non-profit association of 30 dive and snorkeling operations. To receive their guide containing additional dive details send $4.00 to P.O. Box 90295, Honolulu HI 96835.

GETTING THERE. All-expense packages including airfare can greatly simplify planning your trip to Hawaii. Several major airlines fly into Honolulu International Airport. The largest carrier is Continental Airlines. Other flights available from United Air Lines, Northwest Orient, Western, American, Delta, Hawaiian Air, World. Frequent daily flights from Honolulu to the other main islands of Hawaii are offered by Aloha Airlines and Hawaiian Air.

ENTRY REQUIREMENTS. Non-U.S. citizens must have a passport and visa. Canadians must prove place of birth with either a birth certificate or passport.

CLOTHING. A lightweight wetsuit is suggested for diving in Hawaii. Ocean temperatures are 72 to 80° F. Topside is tropical with average air temperatures in the 80's. During winter months a light jacket or sweater is recommended. Light casual clothing is appropriate for most activities. Lower temperatures are found in the mountains.

EXPORT RESTRICTIONS. With the exceptions of pineapple and coconuts, no fruits, seeds, coffee, sugar cane, soils, or plants may be taken from the island.

CURRENCY. U.S. Dollar, credit cards widely accepted.

DIVING EMERGENCY. Twenty-four-hour assistance for SCUBA diving accidents is available from the Hyperbaric Treatment Center, 42 Ahui St. Honolulu, ☎ 523-9155 (or 911). For cases requiring emergency hyperbaric treatment, alert the center immediately after contacting the county's emergency dispatcher. Chambers are also available on Maui and Kauai: Maui Memorial Hospital, Wailuku (☎ 244-9056) or Kauai Veterans Memorial Hospital, Waimea, (☎ 338-9431). If you need emergency medical or rescue services call (Kauai, Oahu, Maui): 911, or "O" for operator. On Lanai ☎ 565-6525 (police) ☎ 565-6411 (ambulance) or "O" for operator.

MARINE FORECASTS. Kauai, ☎ 245-3564; Oahu, 836-3921; Maui, 877- 3477; Hawaii, 935-9883.

NOTE: Snorkelers and divers should use a water-resistant sun screen with a high sun protection factor (SAF) rating to prevent painful sunburn.

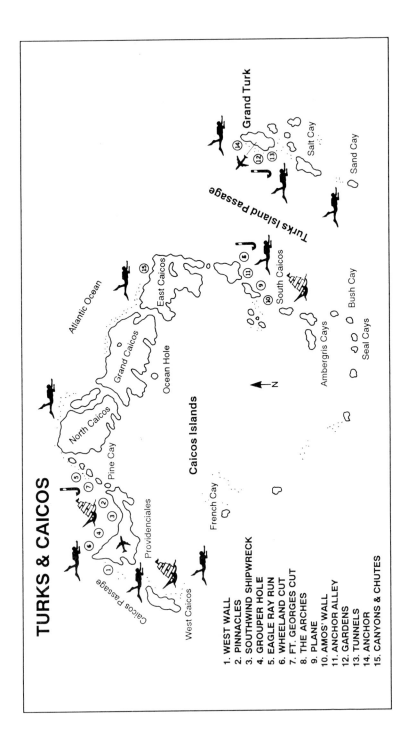

TURKS & CAICOS

Calcos Passage

West Caicos

Providenciales

Pine Cay

North Caicos

Atlantic Ocean

Grand Caicos

Ocean Hole

East Caicos

Caicos Islands

French Cay

N

South Caicos

Ambergris Cays

Seal Cays

Bush Cay

Sand Cay

Salt Cay

Turks Island Passage

Grand Turk

1. WEST WALL
2. PINNACLES
3. SOUTHWIND SHIPWRECK
4. GROUPER HOLE
5. EAGLE RAY RUN
6. WHEELAND CUT
7. FT. GEORGES CUT
8. THE ARCHES
9. PLANE
10. AMOS' WALL
11. ANCHOR ALLEY
12. GARDENS
13. TUNNELS
14. ANCHOR
15. CANYONS & CHUTES

TURKS AND CAICOS

This little-known archipelago is one of the last great diving frontiers. Hundreds of dive sites remain unexplored. Located off the southeastern tip of the Great Bahama Bank, the islands lie well off the beaten path. All are sparsely populated and the cays are fringed with some of the finest and oldest coral communities in the Western Hemisphere. The hundreds of miles of beautiful white beaches are dotted with great snorkeling coves. The vegetation is identical to that of the Bahamas—scrub brush and tall cactus.

The Caicos group consists of six principal islands: West Caicos, Providenciales, North Caicos, Grand Caicos, East Caicos and South Caicos. All offer numerous small cays. The Turks consist of two main islands: Grand Turk and Salt Cay. They are separated from the Caicos by a 22-mile-wide deep- water channel, the Turks Island Passage.

Cockburn Town, the capital of Grand Turk, reflects some of the islands' history in its colorful homes. Some, over 100 years old, are either brightly painted wood frame construction or made from Bermudian stone brought in as ballast by ships seeking salt. Donkey carts clatter through the streets.

A substantial annual rainfall during the late summer and early fall almost dictates that you visit the Turks and Caicos in late winter, spring or early summer. All divers must present a

Area Contributors: Dr. Susan Cropper, DVM; Peggy Becker; Mary Mahoney, *Aviation International News*.

valid C-card before they will be allowed to dive. Spearguns and Hawaiian slings are not permitted in the Turks and Caicos, and treasure hunting is forbidden.

Note: Credit cards and personal checks are not welcome in some of the Turks and Caicos establishments.

PROVIDENCIALES ISLAND AND NORTH CAICOS

The six principal islands of the Caicos and their numerous small cays offer superb wall diving. Along the barrier reef surrounding them you'll find iridescent sea anemones, huge basket sponges and dense gardens of elkhorn coral.

All island activities are centered around the choice dive resorts. Most Provo dive sites are about a 35-minute boat ride from the dive shops.

Best Dives of Provo

☆☆☆☆☆**WEST WALL.** This is actually hundreds of dive sites based on a vertical edge of the continental shelf, with drop-offs beginning at 25 ft and bottoming at 6,000 ft. Divers exploring the West Wall have reported encounters with huge fish, schooling eagle and manta rays, shark and dolphin. During the winter months, humpback whales have been sighted. Forests of black coral start as shallow as 60 ft.

Much of the best terrain has been named—Grand Canyon, Black Coral Forest, Carol's Wall, for example. Visibility is always excellent with sea conditions dependent on the winds and weather. Recommended for experienced divers.

☆☆☆☆**PINNACLES.** Located on the northeast coast of Provo near Grace Bay, the Pinnacles range in depth from 35 to

Club Turkoise, Provo

60 ft. This spur and groove area is home to a mass of Nassau grouper, sea turtles, snapper, sergeant majors, basslets, and schooling grunts. Clump plate corals are dotted with purple and orange sponges, and the many moray eels sometimes seen during daylight hours. Visibility is exceptional.

☆☆☆*SOUTHWIND* **SHIPWRECK.** This 80-ft freighter is a favorite spot for shooting fish photos and dramatic diver portraits. Sunk off Provo's north coast during 1985, the wreck has become home to many tame grouper, as well as barracuda, Spanish hogfish, French angels, horse-eye jacks, damsels, and schools of sergeant majors and yellow tail. The wreck sits on the sand at a 60 ft depth. Visibility is usually good.

☆☆☆**GROUPER HOLE.** Located on the north shore, this dive is a wide sand hole housing a large coral head. Mammoth grouper and jewfish, one exceeding 300 lbs, are residents of this protected spot. Seas are generally calm. Light current may occasionally be encountered.

Best Snorkeling Sites of Provo

☆☆**EAGLE RAY RUN.** Located near Fort George Cay, Eagle Ray Run is the habitat of abundant fish life and shallow gardens of elkhorn coral. Reef depths range from the surface to about 20 ft. This is a super spot for check-out dives and snorkeling. Large eagle rays, turtles, spotted groupers and crustaceans make their home here. Good visibility.

☆☆☆☆☆**WHEELAND CUT.** This area is located on the northwest point just off Navigation Light. A dense shallow elkhorn reef shelters schools of fish, turtles, barracuda, an occasional small shark and a host of critters. Vase sponges and gorgonians thrive in the light current.

☆**FORT GEORGE'S CUT.** At this cut, on the northeastern end of Provo just off Fort George Cay, snorkelers are well protected. This spot is very shallow and a good place for beginning divers. On the bottom, they'll find some old cannons, and around them, small barracuda darting between the shadows.

Dive Operators

NEAL WATSON'S UNDERSEA ADVENTURES on Provo serves the local hotels, offering guided reef trips for divers and snorkelers. Tanks and backpack rentals. ☎ 800-327-8150.

PROVO TURTLE DIVERS has been operating on Provo for 19 years. Owners Art and Mary Pickering offer reef trips—all 15 to 30 minutes away, resort courses. ☎ 809-946-4232.

Accommodations

Note: Some of the hotels on Turks and Caicos close during the summer months. For information, contact the Reservation Center at ☎ 305-667-0966 or your travel agent for availability.

EREBUS INN. This inn is situated on Turtle Cove, a small resort community where you'll find restaurants, shops, dive shops and beaches.

Parrot fish

The only hyperbaric chamber between Miami and Puerto Rico is on the site of the inn. For more information write Erebus Inn, P.O. Box 52-6002, Miami FL 33152. ☎ 809-946-4240/4533. Telex 8436 EREBUS TQ.

THIRD TURTLE INN. This is a small exclusive dive resort situated on a hillside overlooking Turtle Cove and a beautiful snorkeling lagoon. Divers are accommodated in 13 spacious rooms, all with a view of the sea. The rooms are cooled by huge fans and the Trade Winds. Each room is tastefully furnished in tropical wicker furniture with both a double and single bed. Write to The Third Turtle Inn, Hotel Plans, P.O. Box 3875, Oak Brook IL 60522. ☎ 800-323-7600 or 312-655-5678.

CLUB TURKOISE. This is Provo's Club Med. It offers a complete diving program including guided reef trips for diving and snorkeling, resort courses and rentals. For additional information contact Club Med Sales, Inc., 40 West 57th Street, NY NY 10019. ☎ 1-800-CLUB MED.

THE PROSPECT OF WHITBY HOTEL. Located on North Caicos which neighbors Providenciales, this is considered one of the finest hotels around. Newly renovated. Dive/accommodation packages. Reserve through your travel agent.

LEDECK, opened in 1988, features TV, air conditioning, Creole restaurant, pool, balconies, and a dive shop on the premises. Reserve through your travel agent.

TURQUOISE REEF HOTEL is Provo's newest and most complete resort. This newest addition to the Ramada chain is a 230-room hotel complete with casino, full-service dive center, health club, conference center, tennis courts, and three restaurants. Reserve through your travel agent.

SOUTH CAICOS

Countless snorkeling coves and miles of shell-lined beaches make this island a beachcomber's paradise. A herd of wild horses roam the Eastern Ridge.

Dive boat, Provo

Diving and snorkeling on the nearby reefs and uninhabited cays is magnificent, although getting to the reef may be a do-it-yourself deal. Excellent snorkeling exists on the western shores.

Best Dives of South Caicos

☆☆☆☆☆**THE ARCHES.** This reef, beautiful by day, is also a favorite choice for night dives. On one evening exploration BDWH diver Dr. Susan Cropper made friends with two enormous angel fish and saw many large sleeping parrotfish. Stands of elkhorn and brain corals offer a nice background for marine animal photos.

☆☆☆☆**THE PLANE.** The remains of a *Convair 340* offers shelter to six-ft nurse sharks, eagle rays, huge coral crabs, schools of grunts and some big barracuda who like to follow divers around. The plane sits on the edge of a wall and makes an interesting video subject. Seas are generally calm.

☆☆☆☆**AMOS' WALL.** A huge cut in the wall starting in the sand at 65 ft angles down to 130 ft here. Divers have encountered many "cleaning stations" where barracuda and other fish actually line up to have "barber" or "cleaning" shrimp pick parasites from their teeth and scales. Both lavender and clear shrimp have also been observed. Huge eagle rays, sea turtles, big grouper, queen angels, and Spanish hogfish abound.

☆☆☆**ANCHOR ALLEY.** As the name implies, numerous ships have lost their anchors on this spot, probably the result of chaffing against the scattered coral heads, but the real attraction is the fish life. Divers have spotted gray angels appearing to be four ft in diameter along with a number of Nassau grouper, spotted morays, and king-size jacks.

☆☆☆**THE POINT.** Situated at the south end of South Caicos. The Point is a good place for a night dive. Many lobster, crabs, spotted cowfish, morays and parrots are found on the reef along with large butterfly fish and small critters.

GRAND TURK

Grand Turk is the seat of the Turks and Caicos government and is the most densely populated of all the islands. This tiny 10-square-mile island is separated from the Caicos by a 22-mile-wide channel known as the Turks Island Passage.

Best Dives of Grand Turk

The wall at Grand Turk which borders the Continental Shelf drops off to the 7,000-ft Turks Island Passage beginning one quarter-mile offshore. The top of the reef starts at about 35 ft. Schools of manta rays come in to feed on the reef during spring, a period when the waters are rich with a bloom of plankton— free-swimming micro-organisms which are a food source to many species of marine life. Other marine life includes bottle nose dolphins and occasionally, in late winter, humpback whales.

☆☆☆☆☆**THE GARDENS.** This wall dive starts at about 35 ft and slopes off to the depths of the channel. During springtime manta rays are frequently sighted. Marine life is so abundant along this section of the Grand Turk wall that the exquisite beauty of the reef is often overshadowed by the magnificence of the animals.

Mini-critters such as cleaner shrimp and octopi are found in the crevices of the reef. This is a superb area for video and still photography.

☆☆☆☆☆**THE TUNNELS.** Just south of the Gardens are the Tunnels where divers find easy swim-through chutes at depths between 50 and 75 ft. The reef life is similar to that in the Gardens. Six- ft mantas have been sighted here during the spring migration. At 60 ft you'll find a big sandy bowl.

☆☆☆☆**THE ANCHOR.** Just north of the Garden's you'll find the Anchor, one of the prettiest sections of the Grand Turk wall. Here you'll find huge pastel sea fans, dense thickets of soft and hard corals, and some huge tube and barrel sponges. Black coral is found at depth. The reef starts at about 40 ft and drops off.

Best Snorkeling of Grand Turk

Good snorkeling and snorkel-swimming is available off the beaches of the Kittina Hotel and the Salt Raker Inn. Snorkelers will find some nice shallow coral heads as well as juvenile reef fish (angels, barracudas), shells, and small turtles. Depths on the Grand Turk wall, which is accessible only by boat, begin at 25 ft and are fine for experienced free divers, but not recommended for snorkel swimming or novices.

Dive Operators of Grand Turk

BLUE WATER DIVERS. Located in Cockburn Town, Blue Water Divers offers guided reef trips to the Grand Turk Wall. ☎ 809-946-2432. Write to Blue Water Divers, P.O. Box 124, Grand Turk, BWI. Complete dive/accommodation packages available.

OMEGA DIVERS. Located adjacent to the Kittina Hotel, Omega Divers offers guided reef tours. Packages and group rates are available. Write to 8420 S.W. 133 Avenue, Miami FL, ☎ 800-255-1966, 800-843-7544, or 305-385-0779.

Live-Aboard

THE AQUANAUT. Captain Bob Gascione will take you to his personal "best" dives of the Turks and Caicos, alternating between West Caicos from August to December, and Grand Turk sites from January on. The 45-ft motor yacht, *Aquanaut*, carries four to six divers comfortably. ☎ 800-348-9778 (US) or 809-946-2497. Write to P.O. Box 101, Grand Turk, Turks & Caicos Islands.

Purple sea plumes and gorgonians on the wall, Grand Turk

Accommodations—Grand Turk

KITTINA HOTEL. This family-owned resort offers modern, spacious suites, a native restaurant and beach bar, sand beach, and freshwater pool. Dive packages available. For reservations contact your travel agent or write to Turks and Caicos Reservation Center, Franklin International Plaza, 255 Alhambra Circle, Suite 312, Coral Gables, FL 33134. ☎ 305-667-0966. The Reservation Center can also provide additional hotel listings. Please note that many small hotels in the islands close during the summer months.

Other Activities

A few tennis courts are scattered around the islands, but generally the only non-watersport activities are those offered by the individual resorts.

FACTS

RECOMPRESSION CHAMBER. Modern facilities are operated by the Society of Underwater Diving Safety on the island of Providenciales.

GETTING THERE. Weekly flights are available from Miami to Grand Turk and Provo aboard Pan Am (Mon. Tues. Thurs. and Sat. to Provo; Sun. and Fri. to Grand Turk). Some connections are available through Nassau and the Dominican Republic aboard major U.S. carriers. Inter-island transportation is provided by Turks & Caicos National Airlines.

ISLAND TRANSPORTATION. Taxis. Car rentals available on Grand Turk and Provo.

DRIVING. Traffic moves on the left side of the roads.

DOCUMENTS. U.S. and Canadian residents are not required to carry a passport, but will need some identification such as a voter registration card or birth certificate. Passports are required for other nationalities. An onward ticket is required.

CUSTOMS. Cameras and personal dive equipment do not require any special paperwork. No spearguns are allowed on the islands. Possession of drugs brings a strong penalty. Pets and animals should have a current certificate of health from a registered veterinarian.

CURRENCY. The U.S. dollar is legal tender.

Turks and Caicos beach

CLIMATE. 70 to 90°F year-round. Water temperature never below 74°F. Possibility of storms and heavy rainfall in July through November.

CLOTHING. Lightweight, casual. For diving, wet suits are not needed during the summer, but a lightweight wetsuit, shortie or lycra wetskin is a good idea for winter diving or to prevent coral abrasion. Divers should bring all their own personal gear since rental equipment is not widely available.

ELECTRICITY. 120 volt, AC.

TIME. Eastern Standard.

LANGUAGE. English.

TAX. There is a $10 departure tax. Hotels may add a 15 percent service charge and a 5 percent government accommodation tax.

RELIGIOUS SERVICES Roman Catholic, Anglican, Baptist, Methodist, Seventh Day Adventist, Church of God.

FOR ADDITIONAL INFORMATION Contact the Turks and Caicos Tourist Board, 1208 Washington Drive, Centerport NY 11721. ☎ 1-800-441-4419 or 516-673-0150.

ST. CROIX
United States Virgin Islands

Cane Bay

Buck Island

Christiansted

ST. CROIX

1. LONG REEF
2. FREDERIKSTED PIER
3. NORTHSTAR REEF
4. BUTLER BAY
5. SALT RIVER CANYON
6. BUCK ISLAND
7. RAINBOW REEF

UNITED STATES VIRGIN ISLANDS

Discovered by Columbus in 1493, the U.S. Virgin Islands (USVI) comprise three main islands: St. Croix, St. John and St. Thomas. Each island has a distinct personality and flavor, and since they are close together you can choose one island as your vacation base and still catch the fun of the other two.

Dive boats and facilities damaged by Hurricane Hugo in 1989 are in the process of being rebuilt or replaced. Check listings with your dive travel specialist.

ST. CROIX

The largest of the USVI, St. Croix plays host to over 50,000 visiting snorkelers and divers per year, the main attraction being Buck Island National Park—the most famous snorkeling spot in the world. SCUBA divers will find their share of reefs, walls and wrecks to dive.

Picturesque St. Croix, once a Danish territory, is known for its easy going lifestyle and warm hospitality. The streets of Christiansted, the tiny capital, are lined with 18th-century buildings in pastel pinks, blues and yellow. Tropical flowers

---

Area Contributor: Michelle Pugh, Dive Experience, Christiansted.

greet the visitor everywhere. At night, shops, restaurants and nightclubs come alive with indigenous sights and sounds. Gracious and informal, the Cruzans appeal to all visitors.

Much of the best diving and snorkeling around St. Croix is accessible by beach entry.

Best Dives of St. Croix

☆☆☆☆**LONG REEF** is on the outskirts of Christiansted Harbor. This is a nice shallow reef, ideal for snorkeling and for novice divers. It slopes gently from 30 ft to an average depth of 50 ft, reaching 80 ft at some spots. As you swim down the terraces you'll be joined by French angels, parrot fish, lobsters and goatfish. A docile nurse shark is frequently sighted here. The reef is habitat to hundreds of fish and ocean critters. Huge brain and elkhorn coral formations decorate Long Reef.

☆☆☆☆**THE FREDERIKSTED PIER** is the ultimate night dive at St. Croix. The underwater pilings are carpeted with red, yellow and orange sponges, tube worms, and corals. Photographers enjoy shooting a fantasy land of seahorses, octopi, baby morays, parrotfish and tube anemones. Entrance to the dive site is by climbing down a ladder from the pier. Be sure to first see the Harbor Master at the pier. ☎ 772-0174. Diving is prohibited when a ship is in.

☆☆☆☆☆**NORTHSTAR REEF** is a spectacular wall dive at the east end of Davis Bay. Beach entry is possible here but most divers opt for boat access because of the rocky terrain. The wall is covered with beautiful staghorn coral thickets. At about 50 ft, divers may swim to a sandy shelf that leads to a cave. A huge green moray is usually hiding there.

Divers exploring Northstar, a onetime port for 18th-century sailing ships, enjoy swimming among huge anchors. The marine life here is superb. Frequent dolphin visits are reported. An occasional moderate current is encountered at Northstar.

☆☆☆**BUTLER BAY,** located just north of the Frederiksted Pier on the west shore, is the site of three ship wrecks: the 170-ft *Rosaomaira* which sits in 100 ft of water; the 140-ft *Suffolk Maid*, an old fishing trawler which can be seen at a depth of about 90 ft; and the *Northwind*, a retired tugboat at about 60 ft. The wrecks are part of an artificial reef system. All

Grunts under antler coral

three wrecks are havens for goatfish, groupers, snappers, turtles and rays. This site is recommended for intermediate to experienced divers.

☆☆☆SALT RIVER CANYON is a reef and a wall dive on the north shore. When seas are calm, it is an excellent spot for novices. Divers have fun swimming over arches and ledges, around caves and through arches at Salt River Canyon. There's an abundance of fish here and dolphin and turtles are frequently sighted.

Best Snorkeling of St. Croix

☆☆☆☆☆BUCK ISLAND REEF is a snorkelers' paradise. Established by President John F. Kennedy as a national monument and recognized by National Geographic as one of the 10 most beautiful spots in the world, Buck Island Reef continues to capture the hearts of Caribbean tourists.

Buck Island lies just off the coast of St. Croix, the largest and most historic of the USVI. This 850-acre sanctuary houses the world's only underwater national park. Protected from the invasion of spear fishermen and developers, Buck Island remains exactly as it was when Kennedy swam there.

As in most national parks, Buck Island has its own rangers, only here they sport swim trunks and patrol in power boats. There are also the standard park guide markers, but at Buck Island they stand at a depth of 12 ft, embedded in the sands along the ocean floor.

Beginners and experienced snorkelers alike can experience this underwater fantasy in an unusually safe atmosphere. The reefs of Buck Island lie only 100 yds off the coast and no trail is more than 15 ft deep.

As snorkelers enter the park, they are startled to see a blue and white welcoming plaque shimmering below the surface.

Windmill, Christiansted

One marker (number 8) located next to an unusual round coral full of veins inquires, "What would you name this coral?" The next marker says "You are right. Brain Coral." Arrows and signs guide the swimmer along the underwater trail and give the precise names of coral and other growths below the surface. More than 300 species of fish are identified, just as other national parks describe their attractions. One species that audibly demands attention is the small striped grunt, a fish that can be clearly heard underwater. The National Park Service maintains a careful watch, but one familiar park rule— Don't Feed the Animals— does not apply here. Swimmers can feed the fish as often as they like.

Since the reef park is strictly non-commercial, you are advised to rent gear before heading out.

And getting there is half the fun. Most hotels on St. Croix offer a shuttle service to Christiansted where you can select almost any kind of boat imaginable.

Areas of Buck Island Reef away from the snorkeling reef can be dived with scuba gear.

Dive Operators of St. Croix

All of the dive operators on St. Croix require a C-Card.

DIVE EXPERIENCE is located at the Club St. Croix in Christiansted. Owner Michelle Pugh is a diver/medic instructor as well as a PADI instructor. This PADI five star facility offers all certifications including a four day certification, a resort course, rentals, photography equipment. Hotel and dive packages are available. ☎ 800-635-1533, 809-773-3307 or write Estate Golden Rock, Christiansted, St. Croix, USVI 00820.

DIVE ST. CROIX in Christiansted, owned and operated by Peter Hughes Diving/Divi Resorts, offers wall and wreck diving trips. ☎ 800-523-3483 or 809-773-3434.

VIRGIN ISLAND DIVERS is located at the Pan Am Pavilion in Christiansted. All certification ratings and rentals. Beach dives, boat, night and wreck dives aboard any one of four custom dive boats. ☎ 809-773-6045 or write Pan Am Pavilion, Christiansted, St. Croix, USVI 00820.

CARIBBEAN SEA ADVENTURES is in Christiansted at the King Christian Hotel. CSA operates four dive boats and can accommodate groups of up to 20 divers. Rentals. Diver courses plus underwater photography. ☎ 809-773-6011/773-5922 or write P.O. Box 3015, Christiansted, St. Croix, USVI 00820.

UNDERWATER ST. CROIX, at the Green Cay Marina just east of Christiansted, offers dive charters and instruction. Dive packages available with hotel condos or villa. P.O. Box 3608, Christiansted, St. Croix, USVI 00820.

SCUBA TECH at the Salt River Marina is a full-service dive facility. Accommodation packages available. ☎ 800-233-7944 or 809-778-9650; write P.O. Box 5339, St. Croix, USVI 00820.

Accommodations

St. Croix offers a wide range of luxury resorts, villas, condominiums, inns and guest houses.

DIVI ST. CROIX BEACH RESORT is a beach-front hotel complex located on Grapetree Beach. All 86 guestrooms and suites are air-conditioned, and each has a private terrace or balcony with ocean views. ☎ 800-367-DIVI or write to Divi Hotels, 54 Gunderman Rd., Ithaca NY 14850.

THE BUCCANEER HOTEL in Christiansted is a sprawling resort with three beautiful beaches, three restaurants, a spa, shopping arcade, eight tennis courts, an 18-hole golf course and all water sports. ☎ 800-223-1108 or 809-773-2100; write P.O. Box 800, Waccabuc NY 10597.

THE ROYAL DANE HOTEL is a restored Danish town house on the harbor in Frederiksted. Dive packages with Cruzan Divers. ☎ 809-772-2780 or write 13 Strand Street, Frederiksted, St. Croix, USVI 00840.

Condo and Villa Rentals

THE WAVES AT CANE BAY, P.O. Box 1749, Kingshill, St. Croix, USVI 00850. ☎ 809-773-0463.

Dining

THE BRASS PARROT in the Buccaneer Hotel promises a feast to remember. The Haitian chef prepares fine continental cuisine with a touch of the islands. Specialties include conch with hot lime sauce and Shrimp Bahia—giant shrimp sauteed in garlic butter and topped with brandy and pineapple liquor.

CLUB COMANCHE RESTAURANT, located on the second floor of an old Danish town house in Christiansted, offers a livelier, more informal setting. Favorites here are cucumber soup, steak tartar, or roast chicken with oyster stuffing. For dessert try key lime pie.

THE WRECK BAR on Hospital Street is the place for West Indian atmosphere. Opens for dinner 4 PM Monday thru Saturday. Entertainment includes crab races and guitar music. Cash only.

BANANA BAY CLUB features exotic breakfast omelets and pancakes. Local favorites are conch chowder and fried fish. Steel drums after 6:30. Reservations. Major credit cards welcome. ☎ 809-778-9110.

ST. JOHN

St. John, the smallest and most verdant of the USVI, is truly the most "virgin". The island is an unspoiled sanctuary of natural beauty and wildlife.

Two-thirds of the 28-square-mile island and most of its stunning shoreline comprise the Virgin Islands National Park, part of the U.S. National Park system.

Best Dives of St. John

☆☆**CONGO CAY** is a favorite site for dive boats based at St. John and St. Thomas. It is a rocky islet located between them. Visibility is usually good. As with many of the small cays, the rocky submerged areas are home to large schools of fish. The coral mounds, some of which have been beaten up by the sea, are decorated with soft corals and brightly colored sponges. Currents are occasionally strong here.

☆☆**CARVAL ROCK** is a short boat ride from the north end of St. John. Try this dive only if weather and sea conditions permit; recommended for very experienced divers because of strong currents sometimes encountered . The attraction here

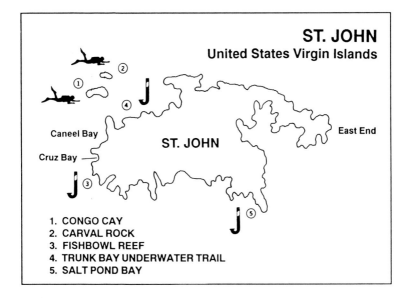

ST. JOHN
United States Virgin Islands

Caneel Bay

Cruz Bay

East End

ST. JOHN

1. CONGO CAY
2. CARVAL ROCK
3. FISHBOWL REEF
4. TRUNK BAY UNDERWATER TRAIL
5. SALT POND BAY

is the schools of very large fish and eagle rays. The submerged part of the rock is covered with sponges, gorgonians, basket stars, and false corals.

☆☆**FISHBOWL REEF,** just south of Cruz Bay is a nice shallow dive for novices and snorkelers. Divers swim along ledges sparkling with beautiful elkhorn and staghorn coral. Soft corals undulate in the shallows. Many kinds of small reef fish are found hiding in the crevices.

Best Snorkeling Sites of St. John

Half-day and full-day snorkeling excursions by boat for exploring outer reefs or shipwrecks, are available.

☆☆☆**TRUNK BAY** on the north shore of the island has a clearly marked underwater trail, with abundant soft and hard

corals, yellowtail, damsel fish, and occasional turtles. The reef is shallow and is just off beautiful Trunk Bay Beach. Top-side here is great for snapshots. Average depths: 10 to 15 ft.

☆☆☆SALT POND BAY at the southeast end of the island is never crowded and is blessed with ample shade trees. Coral reefs stretch from both points of the Bay, offering snorkelers a full day's worth of adventure. Many fish and marine animals make their home here.

Dive Operators

CORAL BAY WATERSPORTS CENTER offers diving rentals, snorkeling gear, sailing, windsurfing, fishing, and parasailing. ☎ 809-776-6857 or write 14 Emmaus, Coral Bay, St. John, USVI.

ST. JOHN WATERSPORTS INC. offers rentals and dive trips. ☎ 809-776-6256. Or write P.O. Box 431, Cruz Bay, St. John, USVI 00830.

CINNAMON BAY WATERSPORTS CENTER, located at Caneel Bay Resort, operates a 42-ft custom dive boat complete with compressor. Dive trips are offered to the outer islands (cays) and reefs and to the wreck of the *R.M.S. Rhone*, an outstanding dive in the nearby British Virgin Islands.

Accommodations

CANEEL BAY RESORT occupies a 170-acre peninsula that adjoins the Virgin Islands National Park. There are 171 guest units in low-profile buildings scattered about the grounds, three restaurants, seven white sand beaches and seven tennis courts. ☎ 800-223-7637 or see your travel agent.

Cinnamon Bay

Campgrounds

Camping/snorkeling trips are popular on St. John. Be sure to take your own gear.

CINNAMON BAY CAMPGROUND , P.O. Box 720, Cruz Bay, St. John, USVI 00830. ☎ 800-223-7637 or 809-776-6330. Dive packages available, windsurfing and sailboat rentals.

MAHO BAY CAMPS , P.O. Box 310, St. John, USVI 00830. ☎ 809-776-6240.

ST. THOMAS

St. Thomas is the second largest of the USVI and site of their capital, Charlotte Amalie. Provincial yet cosmopolitan, modern yet rich in history, St. Thomas can be seen in a day. Divers should save an afternoon for shopping. Duty-free prices and keen competition make St. Thomas a bargain-hunter's dream. In the narrow cobblestone streets and arcades of Charlotte Amalie you'll find designer shops housed in 200-year-old restored warehouses which were once full of molasses and rum.

For those mixing SCUBA diving and sailing, St. Thomas is the home port to a number of charter operators.

Though some beach-entry diving exists here, the prettiest reefs and clearest waters are found around the outer cays. Cruise ship visitors will find an abundance of snorkeling opportunities.

Best Dives of St. Thomas

☆☆☆☆**FRENCH CAP CAY** is well south of St. Thomas, but worth the long boat trip for both divers and snorkelers. This reef complex displays an enormous array of corals, caves, tunnels, and a spectacular sea mount. Visibility is often unlimited. The reef is teeming with fish, rays and critters. Beautiful lavender, orange, and yellow vase and basket sponges grow on the walls. A light current is usually encountered here.

☆☆**CAPELLA ISLAND** is just east of Little Buck Island. The reef here begins at 25 ft. Divers swim down through coral-encrusted canyons to a beautiful rocky bottom where basket sponges, soft corals and pillar coral grow. The visibility, often excellent, is weather-dependent. Fish life is abundant.

☆☆**SABA ISLAND,** a short boat trip from the St. Thomas's harbor, is a favorite one-tank dive. Depths are 20 to 50 ft. The reef at Saba Island is very pretty; divers swim through staghorn thickets and pillar corals. Large boulders cover the bottom which is at a depth of about 50 ft. You may encounter surge; a number of divers have been tossed into the fire coral on the reef.

Best Snorkeling Sites

☆☆**COKI BEACH** on the north shore of St. Thomas is a favorite beach dive and snorkeling site. The beach is adjacent to Coral World, an underwater viewing tower. The reef here ranges in depth from 20 to 50 ft. Divers swim down a sand slope amid schools of snappers, French & queen angels, and an occasional baby shark. This is an excellent first dive also.

☆☆☆*CARTANSER SENIOR,* a 190-ft wreck, sits just off Little Buck Island in 35 ft of water. It is filled with schools of squirrel fish, morays, angels, butterfly fishes, sergeant majors,

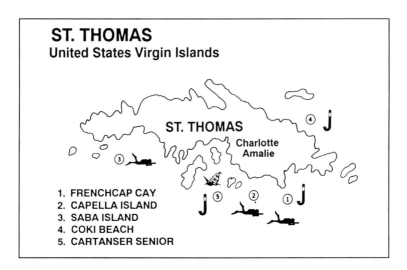

ST. THOMAS
United States Virgin Islands

ST. THOMAS

Charlotte
Amalie

1. FRENCHCAP CAY
2. CAPELLA ISLAND
3. SABA ISLAND
4. COKI BEACH
5. CARTANSER SENIOR

angels and damsels, all of whom are accustomed to being handfed and will approach you looking for a snack. Visibility is often good here.

FRENCH CAP CAY has the best visibility for snorkeling and free diving photography (see overall description above). The reef has many shallow areas full of large sea fans, antler coral, and elkhorn.

St. Thomas Dive Operators

AQUA ACTION at Secret Harbour Beach Hotel features custom dives to area sites. Dive packages. ☎ 809-775-6285 or write P.O. Box 12138, St. Thomas, USVI 00801.

CHRIS SAWYER DIVING CENTER has two locations, one at the Grand Beach Hotel at Coki Beach and the main operation at Compass Point Marina. All gear, including underwater photo equipment, is available for rental. A fast 42-ft dive boat shuttles divers to all the best dives around St. Thomas and its outer islands.

CARIBBEAN DIVERS at Red Hook has boat dives and PADI certification classes. Tel 809-775-6384.

ST. THOMAS DIVING CLUB, at the Bolongo Bay Beach Club, specializes in dive and snorkel excursions to local and neighboring BVI sites. ☎ 809-776-2381.

VIRGIN ISLAND DIVING SCHOOL. If you're arriving by cruise ship, Virgin Island Diving School will pick you up at the dock, take you diving, and drive you back to the ship. Resort courses and SCUBA certification lessons are available. Boat and beach diving for novices and experienced divers around St. Thomas and the outer cays. ☎ 809-774-8687 or write P.O. Box 9707, St. Thomas, USVI 00801.

JOE VOGEL DIVING COMPANY is located on Mandalh Rd near the Mahogany Run Golf Course. Ex Navy diver Joe Vogel and wife Debbie conduct personalized SCUBA tours off the beaches. ☎ 809-775-7610 or write P.O. Box 7322, St. Thomas, USVI 00801.

Accommodations

St. Thomas has a seemingly endless variety of accommodations. You'll find charming antique guesthouses and cozy in-town hotels, resorts on secluded beaches, romantic mountain-top villas, condos, and hotels.

BOLONGO BAY BEACH CLUB offers diving packages in co-operation with the on-premises St. Thomas Diving Club. Bolongo Bay also packages combination vacations with live-aboard cruises to the BVI. ☎ 800-524-4746 or 809-775-1800 or write P.O. Box 7337, St. Thomas, USVI 00801.

STOUFFER GRAND BEACH RESORT, a deluxe beach-front resort is located at Pineapple Beach on the east shores of St. Thomas. It has 315 rooms, two pools, three restaurants, entertainment, and TV. ☎ 800-468- 3571 or write P.O. Box 8267, St. Thomas, USVI 00801.

Live-Aboards

BOLONGO BAY BEACH CLUB offers sailing cruises which visit all the USVI and BVI dive sites. ☎ 800-524- 4746 or 809-775-1800 or write P.O. Box 7337, St. Thomas, USVI 00801.

VIRGIN ISLANDS CHARTER YACHTS will rent you a sailing yacht and teach you how to sail. On some yachts crew includes a divemaster; some also have compressors aboard. Others arrange rendezvous with dive boats. ☎ 800-524-2061 or 809-774-3944. Reserve at least four months in advance.

REGENCY YACHT CHARTERS has several magnificent sailing yachts custom outfitted for SCUBA tours, including the 85-ft ketch, *China Cloud*, for groups. If you're already a sailor, Regency instructors will teach you how to dive; if you're already a diver, they'll teach you to sail. ☎ 800-524-7676, 809-776-5950 or write Long Bay Rd, St. Thomas, USVI 00802.

Sightseeing and Other Activities

The USVI provide opportunities for a wide variety of activities. Check with your hotel or the tourist newspapers (available everywhere) for historic tours, rum factory tours, golf, tennis, deep sea fishing, bird walks, day sails, visits to the new national park on Hassel Island, parasailing, and board sailing.

Check nightclub listings for broken bottle dancing, fire eating, limbo dancing, steel bands, and island entertainment acts. Be sure to see a performance of the Mocko Jumbis on their 17-foot stilts or the Mungo Niles Cultural Native Dancers and Musicians.

Dining

The rich history of the USVI is reflected in the wonderful restaurants. You can dine on the finest continental cuisine or sample exciting local dishes.

HOTEL 1829 was originally built by a sea captain and completed in the year of its name. This is a formal restaurant with an interior resembling an Italian villa. The chef specializes in rack of lamb and various pasta dishes. Located in the heart of the harbor. ☎ 809-776-1829.

BLACKBEARD'S CASTLE is an old observation tower built on a scenic hilltop in Charlotte Amalie. Gourmet seafood is served weekdays at lunch and dinner. ☎ 809-776-1234.

THE CHART HOUSE, located in Frenchtown's historic Villa Olga, serves dinner on a lovely terrace. The favorite here is the 40-dish salad bar. Entrees include ribs, chicken, lobster, fish and shrimp. ☎ 809-774-4262.

Spanish hog fish

TONGA REEF is set on the shore at the Carib Beach Hotel. Diners are served by torchlight beside a glimmering waterfall. Specialties are native fish, steaks and seafood. Entertainment. ☎ 809-774-2525.

FACTS

RECOMPRESSION CHAMBER. St. Thomas.

GETTING THERE. There are daily connecting flights to the USVI from Puerto Rico via Eastern Metro Express, American Eagle, Pan Am, LIAT and Midway Airlines. Pan Am flies direct from New York and Miami; Delta from Chicago to San Juan. Eastern and Midway also arrive non-stop from Miami.

Inter-island connections can be made by ferry, seaplane shuttle or one of the island airlines: LIAT, Virgin Air, Crown Air, Midway Express, Air BVI, Aero Virgin. U.S. citizens take a passport if traveling to the BVI during your vacation.

ISLAND TRANSPORTATION. Taxi service is readily available on all three islands. Taxi rates are determined by law and those rates are available from your driver. Bus service and tours are available on St. Thomas and St. Croix. Car rentals: ABC Auto Rentals, ABC Jeep, Avis, Budget, Hertz.

DRIVING. Traffic keeps to the left on all three islands. A U.S. driver's license is required.

CUSTOMS. U.S. residents are entitled to take home $800 worth of duty-free imports. A 5 percent tax is levied on the next $1000.

CURRENCY. U.S. Dollars, travelers checks, major credit cards. No personal checks accepted.

CLIMATE. Year round temperatures vary from 76 to 82° F.

CLOTHING. Casual, lightweight, with sweaters for winter; jackets and ties needed for some resorts and eating establishments.

ELECTRICITY. 110V AC 60 cycles (same as U.S.).

TIME. Atlantic Standard which is one hour earlier than Eastern Standard.

LANGUAGE. English.

TAXES. No sales tax. 7.5 percent hotel tax. Service charge may apply at some restaurants.

NEWSPAPERS. *St. Thomas This Week, St. Croix This Week.*

RELIGIOUS SERVICES. All denominations.

FOR ADDITIONAL INFORMATION. United States Virgin Islands Division of Tourism, 1270 Avenue of the Americas, NY NY 10020. ☎ 212-582-4520; in Miami 305-591-2070; in Los Angeles 213-739- 0138.

LIVE-ABOARDS AND WORLD WIDE EXPEDITIONS

While most divers choose a vacation resort with spacious accommodations, nightlife and varied top-side activities, a growing segment of the dive community is turning to wilderness expeditions and live-aboard vacations.

The term live-aboard refers to any of various sized sailing or motor yachts and ships which have been custom outfitted into floating dive resorts. Ocean Quest International has turned a 457-ft cruise ship, *Ocean Spirit*, into a luxury dive vessel. A fleet of eight 30-ft dive boats store in the hull. The *M.V. Pacific Nomad*, based in Fiji, stretches out to house a helicopter pad, spacious salons, theaters and lounges.

Live-aboards offer diving 24 hours a day in popular resort areas and at remote, often unexplored reefs such as Isla del Cano, a spectacular snorkeling spot or Cocos Island (both off Costa Rica), or any one of a number of world-wide scenic underwater areas. Live-aboard vacationers are usually experienced SCUBA divers who are willing to trade private baths, showers and living space in return for diving new subsea terrain with promises of exotic wildlife. Tales of gigantic marine life, unmatched visibility, virgin reefs teeming with gigantic mantas, schools of tuna, dolphin and rare oversized tropical fish are being told by returning expeditioners. Of course seeing

Diving the waters of Saba / St. Eustatius

is believing and, with the advent of underwater video equipment, actual footage of the sea's majestic beings is readily available to hook the adventurous diver.

Divers can select from privately arranged tours on small luxury sailboats popular in the USVI and BVI or join a group aboard a large sailing or motor yacht such as the luxurious 110-ft *Sea Dancer* operated by Divi Hotels in the Caribbean or the world-wide fleet operated by See & Sea Travel of San Francisco. Adventurous snorkelers are invited to participate in some scientific expeditions with the Oceanic Society in San Francisco; the lure is swimming with dolphins combined with sailing or discovering isolated beaches and islands.

Custom sailing/snorkeling/diving vacations for families and small private groups can be arranged through many of the sailboat charter companies. Often a dive-instructor-captain can be hired.

Be sure to book far in advance (three to 12 months) and specifically request a diving itinerary. While some of these smaller sailing yachts are equipped with compressors, others must rendezvous with dive boats.

Live-aboard vacations and expeditions are not for everyone. Invitations to non-diving companions are definitely not recommended. Since space does not permit us to detail every tour, we recommend obtaining all the facts from the various operators and tour companies before considering one of these offbeat vacations.

While some of these tours offer guests pampered luxury service, others provide downright rugged adventures in primitive areas. Some entail long tiresome ocean voyages through choppy seas, while others offer short hops through calm seas around popular vacation destinations with ample opportunity to go ashore and hit some night spots. Generally the more remote the location the more rugged the adventure.

Several live-aboard and expedition tour operators are listed under destination chapters throughout this guide. Following are additional companies offering world-wide sea-going expeditions for divers and snorkelers.

PRIVATE SAILING CHARTERS

Regency Yacht Charters

Long Bay Road,
St. Thomas, USVI 00802,
☎ 800-524-7676

See & Sea Travel Service, Inc.

50 Francisco St., Suite 205,
San Francisco CA 94133
☎ 800-DIV-XPRT or 415-434-3400.
Telex 278036 SEAS UR.
FAX 415-434-3409.

Sail-Dive trips for small groups (3-8) to the Red Sea, Fiji, Thailand, Palau, Guadeloupe, or Baja, California, the Maldives (offshore Southern India).

Stevens Yachts

Specializes in remote Caribbean locations.
252 East Avenue,
East Norwalk CT 06855.
☎ 800-638-7044 or 203-866-8989.
Telex 643914PNI STEVENS.

Virgin Islands Charter Yacht League

Flagship-Anchor Way,
St. Thomas, U.S.V.I. 00802.
☎ 800-524-2061 or 809-774-3944.

SNORKELING SAFARIS

Ocean Society Expeditions

Fort Mason Center Building E,
San Francisco CA 94123.
☎ 415-441-1106.
Specializing in remote locations around the globe including
The Galapagos (off Ecuador), Costa Rica, Bahamas, the Sea of
Cortez (Mexico), Truck Lagoon & Palau (Micronesia), Aus-
tralia, Hawaii, and the Seychelles (Indian Ocean) including
Aldabra—a magnificent coral atoll/nature sanctuary and
breeding ground to giant tortoises.

Ocean Voyages

1709 Bridgeway,
Sausalito CA 94965.
☎ 415-332-4681.
Tours to French Polynesia, Hawaii, Grenadines.

Cano Andes Expeditions

310 Madison Ave.,
Suite 1916,
NY NY 10017.☎ 800-242-5554 or 212-286-9415.
Specializes in snorkeling tours to Los Roques, Venezuela,
Balleslas Island, Peru, Argentina, Cahuita National Park,
Costa Rica and (during times of peace) to the primitive San Blas
Islands off Panama.

SCUBA EXPEDITIONS

Sea Dancer/ Peter Hughes Diving

54 Gunderman Road,
Ithaca NY 14850.
☎ 800-367-3484, 800-333-3484
or 607-277-3484.
Telex: 444 2061; Telecopier: 607-277-3624.
Specializing in Caribbean tours.

CEDAM International

Fox Road,
Croton-on-Hudson NY 10520.
☎ 914-271-5365.
Specializing in study programs and unique scientific expeditions, such as collecting artifacts from ancient shipwrecks for museums or mapping the Galapagos. No expedition experience required. Destinations include Hawaii, Key Largo FL, Seychelles, Africa, Galapagos, Belize, Roatan, Honduras—with new areas being added periodically.

Poseidon Venture Tours

359 San Miguel Drive,
Newport Beach CA 92660.
☎ 800-854-9334.
Exotic tours to Fiji, Australia, Roatan, Philippines, Micronesia, Truk, Indonesia, Belize, BVI, Bonaire, Grand Cayman, and the Bahamas.

See & Sea Travel Service, Inc.

50 Francisco St., Suite 205,
San Francisco CA 94133.
☎ 800-DIV-XPRT or 415-434-3400.
Telex 278036 SEAS UR.
FAX 415-434-3409.
Luxury live-aboards in the Cayman Islands, Belize, Curacao, Bonaire, Hawaii, Turks & Caicos, Saba, Galapagos, Fiji, Australia, the Coral Sea Islands, Papua New Guinea, the Philippines, and Sudan (110-ft sailboat).

Ocean Voyages

1709 Bridgeway,
Sausalito CA 94965.
☎ 415-332-4681.
Tours to the Galapagos Islands, Costa Rica, New Zealand, Grenadines, Maldives, Seychelles, Malaysia, French Polynesia and Hawaii.

Lost World Adventures

1189 Autumn Ridge Drive,
Marietta GA 30066.
☎ 404-971-8596.
Specializes in tours to Los Roques Islands, Venezuela and Brazil.

Brazilian Land and SCUBA Tours

5254 Merrick Road, Suite 5,
Massapequa NY.
☎ 800-722-0205 or 516-797-2133.
Specializes in tours to the Bay of Dolphins, Brazil.

Tropical Adventures

170 Denny Way,
Seattle WA 98109.
☎ 800-247-3483 or 206-441-3483.
Specializes in tours to Honduras, Seychelles, Indonesia, Australia, New Guinea, Sea of Cortez, Tonga and Micronesia.

Cano Andes Expeditions

310 Madison Ave., Suite 1916,
New York NY 10017.
☎ 800-242-5554 or 212-286-9415.
Specializes in SCUBA tours to Argentina, Galapagos Islands, and Belize.

International Expeditions Inc.

Suite 104, 1776 Independence Court,
Birmingham AL 35216.
☎ 800-633-4734 or 205-870-5550.
Offers sophisticated dive/archaeological expeditions to Belize and the coastal Barrier Reef.

World Expeditions

291 Geary St.,
San Francisco CA 94101.
☎ 415-362-1046.
Specializes in tours to the Red Sea, Sea of Cortez, Baja California, Seychelles, the Pacific, and Caribbean.

SNORKEL- SWIMMING AND FREE DIVING

Snorkeling was once considered a macho endeavor, useful only for spearfishing. Today the sport has evolved into a family affair with sightseeing and underwater photography being the main focus. Together young and old family members can share the magic of underwater discovery. Anyone in average health who can swim can easily master snorkel swimming. Some snorkelers relish floating on the surface while others work at being able to free dive 30 or more feet below the surface. One Florida Keys dive boat captain, growing impatient with two divers who were lingering over a wreck below, surprised the pair by snorkeling down 50 ft and tapping one on the shoulder—a reminder that it was time to go.

Custom-designed boats for snorkeling trips are available at popular dive vacation spots listed in this guide such as Bermuda, Hawaii, Grand Cayman, United States Virgin Islands or Key Largo, Florida. In some areas underwater trails have been laid out with markers identifying corals and other marine life.

EQUIPMENT

The best place to buy snorkeling equipment is at your local dive shop or specialty retailer.

The basic equipment used in warm water snorkel swimming is a face mask and a snorkel. Divers who wear eyeglasses can

Snorkeling, Bonaire

select from masks that hold their optically corrected lens or choose specially-ground face plates. Contact lenses may be worn with non-prescription masks although many have been lost to the sea. Goggles should *never* be used for breath-hold diving. Your nose must be included inside the air space for pressure equalization.

Ill-fitting, poor quality masks often leak or rip and can quickly sour you on the sport. You'll not regret buying a good quality mask. To check for a proper fit try holding the mask on your face just by inhaling—without using the strap. Be sure to first brush stray hair out of your face. A mask that fits properly will not leak air or fall off. Most important, it should feel comfortable. Do not buy a mask that you cannot try on in the store. If you wear a mustache, expect difficulty in getting a good seal. If shaving is out of the question try a bit of Vaseline or suntan lotion on your face around the area where the mask seals.

Snorkels should be well fitting too. The mouthpiece should be comfortable and easy to grip. The size of the barrel should be commensurate with the size of the diver. Some top-of-the-line snorkels are equipped with a purge valve which is intended to help you clear water from the snorkel. These are more costly than the standard non-purge snorkels. To some divers these are considered a fad and to others a valued new invention. Either will work.

Average cost for a good quality mask is $40, and a snorkel, $20.

Swim fins increase swimming efficiency so much that arm strokes can be completely eliminated. Like a good mask and snorkel, quality fins will last many years and are a worthwhile purchase in terms of comfort and usefulness. A proper fit is critical since poorly fitting fins will soon raise blisters and chafe your skin. If you intend to snorkel in cold water consider open back fins which are worn with a wet suit boot.

Condensation of expired moisture or evaporation from the skin will fog your face mask . To prevent this, first scour the inside of the glass plate with toothpaste (we like Colgate). Before each dive moisten the face plate with saliva, or commercially available anti-fog compounds. We find the commercial products, available in most dive shops, far superior to saliva.

SNORKEL-SWIMMING TIPS TO GET YOU STARTED

Most all dive shops and dive resorts offer inexpensive training which often includes an hour or two in a pool or shallow area.

Beginners should practice using snorkeling equipment in a pool or calm, shallow area. Start by standing in chest deep water with the mask and snorkel in place. The snorkel should be on the left side of the mask. Make sure that your mask strap is properly located on the crown of your head and that you have brushed your hair back so the mask seals properly.

1. Place the snorkel in your mouth and slowly lower your face into the water. Bend at the waist and put your face in the water until your ears are submerged. Then breathe in and out slowly through your snorkel.

2. Hold your breath and tip your head to the side and let a little water into your snorkel. Straighten your head and blast your snorkel clear. Do not yet attempt to re-inhale through the tube. The release of air must be a sudden sharp force that drives the water out. Once you are confident you are effectively clear-

ing the snorkel, the next step is to do the entire process in the water without raising your head to breathe. It is very important to inhale slowly when re-inhaling through a wet snorkel. This maneuver requires a little co-ordination and practice.

3. The final step in learning to breathe properly through the snorkel is to combine all the elements into one technique. When you are ready, lie horizontal in the water with your fingers resting on a stable object (pool side or boat ladder or float). Take a deep breath, hold it and relax. Notice your buoyancy; as you exhale you will sink. As you refill your lungs you'll regain your original buoyant position. The objective is to co-ordinate the exhale and inhale so that you do not get water inside the snorkel by sinking too deeply.

Authors feeding fish in Bonaire

When you feel you have this under control, push away from the side and continue to maintain your balance control by your breathing pattern. As a final test, tip your head to the side occasionally and fill the snorkel during the breath-hold portions of the pattern.

When you snorkel-swim in open water it is a good idea to pace yourself in a swim, rest, swim, rest cycle. This cycle will help keep you from becoming fatigued and give you freedom to roam in almost any water condition and depth.

4. Swim fins serve as an extension to your feet and increase the natural surface area much like the webbed foot of a duck. To accustom yourself to using fins begin by kicking your legs up and down. As you feel the flap of the fin against the water you should widen your kick and take slower strokes. Try and keep your fins underwater. If you're kicking air you will only be wasting energy; and remember no arm strokes are needed— there is plenty of power in your fins. Alternate your leg movements up and down in a kicking motion. In snorkel swimming the arms are not used except to change direction. After you have become comfortable hovering on the surface you may want to try breath-hold diving or free diving, as it is often referred to. This requires learning about pressure. Rigid air spaces such as the sinuses and ears cannot compress or expand and will require equalization by adding air to balance any increase in pressure. You probably have already experienced ear and sinus equalization while driving through the mountains or descending in an airplane. Pressure is first felt by a general tightening sensation in your ears which then disappears, usually with a crisp popping sound. You can help equalize pressure by chewing gum, yawning or swallowing. When you hold your breathe and dive you increase the pressure in the same manner, the difference being that the increase in pressure will be exerted by water instead of air. Because the water is heavier the increase will be rapid and you must learn to develop dependable techniques for quick equalization.

Practice on a ladder. Take a deep breath, hold it and pull yourself down until your head is about two or three feet underwater. Blow out gently through your nose. The mask will instantly loosen and feel normal on your face. To equalize ears and sinuses pinch off your nose by reaching into the finger wells or nose grip pocket in the mask. Blow out through your nose gently and hold the airway closed to prevent any air from escaping. Your ears will pop clear and feel normal. Other methods include yawning by lifting the roof of your mouth and jutting your lower jaw forward. Obviously you don't open your mouth underwater and yawn. Swallowing may also be helpful. Ear clearing is done continuously on the way down. It will not be necessary to clear on the way up. Never dive with a cold, sinus infection or hay fever. If your ears don't clear return immediately to the surface. Never, never wear ear plugs or goggles. Ear plugs block the air space that needs to be equalized and goggles cannot be equalized.

Do's and Don'ts

This chapter cannot cover every possible risk, but you may be assured that few snorkel swimmers ever have serious problems.

Common sense and the basic rule of "look but don't touch" will take care of most worries.

We recommend that first-time snorkel swimmers sign up for a guided tour with a pro dive instructor. In addition the following may be helpful. Never dive alone. Always dive with a buddy. Snorkel during daylight hours only. Check local water conditions—tides and current. Attempts to swim against currents that exceed one knot may produce severe fatigue. Most resort area dive tour operators are familiar with local sea conditions and can offer suggestions on favorable spots.

When anchored in open water, trail a buoyed safety line at least 100 ft long over the stern of the boat. Avoid snorkeling in shipping lanes or heavy traffic areas. Be sure to display a diver's flag to alert other boaters to stay clear of your area. Until you know what you're doing avoid handling marine life and corals. Coral skeletons are frequently razor sharp and can inflict deep painful wounds. Touching or sitting on corals is outlawed in many marine sanctuaries. Fire coral will give you a painful sting, as will jellyfish or sea urchins, when touched. Never poke your hand into holes, caves or crevices; toothy moray eels and some poisonous fish camouflage themselves and hide in coral and holes. Some extremely venomous creatures to watch out for are the stonefish, the lionfish, the cone shell (Pacific), the Portuguese Man-O-War and the fireworm.

Avoid snorkeling in shallow surges especially over coral or rocks, since you can easily be tossed onto them by an incoming wave. Avoid wearing shiny dangling jewelry.

Although exploring a kelp garden, shipwreck or coral reef is fascinating, you can enlarge your underwater outlook by learning about marine life. Once you are able to distinguish the good guys from the no-touch-'ems you'll have fun handfeeding many species of fish. To get in the proper frame of mind pick up a copy of *Touch the Sea* by Dee Scarr.

Two waterproof pictorial fish guidebooks will help you recognize different species. *Fish Watchers Guide to West Atlantic Coral Reefs*, by Charles Chaplin, Livingston Publishing Co., Wynnewood PA and *Guide to Corals and Fishes* by Idez Greenberg, Seahawk Press, Miami FL.

UNDERWATER PHOTO TIPS

Colorful photos of queen angels, turtles, sea lions or diving buddies are now a snap with today's fully automatic submersible cameras.

More and more resort area dive shops offer underwater camera rentals. Two favorites for shallow water are the Minolta 35mm Dual Weathermatic and the Cannon Aquasnappy. Both use 35mm film and have a built-in flash to give you image sharpness and excellent color. They can also be used on land under adverse weather conditions.

The best time to shoot underwater photos is when the sun is high, between 10 AM and 2 PM. Try to fill the frame with your subject. This simplifies composition by reducing the number of elements you are juggling in the frame and focusing attention on your subject. Tight framing also gets you close to the subject, so there is the least amount of water possible between the camera and subject. This gives maximum sharpness and detail.

Shoot towards the surface whenever possible. Shooting down tends to flatten perspective. Surface snorkelers should try to avoid aiming straight down.

If your camera does not have any flash you may be surprised to see your finished photos develop to a monochromatic blue-green. Water filters out red, yellow and orange light. You start to lose it at the surface and by 33 ft it's gone. Flash compensates for this by adding back the warm end of the color spectrum.

Advanced underwater photographers often choose the Nikonos amphibious camera. It is rugged, compact, easy to use, and creates its images through superb Nikon optics. It can be used at any SCUBA depth and offers interchangeable lenses that range from ultra wide to telephoto, automatic exposure, unlimited accessories and the ability to be coupled with powerful strobes.

The other option for professional-quality photographs is to place a standard single lens reflex camera in a waterproof housing. Housings exist for almost every camera and allow the photographer to use any lens or accessory under water that would be used on land. Motor drives, super-wide-angle lenses, extension tubes for ultra-close-up work, even remote triggering devices are available. The only limits to what can be done with housed equipment are your imagination and budget.

The best results with electronic flash are achieved by mounting the strobe up and away from the camera. Extension arms for this purpose are available for use with both camera housings and the Nikonos. If the light is mounted near the camera it will strike suspended particles in the water at a 180° angle to the lens. These particles will light up and can look like a blizzard on film. By moving the light off the camera we change the angle of incidence and the light is reflected away from the camera lens. Good photos can be taken under even extremely murky conditions if we position ourselves or the light so the subject is backlit. Detail will be lost, but the silhouettes will be etched on the film with knife edge sharpness.

With video cameras we need battery-powered flood lights. These are expensive, heavy and generally don't provide a long period of light output or very intense illumination. They are best employed in close-up work and as fill lights. Despite the negatives, they can add a welcome dash of color to otherwise blue-gray scenes.

Surface photography often allows the luxury of shooting subjects of opportunity; underwater you must prepare for the opportunity and exploit it. Just as a good diver plans his dive and dives his plan, so does a successful U/W photographer.

With any camera, whether the simplest or the most sophisticated, cleanliness is next to godliness. Be certain that your O-rings are clean and lightly lubricated with a good quality silicone grease. Check for hairs on the O-ring and the seat. At 80 ft, a single human hair will let water into the camera like an open faucet.

VIDEO EQUIPMENT

Video equipment breaks down into two main categories for the amateur, either 1/2" or 8mm videotape.

The most common video format is VHS 1/2" tape. It is the standard in home VCRs and blank tape is available anywhere that video tape can be found. The Beta 1/2" format gives somewhat better quality but is incompatible with the majority of VCRs and tape can be difficult to find in some areas. If you opt for 1/2" tape, stick with the VHS format.

The equipment for 8mm is light, compact and easy to house. Another advantage is that unlike the 1/2" formats, the industry has established standards for 8mm that will be used by all the manufacturers. This will insure compatibility between different manufacturers and ready availability of tape and equipment.

For additional reading on underwater photography pick up a copy of "Underwater Photography for Everyone" by Flip Schulke.

WHAT ABOUT SHARKS?

Sharks have generated more sensational publicity as a threat to divers than any other animals, even though their bites are among the least frequent of any injuries divers sustain. Two opposing attitudes seem to have predominate: either irrational fear or total fascination.

Paul Sieswerda, collection manager of the New York Aquarium, warns divers about taking either approach to this honored and feared species.

Common sense and a realistic understanding of the animals should be used, he says, adding that "anything with teeth and the capability of biting should be treated with the same respect we give to any large animal having potential to inflict injury".

The vast majority of sharks are inoffensive animals that threaten only small creatures; but, some sharks will bite divers that molest them. Included are such common forms as nurse sharks and swell sharks. These animals appear docile largely because they are so sluggish, but large individuals can seriously injure a diver when provoked. Sieswerda cites an incident with a "harmless" nurse shark as the cause of 22 stitches in his hand—the result of aquarium handling.

The answer to "What about sharks?" from dive masters is usually a shrug of the shoulders. Experience tells us that most sharks are timid animals. Fewer than 100 serious assaults by sharks are reported worldwide each year with the average being closer to 50. Less than 35 percent of these are fatal. Statistics isolating attacks on divers alone are not available; but, they would be far fewer than 50. A majority of those few fatal attacks on man are not by the infamous great white shark biting the diver in two; they are by four- or five-foot sharks causing a major laceration in an arm or leg. Loss of blood due to unavailable immediate medical attention is usually the cause of death.

Overplaying the danger is equally unrealistic. Encounters with dangerous sharks by divers on shallow reefs or shipwrecks are rare. Divers interviewed for this book who have sighted dangerous shark all report the same thing—getting a long look at a shark is tough. When a shark encounters man, it tends to leave the area as suddenly as it appeared.

Sharks are largely pelagic animals found out in deep open water. In general, dangerous sharks are not found in shallow areas where most novice sport diving takes place—certainly not on shallow snorkeling reefs.

Most dive guides agree they would change their line of work if they thought a huge set of jaws were awaiting them on each day's dive.

So use common sense. Avoid diving in areas known as shark breeding grounds. Avoid spearfishing and carrying the bloody catch around on the end of the pole. If you do see a shark, leave the water. Above all do not corner or provoke the shark in any manner.

One crowd of bathers in Miami, fearful after seeing a well-known shark terror movie, clubbed a baby whale to death in the surf, thinking it was a shark.

Our favorite shark danger story comes from a Florida divemaster. A young diver begged to see a shark in the water. Finding one presented quite a problem. The area was largely shallow reefs so shark sightings were rare indeed. Thinking hard, the divemaster remembered a big old nurse shark who could be found sleeping under a ledge on one of the outer reefs. She had been there for years totally ignoring the daily stampede of divers and snorkelers. So he took the young man to that spot and, as luck would have it, there was the shark. Upon seeing it sleeping under the ledge, the young diver became frozen with fear. In a wild panic he backed into a wall of coral putting his hand deep into a hole where a big green moray eel lived. The nurse shark, true to its calm reputation just kept sleeping. But the moray, incensed at the intrusion, defended its home by sinking it's sharp teeth deep into the diver's hand.

MOONLIGHT DIVING

Exploring coral reefs, rocky kelp gardens and ancient ship-wrecks after dark may seem like a feat of daring to new divers. In fact many experienced divers pack up their gear after sunset and never consider a moonlight plunge.

Contrary to the eerie picture one might imagine, night diving offers a whole new magical world to explore. The first phenomenon a diver encounters is bioluminescence, a light produced by chemical reaction in microscopic living organisms. These tiny creatures, not visible to the naked eye, are sensitized by motion and will produce an almost fluorescent light, like a firefly, when touched. Theories as to why they glow range from maintaining contact with other members of their species to mating signals. One shake on the anchor line and the entire length of line will glow. Wave your hand and it becomes illuminated. In one area of Puerto Rico, an entire bay, rich with micro-organisms, is said to visibly glow from the surface after dark.

Once the spell of bioluminescence is broken, another nocturnal world of marine animals will fascinate you. Coral polyps, normally closed during the day, open up to feed at night. Parrotfish spin a transparent veil around themselves as they prepare to sleep. Huge rays, normally hiding during daylight hours, glide by in search for food. On coral reefs basket starfish which resemble a leafless bush by day get up and "walk" around. Eels normally hiding in caves and crevices may be out free swimming. Seals and sea lions roaming kelp gardens may be attracted to your light.

Most resort dive tour operators take guests to special areas for night diving. These areas are frequently shore dives, some being under piers where sea horses or small critters may be viewed. Shallow ship wrecks such as the *Balboa* in Georgetown Harbor, Grand Cayman or the wreck of the *Benwood* in John Pennekamp State Park, Florida are also good choices. Some custom dive boats have underwater spot lights which are reassuring to night divers.

Many captains begin the night dive at sunset to gradually acclimate the divers to darkness. Special safety courses for night diving are offered by many dive shops. Be sure to pick a moonlit night when seas are calm for your introductory night dive. As night diving and underwater navigation requires a bit more skill than day diving most vacationers opt for joining a group with an experienced dive guide rather than exploring on their own.

Many dive operators listed in this guide offer night tours of their best dive sites.

FIRST AID TIPS FOR MINOR DIVING-RELATED INJURIES

Cuts and scrapes on coral reefs, jelly fish stings or first-day-out sunburns can ruin a diving vacation.

Follow up treatment by a physician is recommended. For serious cuts or injuries seek immediate medical assistance.

CORAL CUTS

Coral animals leave behind a hard skeleton, which is frequently razor sharp and capable of inflicting deep, painful wounds. Some living coral have stinging cells similar to those in a jellyfish and produce a sting which rapidly disappears, but may leave itchy welts and reddening.

The most delicate-appearing corals are often the most dangerous. Coral cuts, while usually fairly superficial, can take a long time to heal.

Prevention

Coral should not be handled with bare hands. Wetskins, made of lightweight lycra and ideal for warm water diving or snorkeling, offer a bit of protection. Many marine parks have outlawed wearing gloves to protect the coral. Divers should exercise extreme caution when exploring a reef formation which is subject to heavy surge and wave action or surface and bottom current. It is easy for the unprepared diver or snorkeler to be swept or tumbled across coral. Consequences can be serious. Be prepared.

First Aid

Control local bleeding. Cover with clean dressing.

Treatment of stinging coral wounds: clean wound being sure to remove all foreign particles. A tetanus shot is recommended. Wash with soap and water since live coral is covered with bacteria. Or wash with a baking soda or weak ammonia solution, followed by soap and fresh water. When available, use a cortisone ointment or antihistamine cream. An application of meat tenderizer may speed up the healing process. The venom from stinging sea creatures is a protein, which the tenderizer destroys. Mix the tenderizer with water to make a paste. The wound should be covered with a sterile dressing to prevent infection.

A commercial sea sting kit, available from dive shops, is useful for minor coral scrapes. Severe wounds must be treated by a doctor.

JELLYFISH STINGS

Many marine animals sting, including jellyfish, stinging corals and sea anemones. Most sting injuries are minor and will clear up quickly. The most common are caused by jellyfish. When you come in contact with a jellyfish, you are exposed to literally thousands of minute stinging organs in the tentacles, yet the stinging results only in painful local skin irritation. The Portuguese Man-of-War is an exception and its sting has in rare cases resulted in death.

Prevention

1. Do not handle jellyfish. Even beached or apparently dead specimens may sting.
2. Tentacles of some species may dangle as much as 165 ft. Stay away to prevent contact.
3. Wet suits or protective clothing should be worn when diving in waters where jellyfish are abundant.

First Aid

1. If you're stung, remove any tentacles and attempt to prevent untriggered nematocysts from discharging additional toxins by applying vinegar (acetic acid), 10 percent formalin solution, sodium bicarbonate, boric acid, or xylocaine spray. Vinegar appears to be the most effective in reducing additional nematocyst discharge. DO NOT USE FRESH WATER OR RUB SAND ON THE AREA—you may cause additional nematocyst discharge.

2 Antihistamines or analgesics have been useful in relieving itching and redness. Meat tenderizer may also be useful in relieving the pain.
3. A commercial sea sting kit, available at dive shops,is recommended for jelly fish stings.

SEA URCHIN PUNCTURES

Sea urchins are radial in shape with long spines. They are widespread in the Western Hemisphere. Penetration by the sea urchin spine can cause intense local pain. The spines can go through wetsuits, booties or tennis shoes.

First Aid

1. Large spine fragments may be gently removed but be careful not to break them into smaller fragments that might remain in the wound.
2. Alternately soaking the injured extremity in hot then cold water may help dissolve small fragments.
3. Get medical attention for severe or deep punctures.

Treatment

1. Clean wound.
2. Remove as much of the spine as possible, by first removing those spines which can be grasped with tweezers. Spines which have broken off flush with the skin are nearly impossible to remove and probing around with a needle will only break the spines into little pieces. Most of the spines will be dissolved by the body within a week. Others may fester and can then be removed with tweezers. Some forms have small venomous pinchers which should be removed, and the wound should then be treated as a poisonous sting. Some small fragments may reabsorb. Some divers have found the use of a drawing salve helpful.

In severe cases surgical removal may be required when spines are near nerves and joints. X-rays may be required. Spines can form granulomas months later. Spines may migrate to other sites.

STONEFISH, ZEBRAFISH, AND SCORPIONFISH STINGS

Stings by these fish have been known to cause fatalities. Divers and snorkelers should avoid handling them or any venomous fish.

Venomous fish are often found in holes or crevices or lying well camouflaged on rocky bottoms. Divers should be alert for their presence and should take care to avoid them at all times.

First Aid

1. Get victim out of water
2. Lay patient down
3. Observe for shock
4. Wash wound with salt water (cold) or sterile saline solution.
5. Soak wound in hot water for 30 to 90 minutes (not hotter than 50° C or 120° F.) Use hot compresses if wound is on the face.
6. Get immediate medical assistance.

SUNBURN

Prevention

Some of the most severe sunburns can be received on cloudy days when the sun is not visible. Snorkelers spending a great deal of time floating face down on top of the water are frequent victims of badly sunburned backs and legs. Long- sleeved shirts and long pants are recommended for snorkelers. At the very least a tee shirt should be worn.

Treatment

A variety of sunburn ointments and sprays are commercially available and should be carried in every dive bag. If no special ointment is available, bandages soaked in tannic acid, boric acid, or vinegar will provide some relief. The victim should avoid further exposure until the condition has passed.

SEA LIONS

Sea Lions are normally harmless. However, during the breeding season, large bull sea lions may be irritated and nip divers. Attempts to handle the animal may result in bites. Bites are similar to dog bites and are rarely severe.

Prevention

Look, but don't touch.

DIVERS ALERT NETWORK

The Diving Accident Network (DAN) was formed in 1981 to assist in the treatment of underwater diving accidents by providing a 24-hour telephone emergency number (919) 684-8111. This number, which may be called collect in emergencies, is received at the national DAN headquarters located at Duke University Medical Center. For medical problems, the caller is connected with a physician experienced in diving medicine. The physicians will assist with diagnosis and initial treatment of an injured diver and supervise referral to appropriate recompression chambers while working with regional coordinators throughout the nation.

DAN does not maintain any treatment facility and does not directly provide any form of treatment, but is a service which complements existing medical systems.

DAN support comes from membership and contributions from the diving industry. It is a not-for-profit, tax-exempt, public service organization.

Members of DAN receive a comprehensive emergency first aid book along with a membership card and several decals displaying the emergency phone number. At this writing, membership costs $15 ($20 non U.S. address). Mail should be addressed to: DIVERS ALERT NETWORK Box 3823, Duke University Medical Center, Durham NC 27710.

DAN now offers medical insurance which, for $25 per year, covers recompression chamber and air ambulance costs for diving related accidents. Write to DAN for additional information.

SCUBA CERTIFICATION ORGANIZATIONS

Locations for SCUBA instruction near your home may be obtained from any one of the following organizations.

UNITED STATES

YMCA

(Young Men's Christian Association),
6083-A Oakbrook Parkway,
Norcross GA 30092
Tel: 404-662-5172.

NAUI

(National Association of Underwater Instructors),
P.O. Box 14650,
Montclair CA 91763.

NASDS

(National Association of SCUBA Diving Schools),

P.O. Box 17067,
Long Beach CA 90807.
Tel: 213-595-5361.

PADI

Professional Association of Diving Instructors,
1243 E. Warner Ave.,
Santa Ana CA 92705.
Tel: 800-722-7234 or 714-540-7234.

SSI

(SCUBA Schools International),
2619 Canton Ct.,
Ft. Collins CO 80525.
Tel: 303-482-0883.

IDEA

(International Diving Educators Association),
P.O. Box 17374,
Jacksonville FL 32245.
Tel: 904-744-5554.

CANADA

NAUI

P.O. Box 510,
Etobicoke, Ontario,
Canada M9C 4V5

PADI

243 Mary Street,
Victoria, British Colombia,
Canada V9A 3V8.

ADDITIONAL READING

Additional Adventure Travel Books and Tour Guides from Hunter Publishing

THE OTHER PUERTO RICO
by Kathryn Robinson
Escaping the tourists and the crowds, this guide shows you where to find the secret beaches, unspoiled valleys, jungles and mountains of the island. Aimed at the traveller interested in outdoor adventures, each chapter explores a separate route: down the Espiritu Santo River; the Long Trails of El Yunque; beaches and birds in Guanica; tramping on Mona; scrambling through San Cristobal; on the track of history; the heart of coffee country; Vieques by bike; and many others. Photos throughout, plus a fold-out map.
6" x 9" paperback / 160 pp. / $11.95

THE ADVENTURE GUIDE TO THE VIRGIN ISLANDS
by Harry S. Pariser
The most up-to-date, comprehensive, and colorful guide to both the American and British Virgins—celebrated for their incredible beauty since Columbus first discovered and named the islands in 1493. From St. Croix, St. John, and St. Thomas, to Tortola, Virgin Gorda, and Anegada, all of the islands are covered in depth. Maps of every island and town are included, with historical sections, complete sightseeing details, where to find the best food, and extensive information about hotels in all price ranges—from posh resorts to intimate guesthouses. Whether you are seeking the best walking trails at Cinnamon Bay, a good drugstore in Frederiksted, or a pay telephone on Tortola, this guide will show you the way.
5 3/8" x 8" paperback / 224 pp. / maps and color photos throughout / $13.95

THE ADVENTURE GUIDE TO JAMAICA
by Steve Cohen
How to explore the real Jamaica—away from the high-rise hotels—with an emphasis on walking, canoeing, cycling, and horseback riding. The best places to stay and eat, plus sections on the black market, transportation, where to shop for authentic crafts, ganja, reggae, and everything else the visitor will want to know.
5 3/8" x 8" paperback / 288 pp. / color photos throughout, with fold-out color map / $14.95

PUERTO RICO TRAVEL MAP
1:294,000 scale. Full color map shows all roads. Also includes maps of the Virgin Islands. On the reverse is an extensive text featuring practical information for the visitor.
Map measures approx. 2' x 3' unfolded / $7.95

THE CARIBBEAN TRAVEL MAP
Individual maps of Guadeloupe, Martinique, St. Lucia, St. Martin, St. Barts,
and Dominica, plus an overall map of the islands. Full color cartography shows
features of the terrain as well as all roads. Practical information for the visitor
appears on the reverse.
Map measures approx. 2' x 3' unfolded / $7.95

HISPANIOLA TRAVEL MAP
1:816,000 scale color map of Haiti and the Dominican Republic. Practical travel
information in the margins, plus individual town maps of Port-Au-Prince,
Santo Domingo, and Cap Haitien.
Map measures approx. 2' x 3' unfolded / $7.95

HAWAII: A WALKER'S GUIDE
by Rodney N. Smith
The most scenic walks on all the islands. color photos, and maps.
5 3/8" x 8" paperback / 224 pp. / $13.95

ADVENTURE GUIDE TO THE SOUTH PACIFIC
by Thomas H. Booth
The most up-to-date guide to Tonga, Bora Bora, Moorea, Tahiti, Fiji, the
Solomons, the Cooks & Micronesia. All color with maps.
5 3/8" x 8" / 448 pp. / $15.95

THE ADVENTURE GUIDE TO PUERTO RICO
by Harry S. Pariser
The best all-around guide to the island. History, people & culture, plus what
to see, where to stay, where to dine. All color, with maps.
5 3/8" x 8" paperback / 224 pp. / $13.95

INSIDER'S GUIDES
    AUSTRALIA
    BALI
    HAWAII
    CALIFORNIA
    KENYA
Hundreds of color photos and maps; complete practical information, with
historical background sections. Large fold-out maps included.
6" x 9" paperbacks / 224 pp. / $13.95 each

MACMILLAN CARIBBEAN GUIDES
    ANTIGUA/BARBUDA $11.95
    BAHAMAS $13.95
    CUBA $17.95
    CURACAO $6.95
    GRANADA $11.95
    BERMUDA $12.95
    **SINT MAARTEN/SAINT MARTIN, SAINT-BARTHELEMY, AN-
    GUILLA, SABA, SINT EUSTATIUS** $10.95
    TRINIDAD & TOBAGO $12.95
    NEVIS $10.95

SAINT LUCIA $6.95
ST. KITTS $11.95
BRITISH VIRGIN ISLANDS $11.95
These are comprehensive full-color guides, with practical information, walking tours, history, culture, flora & fauna, even the cuisine of each island detailed.
5 1/2" x 8 1/2" paperbacks/96-288 pp.

MICHAEL'S GUIDES
Included in this series are volumes on:
ARGENTINA & CHILE
ECUADOR, COLOMBIA, & VENEZUELA
BRAZIL
BOLIVIA & PERU
Each is packed with practical detail and many maps. These pocket-sized paperbacks tell you where to stay, where to go, what to buy.
4 1/4" x 8 1/4" paperbacks/200 pp./$7.95 each

ALIVE GUIDES
BUENOS AIRES ALIVE
GUATEMALA ALIVE
RIO ALIVE
VENEZUELA ALIVE
VIRGIN ISLANDS ALIVE
Researched and written by Arnold & Harriet Greenberg, owners of the celebrated Complete Traveller bookstore in New York. These guides are the ultimate source for hotel, restaurant, and shopping information, with individual reviews for thousands of places—which to seek out and which to avoid. Sightseeing information as well.
5" x 7 1/4" paperbacks/296 pp/$10.95 each

HILDEBRAND TRAVEL GUIDES
Among the titles in this series are:
MEXICO 368 pp./$10.95
JAMAICA 128 pp./$8.95
HISPANIOLA 143 pp./$9.95
The New York Times describes the series: "Striking color photographs, concise fact-packed writing, valuable practical information and outstanding cartography, including a fold-out map inside the rear cover."
4 1/2" x 6 3/4" paperbacks

The above books and maps can be found at the best bookstores or you can order directly. Send your check (add $2.50 to cover postage and handling) to:

HUNTER PUBLISHING, INC.
300 RARITAN CENTER PARKWAY
EDISON NJ 08818

Write or call (201) 225-1900 for our free color catalog describing these and many other travel guides and maps to virtually every destination on earth.